Unfinished Tapestry

Memoirs of a Mersea Island Girl

Margherita L Oppezzo

Cover picture taken from a pastel painting
by
Margherita Petrie

'Looking over the Feldy marshes'

First published 2017

ISBN:10: 198126907X
ISBN-13: 978-1981269075

DEDICATION

For my two daughters Jeanette and Tess and my granddaughter Rhiannon in the hope that one of them will pick up the needle and continue to work the tapestry

La Famiglia Italiana

CONTENTS

INTRODUCTION

Telling a life story is like working an elaborately designed tapestry; an ongoing composition that tells of family, past and present; with every event adding colour and intensity to the overall growing picture. Another section of the tapestry is added as each new life is forming in the womb and should be worked with dedication and commitment. There ought to be more than one person working on the design and quality if the fabric is to be enduring, it being an ongoing undertaking. When stitches are missing or badly worked then the durability is weakened and the overall picture remains incomplete.

Years ago most family units were strong and supportive with each member doing their best to hold the structure together. There was usually a 'chief needlewoman/man'; mother, father, grandparent, aunt, uncle or even older sibling to oversee the governing of family affairs. Today the tapestry of the family is becoming unclear, with many sections missing. For future generations there will be no tapestry, no picture, no record of who we were or from whence we came.

There are few family members willing to 'take up the needle' and for those who try, it becomes a huge undertaking.

Every one of us has a story to tell – a continuation of the tapestry; leaving a valuable legacy for future generations.

I am writing my story so as to fulfil the need to leave a colourful picture of my journey through life; taking up the 'needle' from my mother and father, who both left their own inspirational legacies, as did their parents along with previous generations. My mother's love of poetry and

1

creative writing, inherited from the Morgenstern family, on her father's side, which has now, fortunately been passed on to me. My maternal grandmother passed on her love of classical music, to my mother, along with her ability to play the piano, her most favoured instrument. My father with his fine tenor voice, (a legacy inherited from his Father Roberto and his Uncle Giuseppe) singing arias from the Italian operas..

The design of my section of the tapestry, whilst being a most enjoyable exploration, proved to be a very complicated project that may or may not be completed in my lifetime.

Although it became necessary to change some of the names, the story is told with all honesty, some of which will be shocking and very hard to convey whilst other portions are humorous, bringing lightness to the sometimes dark and sinister picture.

My story has to begin with my Grandparents so as to illustrate the formation and emergence of the character that is me. Reaching back into the past has helped me to understand the true characters of my parents and why they were the way they were. One could go on reaching back through past generations, however there must be a beginning and that is going to be with Florence and Mark, my mother's parents and Roberto and Lydia, my father's parents.

Although I don't know a great deal about my grandparents - they died when I was very young – I feel that I had a glimpse of them through the eyes of my parents and the many treasured items of memorabilia and photographs gathered over the years. It is now my pleasing duty to take up the needle and continue the tapestry.

FLORENCE & MARK

Florence Trevillion 1876 – 1952

Mark Morgenstern 1872 - ?

Finding herself pregnant and unmarried at the age of thirty nine, Florence had to give up her stage career where she sang lead contralto in the chorus of the 'D'oyly Carte Opera Company'.

Having studied music since she was a child, Florence's father Joseph, being a highly skilled, self employed sign writer, was able to fund her studies at the Royal Academy of Music in London.

Her mother's health deteriorated after the birth of her son Sydney and by the time Florence left school, it became necessary for her to take on more and more of the daily chores, along with the added responsibility of caring for her very sick mother and increasingly active, younger brother, Sydney. Joseph, whose business venture was becoming extremely successful and therefore very demanding of his time, fully appreciated his daughter's commitment and loyalty during this very difficult period.

After the death of her mother, Florence continued to care for Sydney until he became old enough to join his father's business as an apprentice sign writer. Florence, who by this time, was in her early twenties, was now able to realise her dreams by joining The Royal Academy of Music as a mature student, furthering her studies in all aspects of her favourite subjects, including pianoforte and voice training.

The year was 1904 and Florence, after long hours of study, hard work and practice, graduated, having gained a Degree with Honours.

Whilst still living in her father's house in Lambeth, she enjoyed a bohemian lifestyle as her circle of friends grew and her interests broadened. She spent most of her spare time attending various recitals or visiting lectures and meetings, some of which took place in Hyde Park where many orators stood on their soapboxes, endeavouring to attract the attention of passers-by.

She was quite a plain looking woman, apart from her beautiful auburn hair, worn in a long plait, reaching down to her waist. Her large midnight blue eyes, which, due to short-sightedness, were framed by the obligatory wire framed spectacles. Her clothes reflected her bohemian lifestyle; she wasn't in the least interested in fashion and had very little dress sense and would have chosen not to 'fritter away' hard earned money on unnecessary 'fripperies'. It was much more likely that she spent any spare money on music scores and cheap theatre tickets for a seat in 'the Gods'.

Her one love was her music and being an avid follower of Gilbert and Sullivan, was delighted when she was finally accepted to join the orchestra of the 'D'oyly Carte Opera Company' as a pianist. However, it was not long before it was discovered that not only was Florence an accomplished musician, she also had a rich contralto singing voice and was asked to join the chorus of the many Gilbert and Sullivan productions which she was proud to take part in. I remember my mother telling me of one particular production 'The Mikado' in which Florence was allowed to wear her own silk shawl, which far outshone that of the leading lady. Having been asked to remove the offending garment, she was delighted to swap with the irate Prima Donna, who was only too pleased to accept the kind gesture. It was never returned.

Mark Morgenstern, an immigrant from Dresden in Germany, came to England , in the early 1900s, following in the footsteps of Karl Marx. He settled in London where he found work as a ladies and gents hairdresser in Soho. His strong atheistic and socialist views did not reflect his Jewish upbringing. It was said that his passion was to stand on a soapbox in Hyde Park, whilst expounding his revolutionary Marxist beliefs to passers-by. He was amongst the many orators responsible for that particular area of the park earning the enduring title of 'Speaker's Corner'.

My mother always referred to her father as being Polish I never quite worked out where the Polish influence came into the story. With a name like Morgenstern, Mark's Father, Mayer, a cigar merchant in Dresden, must surely have been German, whilst, perhaps, the very handsome Mark inherited his dark hair and olive skin complexion from his mother who may have been Polish. There was never a mention of her name which may not have been known to my grandmother.

Try as I might, to look into this side of my ancestry, I have no real information to go by. It was only possible to glean the limited amount of information told to my mother by her nanny. It wasn't until years later that my grandmother spoke of her relationship and short lived marriage to Mark who disappeared without trace when my mother was six months old.

Fascinated by his magnetic personality, Florence often found herself drawn into his company in one of the local cafés where they were joined by their mutual circle of friends, as Mark continued to hold court and debate with his likeminded followers. The main subject of the debate was usually socialism and the philosophy, theories and teachings of Karl Marx and Friedrich Engles; fellow German Jews with radical and sometimes alarming political hypotheses. It is my belief that Mark left his home in Germany as a young revolutionary, following in the footsteps of his mentors.

It wasn't long before he and Florence became emotionally involved and at the mature age of nearly forty, she was dismayed by the discovery that she was pregnant. Mark, being a gentleman, 'did the right thing' and they were married in October 1916. My mother, Gwendoline was born the following January. They set up home together in a house purchased by Florence's father Joseph, but she was unwilling to play the part of dedicated housewife and mother and the rebellious Mark, having been used to the domesticity of the typical Jewish family life experienced in his youth, soon became dissatisfied by what he termed, his wife's neglectful obliviousness to his daily needs and spent long periods away from home.

1917 – With the end of the First World War in sight, revolutionary unrest was now engulfing Central and Eastern Europe. With his strong radical beliefs and being a staunch follower of Marx and Engels, it was thought that Mark, with the support of the British Socialist Party, travelled to Russia, where he would possibly have joined in the 'October Revolution; the first large scale attempt by Lenin, the leader of the Bolshevik Party, to put Marxist ideas into practice. This would have been the path that Mark would undoubtedly have chosen when he eventually left Florence and their six month-old daughter. He was never seen or heard of again.

Left alone and facing the daunting task of single parentage, Florence took her father's advice by advertising for a Nanny / Housekeeper.

Joseph, knowing his daughter's musical talents, fortunately had the foresight of choosing a house with adjoining music rooms, which he generously equipped with two pianos; the 'Steinway' baby grand for his daughter's pleasure; only the best was good enough for his beloved daughter. The upright 'Steck' on which Florence was now finding it necessary to teach pianoforte and give voice training to her growing number of students in order to provide an income for the maintenance of her new lifestyle.

Florence's Father Joseph Trevillion

Mark Morgenstern

MISS JESSIE HARRIETTE WALLEN

Now both in their early teens, Jessie and her younger brother William were devastated by the untimely death of their mother. It was only a short time after the sad event that she was to be subjected to the wrath and ill temper of the young, fiery, redhead her father had chosen to be his new bride. He was over fifty when he remarried and his health was not good; however, against doctor's orders, he managed to father several offspring who were either born sickly or just did not survive. The two surviving children, Cecil and Bernard, were very dependent upon their older half sister, who was subjected to a Cinderella type existence for many years. She did however, have a young gentleman friend whom she was hoping to marry, but it was never to be, for whilst serving as a foot soldier during the beginning of the First World War, he was fatally wounded. Not only did she lose her sweetheart, but also at around the same time, her brother William lost his life on one of the western front battlefields in north-eastern France. Jessie was heartbroken. Shock and overwhelming grief had the effect of prematurely turning her hair white.

Eventually, having had enough of her stepmother's incessant bullying, she answered an advertisement in the newspaper, asking for a Nanny/Housekeeper to a Florence Morgenstern and her six months old baby daughter

Miss Jessie Harriett Wallen fitted the bill perfectly.

Her small, frail frame belied her energetic abilities in taking sole charge of all household duties, whilst at the same time, fulfilling the physical and emotional needs of her young charge Gwendoline; thus allowing her employer, when she wasn't busy with her music students and playing musical accompaniment for artists wishing to practice their singing and dancing skills, to resume her hectic lifestyle of a constant round of recitals, concerts, lectures and parties. Florence wasn't in the least bit interested in domesticity and for that matter, wasn't at all maternal, in fact she didn't like small children and was only too glad to pass her increasingly demanding child into the capable hands of the woman with whom she would eventually share the rest of her life.

Miss Wallen soon became a reliable and well respected part of the household, where she became affectionately known as 'Aunty', a title which stayed with her for the duration of her life.

A severe curvature of the thoracic spine from birth, caused her a lot of pain and digestive problems over the years, but she was never heard to complain. Florence's initial doubts were soon allayed when she witnessed the tireless energy of her new found friend and companion and young Gwendoline soon grew to look on her as a second mother.

A high fence, providing a safe play area for Gwendoline, enclosed the small garden plot at the back of the three-story terraced house in .Fairmount Road, Brixton. She could hear the voices of other children in the adjoining garden and finding a particular knot-hole, at her eye level, she peered through whilst watching them at play. She was fascinated as she watched the little boys, standing very close to her spy hole as they aimed at the fence whilst having a pee. One day Aunty caught *her* in the act as she stood on tiptoes, with her knickers around her ankles, aiming at the toilet pan; she could not understand why she hadn't got 'one of those things' to pee through. There were to be many questions needing answers that Aunty would have to cope with as Florence would just shrug and look helpless.

During the summer months, Florence took great pleasure in tending the many pots of her favourite red Geraniums that adorned every available space round the edge of the postage-stamp lawn. It was during those rare occasions when mother and small daughter met on mutual ground and armed with her small watering can, a present from Aunty, Gwendoline tried to draw her mother's attention by watering her flowers. The only tasks Aunty was allowed to undertake in the garden were building various shelving to accommodate the flowerpots or mending the aged fence.

Another of my mother's treasured memories of her mainly uneventful childhood was when the smell of expensive cigar smoke signalled the arrival of her beloved Grandfather, Joseph Trevillion. Little Gwendoline would run into his arms as Aunty proffered a silver ashtray for him to deposit his cigar before lifting the excited child high in the air. She always plumped up the cushions of his favourite armchair in readiness for his large frame, where, landing with a sigh of contentment, he would pull his granddaughter onto his knee. Joseph was a gentle, kind and loving gentleman. The routine never changed from one visit to the next. Jessie knew that his next move would be to press a silver sixpence into the outstretched hand of his granddaughter whilst whispering "There you are Kiddo"

Aunty watched as the small child snuggled against her grandfather's tweed waist-coated chest whilst he stroked her lovely ebony ringlets. The scene never failed to bring a tear as memories of her own dear father sent her scurrying into the small scullery to lay up the tea trolley. She was a good plain cook and there was always homemade fruitcake for tea along with toasted muffins purchased from the muffin man who delivered most days.

The time arrived when Gwendoline had to attend school. Joseph insisted on paying for her education and she was dismayed at finding herself enrolled in a private school for young ladies; she so wanted to be with boys, in fact she wanted to be a boy. Her social skills were limited, as she had not been allowed the opportunity to mix with children of her own age and for the first five years of her life, had known no other companionship than that of the two mature women, her mother and her nanny. She hated school and it showed in her lack of learning skills; in particular arithmetic and any other subject involving numbers. Later in life she was convinced that she suffered "number blindness".

Gwendoline was very much a loner as she got older and spent a lot of time in a world of make-believe playing with her numerous dolls, the favourite of which was a very lifelike, porcelain faced baby doll, purchased with the sixpences given to her by her grandfather. She religiously handed the money over to Aunty who kept it in a lidless china teapot, along with any small change she herself added to the funds. The day finally came when a very excited little girl, accompanied by Aunty, boarded a tram bound for Streatham, where Gwendoline had first spotted the doll in the window of a rather grand toyshop in Streatham High Street. The elderly gentleman owner of the shop gave Aunty a knowing nod as she handed him a small ticket. Unbeknown to the child, she had reserved the doll with a small down-payment, financed by Joseph.

The doll remained in her possession until the need for money in her old age, drove Gwendoline to sell it to an unscrupulous dealer who one day called at her door, looking to make money out of vulnerable elderly folk such as herself.

Felix the Cat was another favourite who survived the onslaught of time, to be played with by my brother and me when, as children, we visited our Grandmother and dear Aunty. I recall my horror at seeing Felix's' hands tied behind his back and demanding that Aunty cut them free, until it was explained that Felix enjoyed walking with his hands behind his back.

"Felix keeps on walking, keeps on walking still. With his hands behind him, you will always find him." She sang a few verses from the popular song written around the favourite cartoon of the time 'Felix the Cat'. All the toys were kept in the three tea chests Aunty had converted into one long seat; she did this by putting hinges on the lids and making one cushion to go along the whole thing. Nothing ever changed and Gwendoline's toys remained in those makeshift toy boxes until my brother and I discovered them many years later. There was a large, brown Teddy bear, and a floppy legged donkey Aunty made from an old

astrakhan coat. Amongst all these was a treasured toy that my grandmother had made for my mother's tenth birthday – a kaleidoscope. When I first discovered it at the bottom of the box, I was awe struck by this magic tube and pestered Aunty to let me take it home – she never did.

Gwendoline's days, sometimes stretching into early evening, were mostly filled with the dulcet sound of her mother playing one of the pianos or the monotonous repetition made by one of her numerous students practicing the scales. Sometimes she heard the rhythmic tapping feet of a dance duo that regularly came to practice their routines, accompanied by her mother playing a jaunty tune on the upright piano. She often crept stealthily to the half open French windows of the music room to watch with excited delight as the handsome, brown skinned duo performed their vigorously lithe tap dance routine; the reflection of their steel toe-caps glinting like darting stars on the shiny surface of the parquet flooring; which was kept up to a high shine by Aunty's diligent efforts. For this purpose, she used her her own recipe beeswax and linseed oil polish, to which she added left over odds and ends of 'Cuticura' and 'Wright's Coal Tar' soaps. Nothing was ever wasted.

Knowing how intolerant Florence could be, Aunty was usually quite cross when she found her small charge in the act of spying, and always whisked her away to another part of the house where she was made to read a book or play quietly with her dolls

Certain aromas trigger childhood memories of my visits with my grandmother and Aunty. A few that spring to mind are the then much used TCP Lotion which added its pungently, unmistakable aroma to the tea caddy and biscuit tin, along with any other dry goods stored in the cupboard of the aged sideboard in the back parlour; the ever present smell of gas; the smell of boiled fish which Aunty purchased from the fish stall on Brixton market for Tiger and Peter, her two tom cats; the overpowering smell of 'Sloans Liniment' used by Aunty to relieve the continuous pain caused by the severe curvature of her thoracic spine. My mother once told me, being unable to reach the affected area, Aunty would simply pour the harsh liniment down her back. I always slept in her room during my visits and one evening, being awake and unbeknown to her, I secretly watched as she prepared herself for bed. I loved sharing her room and was usually asleep by the time she came to bed. Just as my mother did, I loved this very dear lady and the shock of seeing the huge, scabbed burn, caused by the constant use of the liniment had a devastating effect on my young mind

When puberty raised its unfamiliar head, poor Gwendoline, who at the time, was in bed recovering from measles, thought she must be dying and was too ashamed to voice her fears. She was just eleven years old and very naïve. It wasn't until Aunty saw the blood-stained sheet that she told the poor bemused child that it was a very natural part of growing up and there was nothing to fear.

Florence refused to teach her daughter music or pianoforte, as the headstrong child insisted on playing by ear and would not concentrate on her lessons. Gwendoline, unlike her mother, was not and never would be an academic; she had an artistic temperament and her vivid imagination inspired her to write; a talent that stayed with her throughout her life. The name Morgenstern translates as 'morning star' and whilst researching the family names, I read that the name resulted from the fact that they were usually writers and were said to have worked on their manuscripts into the early hours of the morning, working by the light of the morning star. Maybe this romantic view of family history resulted in Gwendoline's lifetime love affair with pen and paper. Added to which, Aunty unceasingly read to her from most of the classics such as the works of Louisa May Alcott, her favourites being 'Little Women' and 'Jo's Boys It was also to become my delight when dear Aunty read to me from the same books, having been kept in pristine condition, along with many other notable tomes such as a second edition of 'Alice's Adventures in Wonderland' by Lewis Carroll; a treasured possession, given to her as a young girl by her brother William.

Showing me a well-worn dictionary, Aunty once told me that, at a very young age, Gwendoline took pleasure in looking up words that were as yet not in her vocabulary. She went on to tell me how, at times, she became quite impatient with the child's relentless questions and not having had a very good education herself, she found it necessary to look up both meaning and spelling.

My mother very rarely spoke about her teenage years; she seemed to cling to the idyllic memories of a sheltered childhood. I don't think she ever wanted to grow up. She was a romantic who saw everything through rose tinted glasses throughout her entire life. It is as though she rebelled against Florence's incessant pessimism and took on board Aunty's pragmatic outlook on life. I remember her telling me when I was a small girl, how she had developed an ability to ignore or push to the back of her mind nasty happening and how I, having just witnessed my favourite kitten being run over by a car, would have to learn to do the same – I never did.

These are but a few of the treasured memories of dear Aunty Jess.

Young Jessie enjoying afternoon tea with Florence's Aunt Matilda.

Florence and baby Gwendoline

Gwendoline with dolls aged four   and aged seven.

ANOTHER DOOMED MARRIAGE

Cecil Wallen became a frequent visitor to his half sister Jessie and was developing quite an attraction to her employer's pretty, eighteen year old daughter who would sit at his feet whilst he told her of his travels (true or false, no one ever found out) The smitten Gwendoline was captivated by this tall auburn haired young man, whose dark blue eyes seemed to search into her soul as his stories of India held her spellbound. She had dreamed of this magical country ever since she was allowed to read 'Mother India', the magazine her mother subscribed to.

Aunty was not happy when after a short courtship; Cecil spoke of marriage and requested an audience with Florence to discuss his proposition. Florence, having had very little experience of the ways of men, was charmed by Cecil's prepossessing manner and thought him worthy of her daughter's hand in marriage.

My mother never spoke of the wedding day.

Florence provided them with a small bed-sitting room at the top of the house.

The marriage was never consummated. From the start, he insisted on Gwendoline sleeping on a small camp bed so that there was no contact between them. He often left her locked in the room, without food or warmth, whilst he went out for hours on end. On his return, he told her that he had been with prostitutes and shocked her with graphic descriptions of his exploits. He threatened her with appalling consequences if she were to mention anything to Jessie or Florence as regards to his behaviour. The facts soon became obvious to both women when they witnessed the gradual decline in Gwendoline's demeanour along with the fact of her asking for money. She eventually plucked up the courage to tell them all that had been happening. Aunty had guessed and felt very responsible, as she had known of his mental instability as a child, but thought however, that on reaching adulthood he had grown into a responsible young man. He had certainly duped them all with his winning ways; but not the police when they arrested him and charged him with vagrancy, the use of foul language and menacing behaviour, along with the charge of assaulting a police officer.

Soon after a harrowing court hearing in which Gwendoline, accompanied by Aunty, had to give evidence against him and along with the doctor's report, Cecil was found to be insane and committed to a mental asylum, where he was to remain for a number of years.

Non-consummation of the marriage would have given Gwendoline a very good case for an immediate annulment of the disastrous marriage, had either her mother or Aunty been aware of the legalities of the situation. There was never any mention of a divorce.

LYDIA & ROBERTO

Lydia Rebecca Richards 1895 - 1940

Roberto Oppezzo 1888 - 1954

All the information in the following chapter was relayed to me, over the years, by my father and my Nonno Roberto; for this I am most grateful and feel honoured to have been blessed with the ability to retell their stories.

Roberto was seventeen when he left the family home in Stroppiana, one of the small villages skirting the rice fields in the region of Vercelli, Northern Italy, to join his older brother Carlo in London in 1905. He could not speak a word of English and having spent the first years of his working life helping with the family rice growing industry, he was now finding it hard to adapt to life in the big city. Soho was to be his home and his place of work for the next few years.

Carlo spoke good English, having worked a number of years as a chef at the famous 'Frascati's Restaurant' in fashionable Soho where he found Roberto a job as a comis-chef. In those days the kitchen and restaurant staff usually outnumbered the customers and with the rise in popularity of Italian and French cuisine, there was plenty of work for the growing number of European immigrants eager to come to England. In the early 1900's London's West End was becoming the stylish place to be and the restaurant trade flourished.

Roberto was soon recognized, not only for his catering skills, but also for his fine tenor voice.

As he progressed through the ranks in the kitchen, his

popularity as a chef grew and he often found himself summoned to the diner's table where he gratefully accepted the many compliments to both himself and other members of the kitchen troupe. Also, after finishing his kitchen duties, he was usually requested to serenade the delighted customers, by singing various arias from popular Italian operas.

His brothers, because of his fastidiousness about his appearance, had always jibed Roberto. He never left the house without his cane or rolled umbrella; his Homburg perched forward and slightly tilted over one eye. In the early days, when returning from work, having divested himself of the only suit he possessed, he religiously laid the neatly folded trousers beneath his mattress and brushed the jacket before placing it on a wooden coat hanger. His shoes were cleaned and wrapped in a soft cloth in readiness for the next day. This routine never changed throughout his life and I will always remember my dear Nonno as being a rather reserved, neatly dressed Italian Gentleman; for that is what he was, a gentle man and a Gentleman.

Lydia Rebecca Richards was born 1895 in the district of Lambeth in London.

Before buying the shop premises in Brick Lane, Soho, her grandfather Frederick Richards, first started 'Richards Fisheries' selling fresh fish from a barrow on Petticoat Lane Market, helped by his young son, also named Frederick, (shortened to Fred). The business prospered and Fredrick's growing family, which consisted mostly of boys, five in all, became delivery boys as soon as their feet were able to reach the pedals of the trade bikes; making deliveries to the growing number of restaurants and hotels around London's West End.

Lydia helped with household tasks when not working in the shop. The work was hard and in the winter, she continuously suffered from chilblains on her feet and hands; the open cracks in her fingers bled and stung with the salt on the cured fish. She was unlike most other girls of her age, having been reared alongside older brothers; one of whom,

Fred, was old enough to be her father. He and his wife Esther had in fact taken her into their family from birth, as living conditions over the shop were very cramped.

Whilst at school, Lydia was constantly being bullied by the other girls, calling her 'Fishy', holding their noses as they chased her. Her only friend was Maria, a pretty Italian girl, who was also bullied for smelling of garlic. They were known as the "Smelly Sisters" and would be constantly called in front of the head teacher for fighting and using bad language; skills, Lydia had undoubtedly learnt from her older brothers. She was glad when she left school at the age of twelve. Her friendship with Maria continued and what little spare time she had was spent visiting her friend who lived with her family in the squalid, cramped conditions of a flat in 'Little Italy', the Italian quarter in Clerkenwell.

Suddenly she was sixteen, street-wise and fiercely independent. Being the youngest child in a large working class family, she was pushed into adulthood too quickly. Her Brother Fred, who had been more like a father to her, was very protective and as he watched her mature into a very pretty young women, it worried him to witness the way men ogled her and the way she danced attendance whilst serving the handsome young Italians, who seemed to attract her most. One young man in particular visited the shop almost daily and Lydia's lovely hazel brown eyes shone back at his admiring glances as she gaily chatted and flirted with him.

Roberto strode briskly down the busy street towards, his favourite fishmongers. He wondered if Lydia, the fishmonger's daughter would be serving in the shop today. The thought of seeing her hastened his step. Not having had much experience with the emotions of the heart and being extremely reserved and shy, added to which his lack of understanding of the complications of the English language, Roberto found it difficult to even begin to approach this desirable young woman. He felt in his heart that at this stage they could only be friends, although she looked older, she was, after all, still only sixteen, information she imparted with the use of finger language and a coy giggle. He so wanted to plant a kiss on her constantly smiling full lips and let loose the mane of plaited auburn hair that reached down the middle of her shapely back to a well corseted twenty two inch waist. She was never alone in the shop; there was always one of her eagle-eyed brothers or her father watching with suspicion, any man tempted to engage her in friendly conversation. However, his fortune changed one afternoon as, deep in thought, Roberto was making his way down the crowded street when he heard his name being called. A breathless Lydia, accompanied by her friend Maria, ran to catch up with him.

"What's the bleedin hurry Roberto? I thought I wouldn't catch up with you"

His surprised and shy reply came as he quickened his pace. "I be quick, Io lavoro in un'ora, must to cook fish."

Lydia smiled coquettishly as he raised his hat and hurried on.

"Where do you live?" she questioned having whispered something to a departing Maria. "I'll come with you. I'm a good cook, especially fish," her short legs having to break into a trot so as to keep up with him. She was barely five feet tall. Roberto, having taken after his mother's side of the family, who were all short, wasn't a great deal taller at Five feet four inches; unlike his brother Carlo who was larger in stature

I was nine when I went down with a severe dose of 'mumps'. Nonno was living with us at the time and as both my parents were out at work, he looked after me whilst I was confined to bed. It was during this time that he shared his memories with me. I was enchanted as he told the romantic story of how he first met Lydia, my grandmother. My Grandfather became a different man as the sweet memories invigorated his usually sad countenance. I never remembered him smiling, but as he went on to tell how Lydia ran to catch up with him, warmth came into his voice along with an almost imperceptible sob.

Arriving at the dingy bed-sit, Roberto hurriedly kicked the pair of scruffy plimsolls that served as slippers, under the small iron framed bed. The drab, neatly folded blankets sat with a pillow on top at the head of the bed. Pushing the dilapidated sash window up as far as it would go so as to let fresh air into the stuffy room; a very nervous Roberto turned his attention to a disappointed Lydia.

"Cor stone the bleedin crows," she gasped "I always imagined you living in a posh apartment."

"Sono solo un immigrate straniero, I try make living, "he said, seeing the disappointed look on her face as her eyes strayed around the room.

Realising she must have hurt his feelings Lydia took Roberto's hand and looking into his kind, pale blue eyes, she apologised.

"Sei molto giovane e bellissima, is not good you here."

She had picked up a few words from the Italian customers over the years and was used to being told how beautiful she was as the young men flirted with her.

"OK then I'll bleedin' go," she teased "but I'll cook yer fish first."

On reaching the age of eighteen and being pregnant with Roberto's child, Lydia's father consented to the marriage which took place 26th December 1913. My father was born 20th July 1914.

Lydia on her wedding day.

It was around the time of the start of the First World War, when Roberto received orders to return to Italy where he was conscripted to serve in the Alpini Regiment, stationed in the Alps, assigned to the task of guarding the mountain passes. It was only a matter of a few months, when flying shrapnel almost fatally injured him; narrowly missing his heart and causing damage to one lung.

Roberto – bottom right.

Nonno, as he continued recounting his story, unbuttoned his shirt showing me the deep scars where the shrapnel had entered his chest and shoulder. "This one she nearly kill me," he said as he guided my finger into the deepest of the scars. "Is nothing to be frightened of, it heal a long time ago."

I loved my Nonno and the sight of those ugly scars made a lasting impression me

He went on to tell me of the birth of his son, my father, and how Lydia, who had remained in London, had to leave the now six month old Federico with her mother so as to make the journey to Roberto's family in Italy where she remained until he was well enough to be discharged from the military hospital. .He was then sent home to convalesce in the family home in Stroppiana.

Whilst there, the family witnessed Lydia's distress at having to leave her baby in the hands of the Richards family who, although well meaning, had a very different approach to bringing up children than the God fearing, mainly female, close knit community she was temporarily a part of.

Roberto's Sister, Margherita, had married into the wealthy Barbonaglia family and her generous husband Giorgio suggested that he financed Lydia's return to England so as to pick up her son and bring him back to Italy where he would be well cared for by his female cousins.

Federico remained in Italy until he was thirteen years old; visited only occasionally by his parents. Lydia having joined Roberto in the catering trade in London where they both worked long, unsocial hours had started to drink heavily.

FEDERICO GIACOMO OPPEZZO
1914 - 1999

Not a lot was ever mentioned about the return journey back to Italy made by Lydia and her now ten or eleven-month old baby Federico. It is unimaginable the hardships they must have endured, especially with the uncertainty of travel during the period when the First War was in progress. All forms of transportation across the English Channel would undoubtedly have been overloaded with troops making the hazardous journey to the battlefields of Belgium and France.

She would have been concerned, not only about how long the voyage would take, but also whether there were going to be any amenities provided, not only for herself, but also for her baby. It had been hard enough when she herself first made the journey, during which time her only thoughts were of Roberto, her seriously injured husband. This journey was going to prove to be very different with not only the care of her small child to consider, but also the added encumbrance of far more luggage. One route she possibly may have taken would have been by rail - SECR – South Eastern and Chatham Railway - from London Victoria to where she would have boarded the ferry at Folkestone. She may even have been fortunate enough to have travelled in one of the three carriages that where actually loaded onto the ferry. Of course this is all pure supposition.

It was1969, I was 25 years old when my father and I had to make a similar journey travelling by boat train to Italy.
My father's cousin Giochino had died of a massive brain aneurysm and by the time we were notified of his untimely death, it was almost too late to attend the funeral which was due to take place in

Vercelli in two days time. Unfortunately there was an airport strike on the day we intended to travel, which meant us making the journey by boat train. The journey by ferry from Harwich to the Hook of Holland took eight hours; luckily it was quite a smooth crossing, however, when I did complain of a little queasiness, my father took me up on deck where he took great pleasure telling me of his war time experiences, when he spent long periods aboard one of the many Second World War troop carriers; which proved to be no hardship to him, as it was during this period that he fell in love with the open sea.

Whilst travelling by night train through Holland, we encountered an extremely drunk German staggering into our carriage. I became very nervous as he lurched over to where I was sitting and falling heavily into the seat beside me, he proceeded to ask my father if he could buy my services. I was later to learn that he mistakenly thought I was travelling with my Italian sugar daddy. My father was able to translate his slurred and garbled intensions using the small amount of pigeon German he had learnt during the war. Giving me a reassuring look, he drew out the small flick-knife that he was never without; a habit taught to him by his uncle Charlie, Lydia's older brother, whilst spending his teenage years in – what was then - the very violent area of London's gangland Soho. Charlie had to quickly toughen up the young Federico by introducing him to the pugilistic art of boxing along with other dubious forms of self-defence.

I was relieved when the obnoxious man, having reached his destination at the Dutch/German border, unsteadily got to his feet and swinging the carriage door wide, almost fell from the still slowly moving train as it drew into the station. My father then made the suggestion that I remove my makeup and put a few rollers in my hair in the hope of rendering me less attractive to any further unpleasant advances.

As the train pulled out of the station, we became aware of a frail, shabbily dressed elderly gentleman peering warily into our carriage before hesitantly sliding open the door. He clutched a small battered violin case to his chest as he sat huddled in the corner of our carriage.

Moments later the carriage door slid assertively open as two tall, uniformed German border guards made their austere entrance from the corridor. Fear seemed to sweep over our fellow traveller as they officiously stood staring down at him whilst brusquely demanding to see his passport. His hand shook violently as he attempted to open his small case; on seeing this, my father came to his rescue by demanding – this time in Italian - that they allowed him time. The look of what first appeared to be menacing on the stern faces of the two officials, now turned to impatience. In the meantime my father proffered our passports, giving the old man time to extricate his papers from beneath a rather battered violin. As the carriage door slid to a noisy close, the look of shear relief and gratitude that the old man aimed in my father's direction along with a thin smile of greeting for me, lead to the telling of a sad yet very interesting story; albeit in broken English peppered with German; told by the now less nervous David Kossoff look alike. It turned out that being Jewish; he spent most of the Second World War in a concentration camp where he lost each of the close members of his family. The only thing that saved him from either hard labour or even worse, the gas chamber, was when his violin was about to be confiscated. A sharp-eyed German officer allowed him to keep the inoffensive instrument with the agreement that he joins the 'camp orchestra'. Having been a professional violinist, he was soon to find himself in the company of other musically talented internees, providing regular recitals for the officers and their families.

A steward had distributed pillows and blankets for the use of my father and me as our journey was going to stretch into the early hours

The conversation between our fellow passenger and dad continued, during which time I fell asleep. I was awoken by my father excitedly requesting that he and I go to the front of the train, where we were to view the soft violet light of dawn turning the delicately misted mountains of the Swiss Alps into the most magical scene that I had ever had the opportunity to experience. It seemed that our elderly travelling companion, on reaching the end of his journey, alighted from the train at a station just before the Swiss border where he hoped to find long lost distant family members, having recently received information regarding their survival.

Time had already run out; we were, by then, too late for the funeral when we eventually reached Milan where we then boarded a train bound for Vercelli.

This was to be my first experience of meeting the Italian side of the family. Dad and I stayed at the Barbonaglia Family home; a large

majestic building standing behind high electric gates, looking down the
the main street of Stoppiana. The house was now solely occupied by
Giochino's elderly mother, my great Aunt - (prozia) - Margherita, after
whom I was named. I was enchanted by this frail, humble, little lady as
she solemnly welcomed us into her home. We were led into a small
sparsely furnished side room where we were served lemon tea in fine bone
china cups and saucers, and ornate silver teaspoons. The rather austere
looking middle aged woman, whom we later learned was the governante
– the Italian equivalent of housekeeper, poured the tea from a silver
teapot and offered a silver salver of dainty biscotti. Dad had to translate
for me as his aunt spoke very little English. I didn't realise that he
spoke fluent Italian. The only words Nonno taught me, when I was a
little girl, were 'Come stai' (How are you?) and 'Molto bene grazie.
(Very well thank you) and how to count up to ten. Having experienced
a great deal of prejudice, especially after the Second World War, Nonno
was afraid of being overheard speaking in Italian.

Now leading us up the grand marble staircase, my great Aunt
showed me into a large, tall windowed room where I was to sleep. Tthe
walls were lined with sliding doors of several wardrobes, all of which were
faced with mirrors. She apologised for the smallness of the bed,
explaining that this had been her son's dressing room. After showing me
into the luxurious marble floored 'bagno privato' scented with the
fragrances emanating from the many bottles of 'dopobarba' imposingly
displayed on the glass shelves mounted on the ornate ceramic tiled walls,
she left me to settle in. My curiosity getting the better of me, I was
amazed as I slid open the first of the wardrobe doors, behind which were
shelves of Cashmere sweaters neatly folded and arranged in colour
sequence; another revealed pristine rows of immaculate shirts; yet another
had racks of multiple pairs of stylish shoes, above which hung expensive
looking suits, jackets and trousers; reminding me of an exclusive, gents
outfitters. I was beginning to believe dad's story of how his cousin had
gained a great deal of his wealth, having been employed by the Mafia as
an accountant.

The memory of that exhausting journey makes me
wonder how Lydia managed to cope, alone with a small child
and at a time of war. Their safe arrival must have been a huge

relief to Roberto and his family.

Roberto was never recalled to rejoin his regiment in the Alps and it took a long time for him to recover from the near fatal injuries he had sustained; by which time the war was at end. Leaving their growing son in the more than capable hands of his female aunts and cousins, Roberto and Lydia were able to return to London. Federico remained in Italy until he was thirteen.

My father told me of the time when a fascist group came to the village in search of a priest and having found his hiding place, they dragged him out onto the piazza and standing him against the church wall, they shot him. The evidence of the horrific event remains etched, by the hail of bullets, on the wall of the small ornate church; the surrounding buildings showing further evidence of previously unwarranted attacks. He was not yet five years old when he witnessed the whole shocking incident from the top floor of the ancient tenement building where his bedroom window looked out onto the piazza below. It was to be one of the many childhood memories that my father shared with my brother and me over the years.

On a slightly lighter note, my father recalled a story told to him by his mother. It was her first experience of Italian hospitality as she found herself being warmly greeted by Roberto's family. During her stay, she fell in love with a beautiful white cat which she thought was a family pet. She had been out visiting other family members, when, on her return she was greeted by a deliciously savoury aroma emanating from the kitchen. She was hungry and enjoyed her supper of what she thought was rabbit stew. When asked why she had left some small titbits on the side of her plate, her answer, "per il gatto" – "for the cat" gave the family much amusement and she was bitterly shocked and nauseated by the reply " è il gatto" – "it *is* the cat" and was equally shocked when they pointed to the white pelt hanging from the washing line. They could be forgiven as food at that time was very scarce, people were going hungry and they wanted to treat their special guest to a good meal. At times Rani - Frogs were also on the menu along with Lumache – Snails, and any small bird unfortunate enough to become ensnared in the net traps that were in general use during those hungry times. Money, along with a great many food items, was in short supply. My father once told us how, as a child, he remembered regularly seeing a huge, water filled cooking pot hung on an iron tripod and suspended over a wood fuelled fire, set up in the middle of the piazza. As the water came to the boil, villagers added whatever edible ingredients they could muster, ranging from garden produce; beans and pulses; meatless bones; even the plentiful large frogs and snails, during the wet season, offered a valuable source of protein. This would then provide the small population of the village with perhaps the only nutritious meal of the day. My father always maintained that this was the origin of Minestrone. Pasta was in short supply due to the shortage of wheat, however, the sacks of rice secreted away from the prying eyes of their enemies, served as a (to quote my father) 'riempitore di stamaco' – stomach filler. He recalled women regularly going without so as to provide for their children and also the priests, who appeared to be the only ones in the villages to be well fed. The women also felt obliged to give what little money they could to the church.

Stroppiana is one of the small villages situated in the province of Vercelli in the north-eastern region of Piedmont, northern Italy. Vercelli, being one of Europe's leading rice producers, is characterised by the spectacular panorama of rice paddies. As a little lad, my father was sent out into the rice paddies, usually accompanied by his friend Felice, armed with a long stick with a piece of fat dangling from a string. His cousin Magdalena taught him that by dangling the fat just above the water whilst making chirruping sounds, he would attract the huge frogs that were plentiful during the wet season. Grabbing the unsuspecting, rather slimy creature, he would then break its legs and put it into the small sack that hung from his shoulder. Magdalena would then skin them alive and remove their legs which were then fried and served up on a bed of risotto.

This would be another of the events of my father's life that always brought tears to his eyes as he recalled the memory triggered by the army of small frogs frequenting his garden pond. Whilst on my weekly visits, weather permitting, we often sat watching the antics of the numerous forms of wildlife – in the all too infrequent absences of 'the dreaded stepmother. As he retold the story, in his now advanced years, he could never come to terms with the cruelty that he had inflicted on what he now thought of as the welcome inhabitants of his well cared for garden pond. However, he would then go on to say how his boyhood efforts were much appreciated by his hungry family.

The placid lifestyle experienced by Federico during those childhood years, could at times be quite austere, due only to the lack of money leading to a shortage of food; however the unconditional love that he received from the mainly female members of the family made up for any shortages.

Margherita, Roberto's sister tried to influence her wealthy husband, Sig. Barbonaglia, to send Federico to the school where he would receive the same privately tutored education as their son Giochino. However, whilst being quite an astute gentleman, her husband knew better than to waste money on a child that showed no apparent interest in education; only wanting to have fun by the river with his friend Felice; whilst his cousin conscientiously worked at his studies. It has to be said that there was an age gap of six years between the two cousins. It was later to prove to have been a bad decision made by his uncle. As he got older, Federico showed great promise in his interest and strong ambition to study Electronics; however, on his return to England it would remain a dream.

Benito Mussolini's strength as a fascist dictator was taking a strong hold. He became obsessed with military training for the very young. On reaching the age of eight, like most boys of that age, Federico was expected to join

Mussolini's Youth - a section of the National Fascist Youth Party. Having witnessed many of the atrocities now being perpetrated by the Fascist extremists, the family felt under a fear fuelled obligation, allowing their still very young cousin to join the organization. The only recollection of that period of his youth my father shared with us as children, was whilst attending one of the

Eight Year old Federico in the Balilla

training camps organized by the 'Balilla', he had a fight with a youth of a similar age to himself; he always maintained that it was one of Mussolini's sons!

For the most part Federico whiled away, what was predominantly, a carefree childhood until at the age of thirteen, he was both surprised and rather dismayed after having been told by his cousins that his parents were shortly to arrive with the intention of taking him back with them on their return to England.

It was to be an enormous culture shock, experienced by the naïve Federico as he ventured into the unfamiliar territory of London's gangland Soho, where he was now to make his home along with a now alcoholic mother and a frequently absent father. He became disillusioned as resentment etched deep scars into his personality, turning him into an angry young man and was to embitter him later in life.

Lydia was finding it progressively more difficult to keep a tight rein on the increasingly rebellious Federico. Roberto, working long, unsocial hours, especially the evening shifts that usually went on long past midnight, was rarely around to discipline his son. Carlo, on the other hand, whilst working different shifts to his brother, and having a sterner attitude towards discipline, was gradually earning the respect of his sister in law and young nephew.

Federico felt more akin to this robust, happy-go-lucky man and began to believe in the fantasy of Carlo being his real father – a belief that he sustained throughout his life. Roberto never gave any praise and always showed complete disinterest in any of his son's activities, saying he was either too tired or in too much of a rush to get back to work.

Possessing a very outgoing and gregarious personality, Lydia soon found the need to make her own social life, which was not always a good thing for Federico, having to accompany his mother to various hostelries. At her request he would find himself pretending to be her younger brother as various gentlemen plied her with alcoholic beverages; after which time, supporting a very drunk mother, they made their way home. He always felt obliged to stand up for her against the usually irate Roberto refusing to pay the taxi fare. Carlo, who at the time lodged with the family, often came to the rescue by placating the situation with his usual big hearted joviality; however, like Roberto, he worked the unsocial hours of the catering trade and was seldom at home. Being fully aware of the rows that ensued due to his mother's incapacity, Federico struggled to put her to bed before the return of his father.

On leaving school and much to Federico's disappointment, his father found him a job in the kitchen of 'Monaco's' Italian restaurant where both he and Carlo now found themselves employed.

The decision to move was made by the irate head chef of 'Frascati's' who, having fallen out of favour with the management, decided to moved his entire kitchen troupe – as was the custom in those days - to 'Monaco's.

Roberto completely disregarded his son's fervent request to become an electrician, saying that he could not afford to support him through his apprenticeship and if the catering trade was good enough for Carlo and himself, then *he* should be grateful to be usefully employed.

Federico's rebellious nature was to be the cause of him losing a countless number of jobs over the next few years, all of which involved the catering trade. His relentless involvement in street fights brought about Roberto's decision to move to a less violent area. The Family moved several times before finally renting a house in Lambeth where Carlo had also moved into a flat in Cranworth Gardens, Brixton and was helpful in finding them suitable accommodation nearby.

The year was 1935 when Carlo suffered a fatal pulmonary embolism at the age of fifty-four. The now twenty one year old Federico was devastated by the loss of the man he had secretly come to look upon as his father.

Deep depression overtook Roberto after the premature death of his brother, and as it also became increasingly obvious to him, due to her reliance on alcohol, he and Lydia were gradually drifting apart. Showing a great deal of disrespect for her husband, she was not a good influence on her son who adored her and for whom he would have willingly laid down his life.

Over the course of time, drink was to take its toll of what was once a beautiful young woman. Witnessing her gradual decline in health, Roberto decided to make yet another move into a house from where, Federico was to meet his future wife Gwendoline, and where, having succumbed to an aggressive form of breast cancer, Lydia would eventually lose her life.

Fedrico Giacomo Oppezzo

Federico with Uncle Carlo

1937 – NEW BEGINNINGS

Continuing to reside in the small bed-sitting room on the top floor of her mother's house, Gwendoline found herself living entirely alone for the first time in her life. Although it held dreadful memories for her, she was determined to put the past behind her, a feature of her personality developed in early childhood. She had the strong desire to prove, both to Aunty and her rather disappointed mother that she could survive, maybe not financially, but emotionally. Physically she was still recovering from the abusive treatment she had endured over the past few weeks. Nonetheless, her recovery was aided by the daily visits from dear Aunty, who, bearing gifts of food and much-needed tender loving care; came, in the hope of easing her own huge burden of guilt; feeling that she should have had the courage to forbid the relationship between her irascible, psychotic half-brother and her beloved Gwendoline before the ill-fated marriage took place.

The dismal view from the small window of the cramped bed sitting room looked out over the back-to-back gardens of neighbouring houses, separated by a seldom-used weed covered ally-way.

The garden of 22 Fairmont Road, Brixton, my grandmother Florence' house, backed onto the garden of one of the houses situated in Beachdale Road where a handsome young man, dressed only in a skimpy pair of training shorts, performed his daily exercise routine. Gwendoline was fascinated and became strangely excited as she watched him perform, what she later learnt was weight training. She was amused by his enactment of a nimble little dance whilst seemingly punching the air. He was totally unaware of his admirer, until one day Gwendoline had the idea of attracting his attention by shaking a brightly coloured duster from her window; it worked and she was delighted when he smiled and waved to her.

Having discovered the ally-way, that separated their gardens, and using it as a discreet meeting place, their relationship flourished into a passionate romance. However, the regular secret liaisons were soon discovered by Florence, who, whilst tending her garden, heard her daughter's rather loudly whispered sweet nothings being answered by the deeper sounds of a man's voice. Pulling open the aged gate that lead into the ally-way, she was both shocked and embarrassed to find her daughter wrapped in the arms of a stranger. Not knowing how to handle the situation and saying nothing, she gently closed the gate, and hurriedly went in search of Aunty.

Acting as mediator between Gwendoline and her tetchy mother, Aunty explained to Florence that maybe it would be in all their interests to bring the new relationship out into the open by inviting the young man to tea.

The rather stilted atmosphere of the first gathering, soon lead to a more relaxed mood when the subject of opera was found to be of mutually shared interest by Florence and Fred – a name by which Federico now wished to be known.

On learning that Fred's Uncle Giuseppe sang with the Lombardi Touring Opera Company and regularly undertook the role of understudy to the great Caruso, along with the distinction of gaining a recording contract with Columbia Records in America; Florence soon found herself captivated by what she had now discovered to be a charismatic young man. Over the weeks that followed, Fred entertained his newfound friends by singing arias from various Italian operas accompanied on the piano by Florence who, being very impressed by his rich tenor voice, agreed to give him professional singing lessons.

Gwendoline was eager for *real* romance and being charmed by his passionate Latin approach to courtship, she fell deeply in love with Freddy – a name she lovingly called him for a number of years.

Freddy

Learning of Gwendoline's unresolved marriage situation, Fred was under the misinformed notion that the marriage was automatically annulled once her husband had been legally sectioned and committed to the lunatic asylum; information that he imparted to Florence and Aunty whilst broaching the subject of his imminent proposal of marriage. In their naivety, they accepted his word.

When the time arrived for Gwendoline to be introduced to Fred's parents, she was both confused and disheartened whilst receiving the 'cold shoulder' from his possessive and disapproving Mother. Later when questioned about her unfriendly attitude, Lydia told her son that not only did she not like her but also didn't trust her. She went on to say that she felt her to be 'too upper crust' for her 'roughty – toughty boy'. However, Fred was adamant in that he loved her and wanted her to eventually become his wife. Not wishing to cause his now ailing mother unnecessary anxiety, together with the development of circumstances beyond their control, the marriage would not take place for a number of years.

Now living in a squalid flat in Wandsworth in the

vicinity of Battersea Power Station, where Fred had found employment, Gwendoline, undaunted by the fact that she was unmarried, was delighted when she discovered that she was two months pregnant. Richard Robert was born 22nd May 1938.

Living conditions in the flat were to prove most unsuitable for the new baby, and with the onset of winter, they decided to move back in with the non-too pleased Florence. Aunty on the other hand, was delighted, not only at having Gwendoline to care for again, but also her now four-month-old baby son. Fred was relieved to now be within easy walking distance of his parents.

Being by nature an outdoor boy, he enjoyed not only the fresh air but also the exercise of cycling to and from work each day, especially having worked long, arduous hours in the suffocating conditions of the coal fired power station.

Since the birth of her grandson Richard, Lydia's health had greatly deteriorated and Roberto was only too pleased to have his son by his side when, in the November, the breast cancer she had so courageously fought against, took her life.

I found it strange, whilst looking at old photographs, to discover one showing the large, ornate gravestone marking the last resting places of Carlo Oppezzo, Roberto's brother, who died in 1935, and Lydia Rebecca Oppezzo in 1938. The ominous space left beneath the two names would, seemingly, have indicated a future addition to the stone. One would have thought that whilst having the stone designed and erected after the death of Lydia, Roberto had chosen to leave the space for the future inclusion of his own name. However, when later stressing his wish to my father that he was to be laid to rest, when the time came, alongside his ancestors in the small cemetery in the village of his birth, Stroppiana, it became obvious that it was unlikely to have been his intension for his name to be included on the gravestone Having left sufficient funds in his will to have his last wish implemented, it was never to be. When the time did finally arrive, Fred had other plans for the money left by his father! I feel that the cemetery in West Mersea, where my Grandfather lies buried, although final, was never and could never be his final resting place.

As the threat of war became a reality, the war department issued advice to householders on the best ways to avoid injury during an air raid; people were known to sleep under the stairs or beneath a dining room table. A metal cage like construction called a Morrison shelter provided limited protection inside the house The erection of an Anderson Bomb Shelter, if there were space enough in the garden or back yard was another alternative. Fred cleared the area beneath the stairs in the cellar of number 22, where he and Aunty arranged makeshift sleeping facilities, along with a small cooking area, equipped with a Primus stove, kettle and small cooking pots. Also a stock of tinned and dried foods were stored and protected against dampness and infestation in an old metal trunk.

Not waiting for his call up papers, Fred signed up voluntarily to serve in the army. At that time, most recruitment processes were very much hit and miss; there mainly being no given method to the selection procedure, people, in particular those with a trade, were often being allocated to the wrong or unsuitable corps. Fred, earnestly wishing to be selected to join a unit offering training in electronics or engineering, was sickened when he found himself once again thrown into catering. It must surely have been as a result of the information he unwittingly gave during his preliminary recruitment interview, showing evidence of his having worked in the catering trade.

During the initial enlistment training period, the experience of which, many men found extremely arduous, Fred however, was in his element. It was during this time, having practiced amateur boxing in his teens, he became 'flyweight' favourite with his regiment. Although being of small build, he proved to be extremely strong.

I remember as a four year old being very proud as he entertained my brother and his friends with acts of great strength. One such feat was whilst holding the leg of a chair with one hand; he lifted it from the floor – with me sitting in it - and held it out at arm's length.

The Army Catering Corps didn't exist until 1941, when leading up to that time, Fred grudgingly served as a cook aboard various troop carriers. His catering skills soon become apparent whilst catering for the officers and crew in the cramped conditions of the ship's galley. Whilst serving in France, he was able to apply his innovative, practical skills by building temporary field kitchens from materials obtained from bombed out buildings. Playing an instrumental part in the rigging up of temporary showers and latrines and making derelict buildings more habitable, he was, at last, being recognised for his self-taught talents; all of which we were all to gain benefit from in the forthcoming years.

1940 - Fred found himself amongst the thousands of allied soldiers being evacuated from the beaches of Dunkirk, swimming for their lives whilst being attacked from the air by the Luftwaffe gunners of the 'Stuka' dive bombers. When, as teenagers we asked dad if he had been frightened, he told us that it was the intimidating sound of the plane's sirens as they flew in low; their machine guns strafing the land and sea with a hail of bullets, and knowing that there was nowhere to shelter. He told us that he really didn't have time to feel fear, even though, all around him, he heard the fearful cries of men being shot as they struggled toward the awaiting flotillas of small vessels which played an heroic role in what became known as 'The Miracle of Dunkirk'.

Being a strong swimmer himself, he ineffectually endeavoured to support those who either couldn't swim or were too badly injured.

Landing safely on the docks at Dover, wrapped only in a blanket provided by The Red Cross, dad told us of his embarrassment as his blanket slipped down whilst being handed a cigarette by a lady of The Salvation Army; giving him a reassuring smile, she told him not to worry as she had sons of a similar age and as his tears of pent up emotion and relief caused him even further embarrassment, she placed a comforting hand on his shoulder as she whispered "God Bless you dear boy."

1941- The formation of the Army Catering Corps at St Omer Barracks, Aldershot gave new meaning to the word catering for Fred. He was now proud to take up the training, with the added advantage of an increase in pay.

Whilst serving at Aldershot, Fred was surprised one day to find himself being summoned by his Commanding Officer, in whose office, he was equally surprised to find Gwendoline sitting with their small son playing quite happily at her feet.

Prompted by the questioning and disapproving looks aimed at him by the rather irate Commanding officer, Fred questioned her as to how and why she had found it necessary to make the long journey to Aldershot. Gwendoline began to cry as she told how she had been terrified when an incendiary bomb fell on a nearby house, killing the folk that she had known since childhood. In fear of her son's and her own life, along with the strong need to be closer to her husband; having obtained the money from her mother, she decided to travel to Aldershot in the hope of finding accommodation near to where he was stationed. She went on to tell of her fruitless search and how panic had driven her to where she now found herself.

Allowing him time to find suitable temporary quarters for his wife and child, the commanding officer gave Fred a day's compassionate leave.

Upton St Leonards, Gloucestershire was to become home for Gwendoline and her small son Richard for just over a year.

Fred, having almost completed his training, was once again aboard a troop carrier – destination unknown. It was to be somewhere along the French coastline, where his regiment joined a beleaguered platoon earnestly attempting to push back the rapid advancement of German armed forces. There had been heavy losses of men and artillery equipment.

Witnessing the desperate need for any form of sustenance, Fred, along with his comrades, endeavoured to set up a makeshift field kitchen with the intention of providing food and hot drinks for the multitude of exhausted, battle weary troops. They only had time to make hot drinks and hand out dry rations to the few, before being ordered to give assistance in manning what was left of the weaponry. Their efforts were useless as they were driven further back towards the coast. It wasn't long before what was left of the platoon, managed to board any available vessel, waiting in readiness to transport them back to various ports along the British coastline.

Fred 1939   1940 in the R.A.C.C.

THE MOVE TO MERSEA ISLAND

1943 - After the nightmare on the beaches of France, Fred was relieved to be stationed back in England at Googerat Barracks in Colchester. He soon found himself billeted on the island of Mersea, ten miles to the south of Colchester; a prosperous farming and fishing village, famous for its oysters and history of smugglers.

A great many vacant properties and holiday chalets were requisitioned by the government so as to provide accommodation for those made homeless as a result of the London bombing raids, also for the families of military personal stationed in the area. Fred helped with the setting up of the army catering facilities at Whitehaven House in Seaview Avenue.

Whilst serving on board ship he became very fond of the sea and was enchanted with this idyllic part of the Essex coastline. During his off duty he went house hunting at which time he came across a small estate of chalets surrounding a picturesque boating lake. The Goings Estate was primarily for summertime holiday makers and most unsuitable for permanent residency; however the housing shortage meant that folk were glad of just a roof over their heads. Fred managed to secure a small rather rundown chalet called 'Deudonne. Gwendolyn having spent a lonely period in Upton St Leonards Gloucestershire whilst Fred was serving overseas was only too pleased to bring her son Richard where he would be close to his father. By the December of that year, Gwendoline fell pregnant with her second child. Before my birth the family moved into 'Littlebury', another chalet on the same estate, where we were to live until dad was demobbed, around the end of 1946.

I was born in the early hours of the eleventh of August 1944 in what was then known as Colchester Public Assistance Institution, previously known as Colchester Union Workhouse and later to be renamed St Mary's Hospital.

During World War Two, an auxiliary maternity unit was set up in the antiquated institution, providing extra facilities for the growing number of military families housed in the area. The dilapidated conditions of the buildings left much to be desired. With the very low standard of hygiene, my mother became very ill after my birth, due to an infection known then as milk fever. She was put on a course of M&B tablets – the precursors to penicillin – to which she had a severe allergic reaction, causing her further suffering. However, as she told me in later years, the saving grace of the extended duration of her stay was the 'wonderful rice puddings provided by the hospital kitchen.

In the early seventies, I was unfortunate in having to do part of my nurse training at St Mary's where conditions hadn't much improved over the years. On Blaxill Ward, known then as 'the skin ward', the sound of crickets beneath the floor, calling to their loved ones, kept the majority of patients awake for most of the night. Whilst on night duty, one was usually alone for part of the night into the early hours of the morning, when the building crescendo of sound would give the dimly lit ward a very eerie feeling. Cockroaches were another pest that on many occasions put the wind up the unfortunately uninitiated, who, in search of a snack, would feel the sickening crunch under foot and hear the scuttling of many tiny feet as the light went on in the dingy ward kitchen. .

Littlebury was cold and damp during the severe winter of 1944, with only paraffin stoves and lamps for cooking, heating and lighting. There was neither electricity nor a water supply to any of the properties; the island did not yet have a gas supply. The only lavatory facilities were, to put it in local-terms, 'bucket and chuck it'.

My mother soon became very run down and was suffering from a bad bout of bronchitis, as was I. One evening it was snowing heavily and the powdery snow was blowing in under the ill-fitting door. She was in tears as she sat breast-feeding me, a blanket wrapped around us both with only the warmth of the 'Aladdin' oil stove to take the chill off the shadowy room. She was crying because she thought she had spilt her sugar ration.

To this day, the smell of fumes from a paraffin stove brings memories of my childhood flooding back; especially the memory of lying in bed in Waterside and watching the white blue flickering flame cast a dancing pattern of light through the vents in the top of the Aladdin oil heater. "A clean wick gives a good clean flame," dad used to say as he expertly shaved the blackened surface of the wick with one of his old razor blades, saved especially for the job. The smell of lighter fuel also triggers memories, when as a little girl, I would stand watching as my father dismantled his cigarette lighter, cleaning the wick and putting in a new flint, he would then top up the wadding filled chamber from the small can of lighter fuel, before reassembling the 'Zippo' lighter, given to him by an American serviceman at the end of the war. It was to become one of his most treasured possessions.

Towards the end of the winter Fred went AWOL (absent without leave) so as to look after my mother and help with us children. He spent his time attempting to make the chalet more weatherproof and draft free. He built a small field kitchen out in the yard, which he did by digging a trench in which he lit a fire; he then placed an old wire rack over the trench. In those days Smiths crisps used to be delivered to the pubs and shops in metal tins- 24 packets to a tin. Fred was able to obtain the empty tins from the NAAFI canteen at the barracks. It was one of those tins placed on its side over the fire; that acted as a makeshift oven; the lid, acting as the oven door, was held in place with a brick; further bricks and large stones, along with clods of earth, encased the three sides and top of the oven. The fire was fed with driftwood collected from the beach and surrounding area. Another tin was sunk into the ground in a shaded part of the yard, providing a very efficient cold storage, with the lid kept in place by heavy stones keeping out inquisitive animals and vermin - and it worked! Whatever we didn't have, dad would ingeniously make, he was a very resourcefully clever man; however, not clever enough to avoid getting arrested by the military police when they finally caught up with him. Expecting to serve at least fifty eight days in detention at Colchester's MCTC (Military Corrective Training Centre), more commonly known as 'the glass house', he was both relieved and surprised at the shorter sentence of twenty eight days; only to be disappointed when told that it was to be the barracks at Chatham, which turned out to be a physically harsher sentence to endure.

My brother Richard (Dick), being a very adventurous six year old, loved to play around the old boating lake with his pals. The small dinghies, having given so much pleasure before the war, had all been destroyed in the eventuality of the invading enemy using them as a means of escape! When the droning engine of an approaching Doodlebug (German V1 flying bomb) was heard, Richard would run out of the chalet so as to watch as it passed over and according to my mother, it would always be when she was bathing or feeding me. The daunting prospect of having to leave me whilst going in search of her son proved to be the cause of her having many restless nights and haunted dreams. However, her prayers for his safe return were always answered when an excited little boy, totally unaware of the reason for the tears of relief shed by his doting mother, ran in through the open door.

I must have been about two when we moved into 'Waterside', part of a five hundred year old group of cottages, reported to have been one of the oldest dwellings on the island, situated in the 'old city' area at the bottom of Coast Road. Dad had been to see Bernard Cudmore whose father Bobby owned a lot of very run-down properties, including the Cudmore family home, with a small shop taking up one of the downstairs rooms, where anything from mousetrap cheese to mousetraps could be purchased from early morning to late in the evening, seven days a week.

Bernard said that the cottage was in need of some attention, but if dad could make it habitable, it was his for a small rent. Having obtained the key, he immediately moved in and slept there so as to spend as much of his spare time putting it right.

Being a very resourceful, practical man, with the ability to turn his hand to most things, dad soon had the cottage ready for us to move into. There were bits and pieces of furniture already there and he was able to gather other necessary items from one source or another. He was always on the lookout for anything going free that could be put to good use.

Wyatt's boat sheds, Charlie Prigg's shram pile, and Waterside & Smuggler's Way.

Compared to the cramped conditions of 'Littlebury' with only the main living area and one small bedroom, 'Waterside' had the luxury of a separate kitchen with an electric cooker!;
a good sized living room with an open fireplace and amongst other pieces of shabby furniture - to my mother's delight - a

very ancient piano. The winding staircase led up to two bedrooms, one leading into the other. Every room had strangely shaped beams which were painted with a mixture of tar and black varnish and were reported to have once been old ship's timbers. I can still recall the tar like smell that pervaded the house; it wasn't an unpleasant smell, unlike the foul odour of a decaying rat corpse that occasionally used to occur after dad had laid poison under the floorboards. He then had to go round pulling up the floorboards in search of the offending remains; never finding anything, - apart from an assortment of small items that had slipped between the gaps, – but always in the hope of finding something valuable, maybe a gold doubloon or two lost by one of 'Watersides' long past resident smugglers.

The rats, which were to be our constantly unwelcome guests, were often heard scrabbling about and squeaking their protests as the occasional high, spring tide flowed in beneath the living-room floor, where it was thought to be their main place of residency.

Due to a kidney infection, my brother Dick was prescribed M&B tablets to which he suffered the same allergic reaction experienced by our mother during the period of her confinement at St Mary's Hospital at the time of my birth. A camp-bed was set up in the living-room, where the fire, having been banked up with coal dust and cinders, stayed in all night, providing him with a comparatively warm place to sleep. He remembered lying watching the young rats as they played, silhouetted against the glowing embers of the fire. He was fascinated by their seemingly harmless antics and was totally unaware of just how dangerous these creatures could be. According to my mother, my cot was not out of bounds to them either.

Large, hairy-legged spiders were also in residence and would always emerge when Nannie, my elderly grandmother, was on one of her rare visits from where she lived in London. One memorable evening she was sitting happily playing the piano, having previously attempted to tune the antiquated instrument. We were all gathered around singing when all at once she jumped up screaming as a huge ' Sidney' - a name we gave to large hairy legged spiders - ran over her foot. Dad put on a good show of gathering the offending beastie into his hanky and rushing with it to the open window knowing full well that 'Sidney' had scampered back to his dusty hiding place under the piano, awaiting the next opportunity to scare. Other scary creatures were the 'Billy Witches' or 'May Bugs' which, as their name suggests, always arrived in the month of May. These huge, brown, flying beetles seemed mostly to be active at night and being attracted to the light would fly in through the open window, where they noisily buzzed around the naked light bulb (the loud buzzing was made by their wings) and then crash in a heap to the floor, where my brave father would gather them up in a cloth and throw them back out through the window. He was the only member of the family who was not afraid of creepy crawlies, in fact very little, if anything, ever seemed to frighten him.

There was no mains water supply to any of the properties and two ramshackle privies along with a single standpipe tap, situated at the back of 'Waterside' and the adjoining 'Smuggler's Way', along with two other cottages, had to serve the residents of all four dwellings.

As a small girl I remember being very frightened of the dark and dreaded the journey round the back of the cottages to where the privies stood. I often bumped into old Nellie Prigg mumbling away to herself as she slammed the rickety door of the privy, causing the door, behind which I sat, to rattle on its rusty hinges. She often let out a cackle of laughter and went into a spasm of coughing as she sat in the darkness of her cubicle, sucking on her clay pipe. She once told my mother, "Good ol baccy smoke is the best cure fer the stink yer a makin".

Dad used to say that she wasn't the full shilling.

The Privies

Having performed the quickest pee I could, I made a hasty escape, leaving the door swinging on its hinges. As I ran across the yard, I often saw Charlie, Nellie's husband, at the window of their cottage. It was one of those rare occasions when one would see him without his cap and false teeth; the dim light cast by the flame of a flickering candle, gave his sallow skinned, gaunt face, framed by wisps of unkempt hair, a ghostly appearance as he peered into an old piece of mirror propped up against the grimy window; the blade of his cut-throat razor glinting as he performed his evening ablutions, in preparation of attending the local council meeting on which he served as a councillor. Whenever I see 'Mr Punch', I always think of Charlie, for without his teeth, the tip of his large nose used to nearly touch his protruding, badly shaven chin. However, when he was out and about, he always looked the true country gent; his tweed jacket covering a non-too clean stiff collared shirt and a rather grubby tie; his cavalry twill trouser bottoms just touching heavy duty brogues or tucked into Wellington boots when he was bagging and weighing up the shram (*). On the other hand I don't ever remember seeing Nellie in anything other than her sackcloth apron, tied round her waist, covering various hand-me-down, ill fitting dresses, over which she wore an assortment of shabby, dirty cardigans, with holes showing her grubby, cornified elbows. Wellington boots with thick lisle stockings folded over the tops almost completed her wardrobe. In the winter a grimy flat cap covered her nicotine stained hair, which she always wore with its long plaits wound round her ears. A button-less ex-army overcoat tied at the waist by a thin length of rope kept out the chill of winter. It was more than likely that Charlie had been issued with the so named 'greatcoat' whilst serving during the First World War.

"Et wor too bloody long fer us, so I het to cut the bottom orf," she explained when my mother asked why the bottom of the coat was so frayed, "doo I heda ended up on me arse," she always let out a mischievous cackle knowing my mother's dislike of bad language.

She was never without the small battered satchel that hung across her shoulder. One day, her curiosity getting the better of her, my mother plucked up the courage to ask, "Nellie dear you're never without your little bag, what have you got in it that is so precious to you?"

"As got me bacca n me pipe n a bit a ol plug," she chortled, "an I hev to keep me bit a cash out o his sight cos he ont let me hev me own money, mean ol buggar," her tone usually became harsh when she spoke of her husband. "Mind yeu, the Cudmas olus let me hev things on tick when I needs it." Her hen like cackle never ceased to amuse my mother.

Leaning against the door of his prized possession and having finished the bagging up, Charlie would then light up his pipe and watch as poor Nellie struggled to load the heavy sacks into the back of the cumbersome old 'Dodge Shooting Brake'. Clambering in beside the two scruffy mongrel dogs, she lit up her clay pipe as she settled herself in readiness for the delivery journey to the local farms, or even further afield, into Colchester on market days. She never travelled in the front, that seat was reserved for a large basket of ducks and hens eggs, whereas she was always seen bobbing along in the back, swaying from side to side so as to avoid the lifeless ducks and cockerels hanging by their necks from pieces of string threaded through the broom-handle which extended across the interior of the vehicle. It was said that she used to pee into an empty tin can and empty it out of the window as they were going along. Locals knew better than to get too close whilst following behind on their bikes; there were stories of a few near misses!

(*)Sham (chicken grit made from crushed oyster shells) was made by feeding the shells into an antiquated crusher that looked a bit like a much larger version of the old-fashioned 'Spong' meat grinder that clamped onto the kitchen table.

My mother was doing the daily water collection at the standpipe tap when Nellie approached carrying a lifeless chicken by its wing.

"Aw I hent arf glad to see yeu missus," she squawked, "is fred about?"

"Why Nellie dear, what on earth is the matter?" she always addressed her as 'Nellie dear'. "No he's at work and I'm not expecting him back until about six." As she said this the partly plucked bird showed signs of life as it began to flap its other wing; this upset my soft hearted mother. "For goodness sake Nellie dear, the poor thing is still alive."

"Aw I can't git et to die, at keeps a cumin round an Charlie'll be right riled if et hint ready fer is tea."

"But Nellie dear you've killed and prepared hundreds of chickens in your time."

"Not with a thumb like this un I hent," she squawked holding up a very swollen thumb, "I spose I'll jest hev to take an axe to the bloody thing," she continued calling over her shoulder as she walked back to her cottage.

Many such encounters took place at the standpipe tap.

"I really think she is a very lonely soul and watches out for me," I overheard mum telling dad that evening. "She always seems to have some excuse to come out whilst I'm at the tap."

One evening, dad had just arrived home from work and mum was dishing up our supper when there was a loud knock on the door.

"Is yer ol man about missus?" Charlie Prigg stood in the doorway. "Ass Nellie, I think the ol gal hes snuffed it," he said looking very worried. "Can yeu come round cos I don't rightly know what to do," he said as dad appeared from the sitting room.

"The old girl has had her own back on the mean old so and so," dad said when he got back. "She wasn't dead at all; I thought she *was* when I saw her laying there like a corpse and then she sat up and let out her usual cackle. Charlie nearly jumped out of his skin; it gave me a scare too. When she had finished cackling, she told him that she wanted to teach him a lesson after she overheard him telling his 'posh ol council mates' that she was his maid servant."

Dad went on to tell us how she was wearing something resembling a nightdress and having whitened her face with flour, had smudged soot round her eyes.

"What was it like in there?" my mother asked.

"Couldn't see a lot; the only light was from the candle Charlie was carrying; there's no floor boards downstairs and the smell was really bad," dad said as he filled the enamel washing bowl with hot water from the kettle and scrubbed his hands with carbolic soap. "I can't imagine how they survive in such conditions."

One afternoon it was pouring with rain and my brother and his pals were all recklessly playing in the tumbledown end of 'Smuggler's way; I say reckless because the staircase leading up to where they made their hideout was very rickety and they had to pick their way over the rotting floorboards upstairs. Mum had sent me to call Dick in for dinner when I heard Nellie shouting at them all. "Come outa there yeu little buggers, as dangerous, at'l collapse on yer one day. Gew an git yer mother gal," she said, spotting me.

"Dick you come down here at once, you know you're not allowed up there," my mother called out when she saw the boys mischievous faces looking out from where there once had been a window frame.

"They gits up thar t smoke," Nellie said sniffing the air.

"Oh Nellie don't let Fred hear you say that, please," my mother pleaded, "he'll give him a thrashing if he finds his little jar of saved dog-ends empty again. Dad always saved his dog-ends in a small brass topped glass jar, in readiness for when he ran out of tobacco; a trick he learnt whilst serving in the army.

I wanted t see yeu anyway missus, she said holding on to her swollen cheek. "yeu got anythen fer a tooth ache cos as a killen me?"
Hearing this I was surprised because she showed no sign of having any teeth in her dottle stained mouth. Us kids used to call her 'gummy nellie' and 'liquorice gob' amongst other unkind names.

"Come round to the cottage, I've got just the thing for that Nellie dear."

"How can a few bits o old stick help wi this ere pain I'm a suffrin?" she squawked as she closely examined the cloves.mum handed her. "I hint a one fer all this ere fancy stuff, I'll jest hev t git Charlie t git out the pliers like he hes fer all the rest on em"

"No sense, no feeling, poor old dear," dad said when mum told him the story.

On another occasion, I was with mum at the tap when she was washing some fish which Bernard's brother Jack, who was one of the local fishermen, had given her. As usual, Nellie, having spied my mother, trundled towards her gnawing on a piece of 'plug' – chewing tobacco.

"What yeu got thar missus?" brown spittle oozing from the corners of her mouth as she spoke.

"Some nice fresh skate wings for our tea Nellie dear."

"Aw my Charlie ont eat that ol skate, e reckons the ooks git caught in his gums."

"But the hooks come away when you skin it."

"I hent got time fer all that thar fancy cooken, he ont preciate et anyways."

"Fred would always skin it for you in return for a few eggs." Mum was becoming increasingly crafty, a trait she picked up from dad.

"At'll take more n skinnen a bit of ol fish to git im ter part wi anythen mean ol bugger wouldn't gi yer the drippins from is big ol snout."

Although being dismayed by her bad language, my mother always spoke of Nellie as 'a kindly soul, if a little unconventional at times.' Dad said that she suffered from, what was locally termed, 'Mersea madness' due to inbreeding.

He later quoted this to Clem Smith, a 'born and bred' islander who was known to complain about 'all these ere fureners a cumin to the island', to which dad added that if it wasn't for the introduction of new blood there would have been even more cases of the so called 'Mersea madness'.

In those days there certainly appeared to be more, dare I say — with tongue in cheek — eccentric characters on the island? Transport being what it was, many of the locals, more especially in later years, the elderly, rarely left the island.

Nellie

Charlie Prigg

56

THE PAINFUL TRUTH

It was to be one of those rare moments in time which had the effect of galvanising, with full impact, its impression on the immature mind of a child; the initiation of a novice.

I was four and Paul was just over three. We were playing in one of 'Admiral' Bill Wyatt's boat-sheds, which lay along the shoreline just in front of his boat-building workshop. Although we weren't supposed too, we often played there when it was bad weather; it was worth risking the ticking off we usually got from the old admiral, if and when we were caught.

There was just enough space for us to scramble under the sea damaged door into the murky dampness, where we climbed into a dingy where, in the half light, we became pirates of the high seas. Sometimes we planned to run away and live happily ever after on 'The Ray'. Today was to be the last time we would visit our refuge. We hadn't been there long when I heard my mother's impatient call.

"What were you doing in there?"she asked as I struggled out from beneath the door "You know I have to go to work," she was plainly angry, "who was in there with you?" she asked lifting me into my little seat on the back of her bicycle.

"Paul Baker" I replied a little gingerly; she didn't like me playing with 'the Bakers'.

Paul and Valerie Baker used to come down from London's East End during the school holidays to visit with their grandparents Ma and Pa Miles who lived in the cottage next door to Nellie and Charlie Prigg. Having been bombed out of their home during the London Blitz, they were among the lucky few to be evacuated into vacant properties along the Essex coastline, which included Mersea Island.

Valerie, Paul's sister, was five years older than him and was a very pretty girl, with the fine bone structure of her mother Rene and the raven black hair of her father George. Paul was a little blonde rebel of a boy and didn't change much over the years. Rene and Valerie were always immaculately dressed in their London clothes. I remember watching them as they walked down Coast Road towards 'Waterside', having just got off the bus at the 'Yacht Club. I always stood looking out of my bedroom window where I excitedly awaited their arrival. The first thing to impress me was Rene's very finely plucked eyebrows and heavily made up face, which always looked very stern and unapproachable as she teetered along on very high heels. George was short and stocky and not particularly good looking but he was always smiling and he and my dad were good friends. Mum didn't particularly like the family as she thought them to be 'brash and common' and used a lot of what she termed 'lavatorial language'.

Looking back I think my mother could have been a little envious of Rene's ever changing wardrobe; whereas, *she* always had to make do and mend as money was very short. She never looked shabby and with her lovely dark hair, dancing brown eyes and flawless olive skin, would easily have knocked the spots off Rene, had she been able to afford the luxury of stylish clothes and shoes.

"What were you doing in there?" she asked hurriedly strapping me into my seat "You know you're not allowed in the sheds." Her voice was shrill as it always was when she was stressed.

"Paul was showing me his willy," I answered in all innocence.

Seldom did my mother show me any sign of passion, be it in anger or love and the obscure memory of that slap across my face remains like a haunting echo shouting back over the ravine dividing the then from the now. There was no message in the act, only questions. Why did she punish me for telling the truth? Was this the way it was always going to be? I couldn't have known then but this was the first of numerous punishments I would receive for endeavouring to be honest.

There were to be many unforgettable events in my life where my desire for the truth would override the nagging need to lie. My initial lesson just didn't sink in and as a result, would always end in not necessarily physical, but a far more agonizing type of pain, that which scars the mind. Maybe that sting on the cheek instilled a rebellious notion that I wasn't going to let her weaken my resolve to tell the truth at any cost.

Throughout my life the truth would inevitably *slap me in the face*

THE PRIOR SAGA

August 1950 – I had just had my sixth birthday.

Three people ambled down Coast road towards where I sat sunning myself on the doorstep of 'Waterside'. I knew we were expecting visitors because I was in my best frock, having had my face and hands washed and my hair brushed. Dad was now using my washing-water, as otherwise it would have meant another trip to the standpipe tap to refill up the water bucket. The large aluminium kettle, having been filled in readiness for making tea, sat on the primus stove, hissing out clouds of steam.

"Gwenny, I think this must be them coming now." Dad shouted as he emptied the washbasin down the drain outside.

Mum appeared, dressed in one of the only presentable summer frocks she owned. Two tortoiseshell hair slides swept her shining, black hair away from her pretty face.

"Wow! You look smashing love; we should have visitors more often," dad said slipping an arm around her slim waist.

"Aw Freddie, behave yourself, they'll be here in a minute" she giggled as she pushed his arm away. It made me feel warm inside when they showed each other affection.

I had just started school when my mother found full time employment as a delivery girl with the Colchester Co-op Bakery. In those days, the transport for various trades, was usually horse-drawn and I can remember my excitement when, during school holidays, I occasionally accompanied her on the delivery rounds. The huge shire horse, with his feathery feet, swishing tail and leather blinkered eyes, fascinated me as he trotted along, periodically tossing back his head in an attempt at retrieving the oats in the bottom of his nosebag.

Previous to that, before I started school, she managed to find part-time work as a chambermaid at The Victory Hotel further up Coast Road and also did a cleaning job for Mrs Passadora who owned a large house in Firs Chase. My mother went to work for two reasons – one vital reason was money or lack of it; the second being purely social, she loved being involved with people and enjoyed a good chat.

My father was jobless after being demobbed from the army and having made the choice to settle with the family on Mersea Island, he was unable to find full time work. It would have meant a ten-mile journey into Colchester and having no transport of his own and no spare money for the bus fare, he took on odd jobs like gardening and window cleaning and helping Ses Hewes clean chimneys.

Whilst working for the Co-op, my mother met twenty one year old John Prior. He was nine years younger than her and lived with his mother Ida and common law stepfather George Blackmore in a small semi-detached house in Priory Street, Colchester.

I gloomily watched as the Prior Family approached.

The busses from Colchester ran every half hour; the one on the hour only went as far as the bus station up in the village and the one on the half hour came down Coast Road as far as the Yacht Club. Ida would never have made it if it meant her having to walk any distance.

"Hello, you'll be little Rita." Ida was the first to speak in a falsely, supercilious manner. I was filled with horror as I thought she was going to kiss me. Wisps of greasy, grey hair, having escaped from beneath her grubby felt hat, clung to the pasty skin of her moon-like face, glistening with sweat. I was able to ward off the ensuing assault by shielding my face with my Teddy.

George quietly smiled at me as Ida rudely jerked him to one side, whilst at the same time pushing her son in my direction. He reached down to shake my hand. I still recall how his handshake felt unpleasantly clammy and weak in comparison to the rough, dry skin of my father's strong hands. Stepping forward he shook my father's outstretched hand as a beaming Gwenny introduced them.

He looked puny compared to my father and although tanned, he wasn't what one might have thought of as handsome. Like his mother, he had a very large nose accentuating the close togetherness of his watery blue eyes. He had the annoying habit of tossing his head back whilst running his fingers through a mop of greasy blond hair. I took an instant dislike to him, and his mother; I think the feelings were mutual.

I refer to them as 'the Priors' but in fact it was only John who went under that name, which was Ida's maiden name, for she had never married, and had taken the name Blackmore since George Blackmore had become her lodger. They also never married, yet her uncaring and hostile attitude towards him made one question why he had remained with her. Ida was short, stout and middle-aged. She had a large nose and small close-together eyes. Her greasy, grey hair was constantly imprisoned in a hairnet. She never left the house without donning one of her sundry collection of dishevelled felt hats. Never looking clean, her shabby clothes all appeared to be two sizes too small with her petticoat always showing beneath her skirt. Thick Lyle stockings wrinkled their way towards the down-at-heel shoes.

The visits were to become a regular event throughout the summer months. I dreaded it. My brother found any excuse to be out with his friends and resented the consequential rows that almost always ensued after their departure.

If the tide was up, dad took my brother and me swimming. My mother hated the water and stayed to keep the Priors happy and prepare the tea. John was no swimmer and preferred the company of my mother.

During the early days of their visits, there was no obvious evidence of the start of an affair. Although by nature, a very jealous man, dad was also quite vain about his appearance and would undoubtedly have thought it highly unlikely for this 'scrawny weakling' to ever threaten, what he thought of as the ongoing love affair between himself and his doting wife. Time was to prove him wrong and he became increasingly suspicious. He told me in later years, how, on returning from one of his swims, he found my mother giggling as John was supposedly tickling her. I think Ida was well aware of what was going on. George usually slept for most of the visit, only waking up when he heard the clatter of teacups.

With dad now having found himself a job working for The Eastern Electricity Board in Colchester and with my mother now working full time, it was agreed that I would stay with Ida during the school holidays. The only nice memories of those dreaded occasions was being allowed to play with the neighbour's children, Anne and Richard Garrard; both around my age; that is, when I wasn't being hauled off to visit with Ida's relatives who never seemed very pleased to see her. She always came away in a bad mood which was invariably aimed at me. She was very heavy handed. I was made to sit on the wooden draining board whilst she gave me a wash before bed. She would grit her teeth, whilst scrubbing me so hard that it made me squirm, causing her to shout and tell me to 'sit still or you'll get a slap'. I became very frightened of her and couldn't wait for Friday nights when Dad picked me up after he had finished work. Her excuse for my bruises was that I had fallen over whilst playing rough games with the Garrard children.

"You know what kids are like, always falling over when they get together," she lied. I didn't dare tell him what really happened – the pinches and the slaps.

Johnny – as my mother called him (Uncle John to me), usually arrived home around four thirty; sometimes accompanied by my mother if the round had finished early. He was always sent out again to purchase items of food that Ida had conveniently run out of. I heard dad once say that he was tied to his mother's apron strings. I never fully understood what that meant. When I asked if I could go home with my mother, the answer was always disappointingly the same and brought on floods of tears. I instinctively knew, by the harsh look flashed my way by Ida that I would later pay dearly for my tearful request.

"Go out in the garden and play," my mother coldly ordered, "you are disturbing Uncle John, he is trying to cash up."

Watching as he emptied the leather cash bag onto the table, I was amazed by the speed at which he slid the individual coins into the palm of his hand, making little piles as he counted; it all seemed such a lot of money.

"Why do you always need to walk her to the bus?" Ida demanded "Don't you be long boy, I'll be getting the tea ready soon," she shouted as mum and Johnny left.

"You don't want to be a telling your dad that she's been here," Ida ordered, "it would only cause a row." I never understood what she meant; the only thing I could think of was that dad would be cross that mum hadn't brought me home with her.

My only joy was when dear Uncle George arrived home from work each evening. Whilst waiting for his tea, which usually involved chips, he would lift me onto his lap, and tell me stories about the East End in London where he spent his childhood. How the family holidays were always spent hop picking in Kent. When I asked about his mummy and daddy, I remember the look in his tear filled eyes as he quickly changed the subject.

"Why don't you tell the nosy little so and so," Ida piped up, "then she'll know how lucky she is to still have her mum and dad.

Lifting me from his lap, Uncle George went out into the back yard to smoke a cigarette.

"They was all bombed to bits in London during the war," she never minced her words. "He was away fighting and didn't know till he got back and saw the whole house had been flattened; even lost his wife and baby girl, so you think yer self lucky young lady. George yer egg an chips is ready mate."

I ran upstairs not wanting to look him in the face when he came back in from the yard. I thought I had made him cry by being 'a nosy little so and so.' Later I heard him creep into where I pretended to be asleep. He stroked my hair and whispered "Night night little un." I loved Uncle George.

One day, by a stroke of luck, the Garrards and me went down with German measles. I felt very poorly and Ida gave me some medicine that tasted horrible and made me gag. When dad arrived to take me home, there was a hell of a row

"You had no bloody right giving my kid any medicine without my permission" he said, comfortingly hugging me in his arms and slamming out of the door.

From then on I was left in the care of my brother, much to his annoyance. But there was always Ruthie.

The Family

Nannie, me and Dick

Nonno, me and Dick

VIRGINIA RUTH CARPENTER
'Ruthie"

Ruthie lived with her grandmother Florrie in a small cottage up 'The Lane' in what was and still is known as the 'Old City' area, just off Coast Road.

Florrie had brought seven children into the world, six girls and one boy. Stella, Ruthie's mother, was the youngest and most rebellious. She loved the good life and her good looks and frivolous nature attracted many male suitors, one of which was to be the father of her illegitimate baby. She had a tendency for head-in-the-clouds romanticism and attributed the olive skinned complexion and mop of ebony ringlets to the questionable origins of the father of her child. Depending on the listener, she would tell of "Spanish sea captains" and "Romany princes" along with a "rich Italian Count". Ruthie was never to learn the real truth. She was thirteen when it was finally revealed that the woman she had been lead to believe was her Aunty Stella, was in fact her mother.

Florrie was a devout Christian and regularly attended the meetings held in the small Assembly Hall, halfway up 'The Lane'. She was easily influenced by the prejudicial advice given by two sanctimonious, busybody spinsters who took it upon themselves to supervise the services along with all those attending.

"Only bad girls have illegitimate babies" the Brand sisters spitefully alleged. "You must send her into a convent where they know how to deal with sinners like your daughter. She must pay for her sins by having the child adopted."

Stella *was* sent away to a convent, somewhere in Kent, and having given birth to a healthy baby girl, defied the adoption agreement by smuggling her new infant out of the confines of the convent and with great difficulty, made her way back to her mother's cottage in Mersea.

At first Florrie refused to have anything to do with her new grandchild, however, Stella's older sister Gladys was able to persuade her, along with the promise that she and her husband Ed would finance the child's upbringing. They all agreed that it was best not reveal to Ruthie the true identity of her wayward mother until she was old enough to fully understand.

I was about eighteen months old when seven-year old Ruthie spotted me sitting on the doorstep of 'Waterside' nursing Mimi our pure white cat. Hearing a row going on in the cottage between my mother and father, she decided to take me for a walk over the sea wall. It was to be the first of many adventures which we were to share over the next few years.

During the school summer holidays, she usually accompanied us when dad and mum took us for a picnic over the sea wall where Ruthie helped mum to pick blackberries and if the tide was up, dad and Dick had a swim. She didn't enjoy much of a family life and liked nothing better than to join in with the fun which dad always created around him. Gypsy our small mongrel dog always managed to get trapped down a rabbit burrow whilst in hot pursuit of baby rabbits; dad would then send Dick and Ruthie back to the cottage for a spade so as to dig out our pitifully yelping dog.

Forming a circle around Ruthie, the 'captain' of our gang, we all sat spellbound as she told seafaring stories of pirates, smugglers and mermaids. She loved an audience and thoroughly enjoyed seeing the look of anticipated wonderment on our upturned faces. Sometimes she entertained us by playing her mouth organ and singing the rude shanty songs taught to her by Uncle Ed when he'd imbibed in too much rum. Florrie often caught her in the act and chastised her for her use of 'un-Christian profanities', ordering her back to the cottage. She always escaped soon after.

Ruthie had the most inventive imagination that was put to good use in later years, when she entertained a captive audience in the local pubs by telling many of her short stories and anecdotes along with a great many of her poems and songs of Mersea, 'her beloved island'

We enjoyed a 'Swallows & Amazons' type of existence. There were times when, having borrowed Uncle Ed's large skiff (dinghy), she would row us all over to the 'Ray', (the small uninhabited island just off Mersea). Sid Mussett, one of Ruthie's cousins, sometimes rigged up a makeshift mast and on one occasion got a hiding for making a sail out of his mother's best tablecloth.

Once there, we were all given jobs to do, one of which was to collect twigs and bits of driftwood in readiness for lighting a fire on the small stretch of sandy beach. We knew better than to light a fire further on land as there had been destructive fires caused by picnickers in the past. Ruthie never let any of us use her small, very sharp penknife to gut the small fish, which the boys had caught as we made our way over to the island; that was her job. My job was to thread a thin stick, sharpened at one end, from head to tail of each fish, which was then held over the fire by one of the older girls. The deliciously smoky flavour and aroma remains in my memory to this day.

The outgoing tide meant a hasty retreat, or we would have been marooned for ten or eleven hours, depending on the level of the next incoming tide. It *was* possible at low tide to reach the 'Strood' – the road separating Mersea from the mainland – but it meant the hazardous task of jumping the creeks; an undertaking Ruthie was well capable of herself, but was unwilling to risk it whilst having to carry me. She knew that I was terrified of getting stuck in the foul smelling, sucking mud.

Most of Ruthie's relatives were involved in the island's thriving oyster and fishing industry. She loved the sea and at an early age, became very skilled at handling a boat using oars, sail or later, an outboard motor.

She was always there for me, even into adulthood. She taught me many of the joys of childhood and will always remain 'my Ruthie'.

In 1986 I felt impelled to write this poem having spent the day with Ruthie. I stopped the car on the 'Strood' and watched as Ray Island became a deep purple silhouette against a skyline turned pink by the setting sun.

RUTH

Ruth, author of a thousand memories.
Empress of the island of lost dreams.
As I sit and look out over 'The Ray',
I remember times of joy and play,
Of romps on marshes thick with weed,
Of scrumping fruit for youthful greed.
Promises given, never to be broken,
Oaths to the leader solemnly spoken.
Sounds that always spring to mind,
Sweet sounds carried on calling wind,
The Curlew greets the sleepy dusk,
A lullaby is his sweet task.
The splash of oar on ebbing tide,
Offering all who wish a ride.
The tiny craft across the mind,
With thoughts together we shall find
Completeness of life's meanings true,
You the captain, we the crew.
Oh you the ruler of my past,
Who cared and shared in worries vast;
Hold on to memories that were also mine,
Relive them with the passing of time.

Look not on a friend and see only the flesh that covers the bone, look deeper, not with your eyes, but let your soul be your sight. Listen, not to the sound of the spoken word, but open your heart to the dulcet call of true friendship and understanding.

THE DOWNWARD SPIRAL

1952. The move from Waterside took place soon after my eighth birthday.

Ruthie took me for a walk along the sea wall where we sat looking out over at 'The Ray'. I cried; she comforted.

"Will I still be in the gang?" I asked through my tears.

"There ont be a gang no more I've got a job helping Uncle Ed bringing some of the boats in to the mud berths, ready to lay up for the winter. He reckons there'll be plenty to do, what with scraping off the barnacles and repainting the hulls," she said with a proud air to her voice. "An then thars the riggin, that all hes to be treated."

I remember feeling crestfallen. Who would be there when I needed to escape from my brother's impatient taunting and my father's aggressive mood swings if I was going to be miles away down Seaview Avenue – well it seemed like miles away.

What about the regatta next week? We always met up at the fair held in the field behind The Victory Hotel; and the fireworks, I couldn't miss the thrill of the fireworks.

Dick played the bugle in the Sea Cadet Band; I couldn't miss the proud making time of seeing my handsome brother in his smart uniform as the band led the cavalcade of colourful floats down Coast Road; and watching from my vantage point on dad's shoulders as they played 'The Last Post' at the end of the firework display.

"We can't move until the end of the month" I overheard dad telling my mother that evening. "The flat won't become empty till then."

"Slow down little un, stop a holleren," Ruthie said as I breathlessly ran past a surprised Florrie.

"Cawd I though yer legs hed caught fire gel," the unflappable Florrie said handing me a piece of her freshly made treacle toffee. "Now yuew jest set yerself down, chew on that and calm down while the gel finishes her tea." Ruthie was always 'the gel' to Florrie.

"...and I *will* be here for the Regatta after all," I excitedly finished telling her my news as we sat in our favourite spot on the sea wall.

Dick and friends in the Mersea Sea Cadets

"See them," Ruthie said pointing to the shafts of golden light as the last sliver of the setting sun slid down behind the marshes of 'The Feldy', "thas the ol sun holding on to the sky. You watch he'll stretch his fingers through them pink clouds; he never wants to goo to bed." Breaking the spell, she went on to say, "I jes knew your dad wouldn't miss this year's regatta cos Dick's a playin a bugle solo, 'The Last Post', from the balcony of The Yacht Club.

Looking back, I realise that this was the end of the most joyously contented era of my young life. Things were never to be the same.

Fairhaven House, a large, distinctive Edwardian building towards the end of Seaview Avenue, has seen many changes since it was built in 1906. It was originally known as 'Mrs Weaver's Home of Rest', and later became 'Fairhaven Boarding House. During the Second World War, the army commandeered the house along with many other properties on the island, specifically for the use of military personnel. It was later renamed Fairhaven House and was divided into three flats, offering accommodation for those waiting to be re-housed by the local council. When *we* moved there in 1952, three other families shared the house whilst awaiting the completion of several new council houses. We were lucky in having four large rooms on the first floor. The living room had a large bay window providing a clear view down the Avenue to the estuary of the River Blackwater. During a storm, we would stand and watch as lightning lit up the whole of the blue grey sky, jaggedly forking into the wind-swept waves. We were never afraid as dad told us amusing stories about the devil having a fight with his wife and the thunder was when she threw a saucepan at him.

"If you look hard enough you'll see his white horses riding the waves."

We hardly ever used the living-room in the winter as it was difficult to heat and there wasn't enough money to buy coal for the open fire. Dick and I shared the large room facing the Avenue and Nonno or Nannie slept on a camp-bed in the same room when either of them came to stay. Mum and dad's bedroom was much smaller and also had a view of the sea. The north facing kitchen was always dark and cold, winter and summer and the walls ran with condensation when any cooking or washing was taking place. However, the one good feature was its size, giving space for a dining room table and four chairs along with a battered old armchair where dad used to sit after supper. With the high ceilings, the Aladdin paraffin heater barley took the winter chill off any of the rooms.

It was early December and Nonno, my grandfather was on one of his visits, when my brother and I, on arriving home from school, found him sound asleep in the old armchair. He must have turned the Aladdin flame up too high causing it to smoke; both he and the room hung with greasy black soot. Dad said that if it had been any longer the fumes would have killed him. It took a lot of hard work and buckets of hot soapy water to clean up the mess and dad had to help Nonno clean up in the bath. Luckily we now had the luxury of a bathroom and separate toilet.

It was during the time of Nonno's visit that a telegram arrived; for some reason I hadn't gone to school that day.

"Your mother, she is dead," he told me without showing any sign of emotion; seeing my bemused look of disbelief and realizing his mistake, he quickly added, "no it is Florence, your grandmother she is dead," once again said without emotion. "She does it on purpose I think. She never like it when I come to stay."

I remember thinking as I buried my face in the old armchair cushion, how could she have died on purpose, can people die on purpose? I couldn't find tears for a woman who had always seemed distant and unfriendly.

My mother sank to the floor and cried out, making a sound like our dog Gypsy used to do when she became stuck whilst chasing a rabbit down its burrow on the sea wall. I had never seen my mother cry before.

Dad took over and quickly gave us our tea, having sent mum to lie down whilst he made the arrangements. Dick was sent to the phone box up the Avenue, where he rang Vin Thorp, who ran the local taxi service.

"You'll have to stay here and look after Nonno," dad said "we can't leave him here alone boy," he added as he saw the look of disappointment on my brother's face.

Thick freezing fog made the journey to Colchester hazardous and slow, with dad continuously having to get out of the car to clear the windscreen whilst Vin kept the engine running. North Station was eerily deserted when we eventually arrived. We sat, for what seemed to me like hours, huddled around the small open fire in the dimly lit waiting room.

"Sorry folks, the trains are all running late" the stationmaster said, shovelling more coke on the fire, "there should be one along in an hour or so," he said as he went out; the draft, causing the fire to belch out choking coke fumes as he closed the door behind him.

When the train approached the outskirts of London, the fog had turned to dense, unyielding smog.

"Cor blimey, it's a real 'pea-souper' out there," dad said wiping his gloved hand over the misted carriage window, "we'll be lucky to get across London tonight but don't worry love, we'll do our best," he said seeing the distraught look on my mother's face as he put a reassuring arm around both of us. The choking smog hung over Liverpool Street station like a dirty yellow blanket.

"There are no busses or taxies running tonight folks," porters called out as they held yellow oil lamps aloft, guiding the few disembarking passengers towards the barrier. "There is a nice fire in both waiting rooms where you can get a hot drink."

The fuggy air of the crowded waiting room was almost as bad as it was outside, but at least it was warmer. Dad led us over towards the fire where several tramps sat in all the available comfortable chairs. Spotting us, two of them gave up their seats and sat on their various bundles. I had never seen a tramp before and found myself wondering why they were so dirty and scruffy. I was fascinated by one of them who wore odd shoes, one brown and one black, both without laces. Dad told me not to stare. They were toasting chestnuts on a coal shovel balanced on the hot embers of the dwindling fire. 'Mr odd shoes' offered me a toasted nut from the end of his penknife. I wanted to take it, but looked to dad for approval. Giving me a nod, he thanked the toothless, smiling 'Mr odd shoes' who dropped the hot morsel into my gloved hand. Dad peeled it for me; it was then deliciously followed by more of the same.

I was sitting sleepily on dad's lap, when two young police constables stood looking questioningly over to where we sat. 'Mr odd shoes' murmured something unrepeatable as the others began to gather their belongings.

"Ok lads," one of the policemen said, "you don't have to move on tonight, the weather isn't fit for dogs!" This caused more disgruntled murmurings from the other tramps. "What are you all doing here?" the young officer looked very tall as he aimed the question at my dad. Having explained all, we were then invited to wait in the police station. "You'll be more comfortable up here," he said leading us up the iron staircase. "Can I make you some tea? What about you young lady, do you like eggs?" My answer was a look of sheer delight. Taking my hand he led me into a huge kitchen where breakfasts were being prepared; I say breakfast, but it felt like the middle of the night to me. Lifting me onto his shoulders for a better view of the huge frying pan full of sizzling eggs, he asked the cook to make some fried egg sandwiches.

Carrying a bottle of tomato sauce, I followed my 'prince charming' back to where mum and dad were now sitting at a table in the warm Canteen. Placing the tray of sandwiches and mugs of tea onto the scrubbed wooden table, he drew up a chair and lifted me onto his lap. I fell in love.

"Hi, I'm Constable Tim Brewster," he said shaking dad and mum by the hand as they introduced themselves. "What's your name young lady?"

"This is our daughter Margherita, named after my father's sister," dad said answering for me. "We always call her Rita for short."

"Well I like that pretty name so will you mind if I call you by your proper name?" he smiled at me over his mug of tea. He had such kind eyes.

"When do you go off duty?" Dad asked.

"I finished at midnight, but like you, I can't go anywhere."

I must have fallen asleep during the grown up conversation.

I was lying on an old leather settee in the corner of the canteen, with a heavy overcoat keeping me warm, when I was awakened by the sound of noisy chatter and laughter. Cigarette smoke hung heavily on the air. Uniformed men occupied all the tables tucking into plates of fried breakfasts and steaming mugs of tea. Tim wasn't amongst them.

It was barely daylight when we sat on the top deck of the 133 London bus bound for Steatham, calling at Brixton on the way.

"Tim said to tell you goodbye" dad said when I asked about our new policeman friend. "He has given us his address so that you can write and thank him."

Mum looked sad and weary as she laid her head on dad's shoulder.

It was around ten-o-clock and with the cold light of day the smog seemed less dense as we alighted from the bus at 'The White Horse' public house on Brixton Hill. The bomb-site at the entrance to Fairmount Road always frightened me. I had overheard my mother telling the story of the night that an incendiary bomb completely obliterated two terraced houses and how a raging fire caused severe damage to the neighbouring house. Ten people were killed that night. One surviving child was found beneath a heap of rubble, miraculously saved by an iron bed frame carrying three sleeping children from top to bottom of the disintegrating building. The badly charred bed clothes were held in place by a smouldering roof timber and brick rubble, where two of the children, looking as though still asleep, lay dead beside their surviving sibling. My mother said that one of the rescue team, when describing the scene, was heard to say that if it hadn't been for the roof timber which lay across two of the children, they would probably all have survived.

As the front door of number 22 opened, my mother fell into the arms of a very frail looking Aunty Jess, who always looked old, but today she seemed thinner and more lined. She ushered us all into the back parlour where the table was daintily set in readiness for our breakfast. Nothing seemed to have changed, the familiar aromas of boiled fish, gas, and Sloan's Liniment hung heavily in the air.

My mother tearfully asked Aunty if she could go up to see my grandmother. I was the cause of further tears when I questioningly said "But daddy you said Nannie wasn't here anymore."

Much of what happened over the next few days is a blur, however, I do recall the day when two of Nannie's music students arrived with a wreath. My mother got half way down the hall to answer the door and fainted. Thinking she too had died, I screamed and ran upstairs.

"Don't worry love, she'll be alright," dad breathlessly said as he carried her up past where I was sitting on the top stair. "Mummy just needs a little rest," he said on his return, "come on we'll go and do a bit of shopping, shall we go to the market?" He knew how I loved Brixton market where Aunty always took me when I visited during school holidays.

The wreath lay on the hall floor. It was in the shape of a music score. I was fascinated by the treble clef followed by lines of music. Nannie always signed her correspondence with a treble clef following her name.

We stayed until after the funeral, during which time I was given my mother's dolls to play with. I remember thinking how ugly and tatty they were and their peculiarly musty smell. Aunty Jess explained that the smell came from the varnished Papier Mache heads and arms, combined with the glue used to stick on the hair. Either way, I didn't take to the poor things and preferred to play with Felix the Cat who was losing some of his woody filling through a hole in the back of his hard body; not what you would call a cuddly toy, but I loved him. In an attempt at keeping me occupied, Aunty lined up all the dolls, in their now freshly laundered clothes, along with the large brown bear that she had made for my mother when she was a little girl, and of course Felix. I served them all tea and small pieces of biscuit from a miniature china tea set, also having belonged to my mother. There was also an assortment of small, aluminium cooking pots and tiny items of cutlery. Dear Aunty had treasured everything from the childhood days of her beloved Gwendoline.

My father, much to my Mother's dismay, busied himself going through all Nannie's cupboards and drawers. He finally found what he was searching for hidden behind a large picture - a great deal of money. Nannie didn't trust or believe in banks.

"I knew she would do something like that." He said, jubilantly holding up a fistful of large, white five-pound notes. "There has to be more stashed away somewhere."

"Please Fred, not now, it will upset Aunty," my mother

pleaded.

Aunty was in the scullery preparing the supper. Seeing the familiar look on my father's face and fearing that there was going to be a row, I went to help her.

Tiger, Aunty's large tabby cat, sat expectantly on the chair beside the cooker, I knew better than to stroke him, having learnt a previous painful lesson from his well aimed needle clad paw. He always seemed to be scowling and would let out a deep growl of disapproval if you got too close. His only love was Aunty; she could do anything with him.

It was our last evening, and dad was cooking the steaks that he had purchased from the horsemeat stall on Brixton market. I can still recall the sickly sweet smell as he fried the meat. I hasten to add, Aunty and I had a fried egg each; her poor digestion couldn't cope with the rather rich meat and I was put off by the thought of eating a horse.

During supper, dad brought up the subject of letting part of the house out as flats as it would be too big for Aunty to cope with. He suggested that he and his friend George Baker, who was a plumber by trade, could do most of the work themselves.

"Does that mean that Valerie and Paul can come and play?" I excitedly interrupted.

I knew the answer by the look of disapproval my mother shot in my direction and by dad going on to say, "I can meet George here, he's only got to come from The Oval; we could get the job done in a weekend," seeing my look of disappointment he went on to say, "they'll probably be visiting Ma and Pa Miles in Mersea so you'll be able to see them there."

The Bakers came down most weekends if the weather was fine, however, I knew I wouldn't be able to see them anymore as it was too far to walk from where we now lived in Seaview Avenue, but I knew better than to argue with my father

It was early spring when dad and George were able to make a start on what became a longer job than was first expected. A friend that George had met through the building trade was an electrician and was brought in to lay on an electrical supply; there only ever having been gas for lighting, cooking and heating the water.

Aunty was thrilled with the idea of not having to 'fiddle about changing crumbly gas mantles' and having instant light at the flick of a switch, "I shan't know myself I'll be so posh."

On the ground floor one of the two adjoining rooms, at the front, became a bed-sit. The separating double doors of the back room, against which stood a heavy oak chest, were firmly locked; this was to be Aunty's bedroom, which I was to share when I came to stay.

The two rooms were originally used by Nannie, as music rooms; the front room, which was always kept locked, had a luxurious 'Wilton' carpet and was – to quote Nannie – 'out of bounds to 'children and tradesmen' A Steinway baby grand piano, stood in front of the tall casement windows exhibiting its highly polished magnificence. Matching the blues and greys of the carpet, a large three-piece suite, upholstered in uncut moquette, offered seating for Nannie's 'special guests'.

In stark contrast to the opulence of the adjoining room, the only furniture in the parquet floored back room, was an elaborate double-seated piano stool, where Nannie sat beside one of her many students whilst they practiced on the 'Steck' upright piano. We were given permission to play the austere looking instrument, having first been ordered by our strict grandmother to "Thoroughly scrub your sticky fingers." Dad loved nothing better than to hammer out Boogie Woogie; his foot permanently on the loud pedal. Both he and my mother only played by ear and this always infuriated Nannie. When my mother was a little girl, her mother, being a professional musician, tried giving her piano lessons; and with elevated expectations of her young daughter, she soon became impatient with the 'impetuous child' always wanting to rush ahead; not concentrating on practicing the scales or learning to read music. Whilst Nannie was out teaching, Aunty sat beside the young Gwendoline whilst she endeavoured to play simple tunes.

This was the first time I had entered the mysterious

front room. It was like another world, my bare feet sinking into the thick pile of the carpet and feeling swamped as I clambered into the largeness of the sofa, my feet barely reaching the front of the seat. In the corner of the room stood a strange wooden contraption that for some reason reminded me of a frog. I was later to learn that it was 3D slide viewer. I had to stand on a pile of books, thus enabling me to peer into the binocular like eyepieces. A slide had been left in and I was amazed by what I saw, a picture of camels looking as though I could reach out and touch them. I found a lot more slides in a wooden box standing beside the viewer; I soon found out how to change them.

"*Here* you are," Aunty said with a chuckle "come on love your tea is ready." She had a job prising me away from my newfound plaything that I named 'Frog'. I later learned why, when spotting that I had been rifling through the slides, she hastily replaced the strewn contents back into the box and put it on a high shelf of the bookcase.

"Wow! Some of those slides are a bit suggestive, loads of pictures of naked women in all different poses," I heard dad tell mum that evening.

"Why, what do you mean suggestive," she asked, looking worriedly in my direction. "Aw Fred, careful what you say, we don't want to give the child the wrong impression; after all it's only a form of art."

"Oh is that what you call it," dad said with a chuckle.
I didn't see any naked women and the camels all had their fur coats on.

The furniture from the front room was eventually moved down to Mersea where it was stored in the sparsely furnished front room of Fairhaven House along with the upright piano. Much to my mother's sorrow, the Baby Grand had to be sold as transporting it would have cost too much, and besides, getting it up the stairs leading up to our flat would have proved impossible.

Mr Wilkinson, a retired, elderly bachelor moved into the now empty front room, bringing with him his own furniture. The only time he found it necessary to use the scullery, which he shared with aunty, was when he made marmalade or needed to boil a joint of bacon. The rest of the time he used a gas ring in his room.

"He's such a quiet gentleman, one would hardly know he was there, Aunty told me when I was on one of my visits. "I never see him using the sink to do his washing up; I think he creeps in when I've gone to bed. I know he has a younger sister who lives in Norwood, she probably does his bits and pieces of washing." Aunty was quite deaf and probably wouldn't have heard him.

I wondered what he did when he needed to use the toilet. Apart from the one upstairs, there was an outside privy which had to be flushed with a bucket of water from the rain-but, a job that Aunty always did last thing in the evening. I remember sitting on the wooden bench-like seat hoping that the spiders wouldn't come down from their webs in the roof and 'bite you on the bum' as dad used to say when I had sat there too long. I hated having to use the newspaper squares which aunty threaded on a piece of string where they hung from a hook on the door. I couldn't imagine Mr Wilkinson using the privy; he must have crept upstairs to where the 'Izal' toilet roll had a nice disinfectant smell, even if it was more scratchy than The Daily Mirror!

During the following summer a small parcel arrived at Fairhaven House, it was addressed to me. Mrs Sibley, a rather austere widow, lived in one of the two flats on the ground floor with her three children, Margaret, Sheila and Oswald. She kept herself to herself, apart from when she came out to complain about the noise we made running up and down the bare wooden staircase. Her children were never allowed to come out to play; anyway, like their old fashioned mother, they were all a bit strange and very shy. Oswald had webbed fingers and when my brother saw this he told me that they were all from another planet, like the characters in his favourite comic, 'The Eagle'.

"Don't make a habit of this," she said as she

disapprovingly handed me my parcel, "I'm not here to fetch and carry for your family."

I had never received anything by post, not even a birthday card and was so excited I ran upstairs without saying thank you.

"Rude, noisy child" she shouted after me.

Hastily unwrapping the parcel a small card announced that it was from Tim, our policeman friend and his new wife Beverly. I opened the box to find a piece of iced cake nestled in lacy paper; a small silver horseshoe lay beside it. Puzzled by the smallness of the cake, mum explained to me later that it was just a keepsake, sent to all those unable to attend the wedding. I was impatient to eat the sugary icing and allowed the rest of the family to share, what I thought was, burnt fruitcake. Tim had been living in the upstairs flat at Fairmount Road since dad had informed him that it was ready to rent. He religiously spent most of his off duty decorating and furnishing the flat prior to his wedding.

The school holidays were nearing an end when a letter arrived, requesting my parent's permission for me to stay with Tim and his new wife Beverly for the weekend.

It was Saturday morning and dad was able to accompany me to where I was to catch the eleven fifteen train from North Station in Colchester.

"Now you behave yourself on the train" dad ordered as he closed the door of the 'Ladies only' compartment. "Tim will meet you at Liverpool Street."

The whistle blew and as the train slowly moved, dad ran along the platform waving and blowing me kisses until he disappeared into a cloud of smoky steam. My initial feelings of nervousness were soon washed away by waves of excitement. I felt quite grown up until asked by an elderly lady traveller how old I was.

"I'm nine now." I replied trying to sit taller in my seat.

"You shouldn't be travelling alone at your age," she said, giving me a disapproving look over the top of her glasses; reminding me of the way my grandmother Florence used to look, when she caught me misbehaving.

"Oh I'm quite safe; a policeman is meeting me off the train at Liverpool Street Station."

Her look of alarm triggered by the shock of my statement rendered her speechless for the rest of the journey. I didn't care. I became lost in a peppermint-flavoured reverie of thoughts as I delved into the bag of mint humbugs, a parting gift from dad.

I thought of how jealous I had felt when I was told that I couldn't join my brother and his friend Roger Sheldrake when they went up to London to watch the Queen's Coronation procession. But now, here I was, travelling all alone on the train to the big city where I was going to be met by my prince charming.

The smoky hot breath of the engine momentarily blotted out my view as the changing scenery speedily passed by the dirty carriage widow.

This was to be the beginning of my ongoing romance with travelling by steam train. I loved the clickety-clack of the wheels over the jointed track; the sound of the powerful engine puffing its way out of the station as it noisily gathered speed; the whistle announcing its presence on the line, and the familiar smell of the combination of coal smoke and steam.

Tim, having purchased a platform ticket, walked slowly along, peering into each carriage; his look of concern changed into a huge smile as he spotted me leaning out of my compartment window. I felt a pang of disappointment when I saw that he was not in uniform, but that soon disappeared when throwing open the door, he gave me a kiss as he lifted me from the train.

"Are you the policeman this young lady said was coming to meet her?" my travelling companion rather mockingly queried as he reached in for my case.

"Off duty today madam," he replied as he gentlemanly helped her with her luggage.

I remember giving her a 'cheeky little girl grin' of smugness as she strode past.

"Beverly is at work but she will be there this afternoon, he said as though reading my thoughts. "Are you hungry little un?" he seemed a long way up as I smiled and nodded my reply. "Fancy an egg sandwich? I remember that was your favourite!" He grabbed my hand as we mounted the familiar iron staircase to the police canteen.

"Have you ever heard of Sweeny Todd the barber?" he asked as we finished our sandwiches.

We sat on the top deck of the big, red London bus, making its way to Fleet Street, as he told me the gruesome story.

"You mustn't worry, it's only a story," he said when he saw the look of shock on my face. I dimly remember him pointing out a barber shop with a pie shop on the opposite side of the road. I don't think it would have occurred to Tim that it wasn't a suitable story to tell a nine year old girl. Beverly told him so when we arrived back. However the cream cakes Tim bought for tea soon had her smiling as she laid the table.

Beverly was training to be a nurse at St Thomas' Hospital and thought it would be a nice treat to take me on the tube to Westminster the following day, so as to show me Big Ben, near to where she worked. We then sat by the River Thames and enjoyed a pick-nick lunch, followed by a walk to St James's Park where Tim bought us all ice-creams.

By late afternoon I was sad to be waving them goodbye; Beverly blew me kisses and Tim, with his arm round her shoulder, gave me a huge grin as my train slowly started to move.

THE MOVE TO WINDSOR ROAD

The downward spiral of life changing events continued when I changed schools; the reason for which I am unsure. My brother, now having left school, had started his apprenticeship at MG Electrics, in Colchester, next door to the 'Regal' cinema in Crouch Street. I missed my big brother protecting me from the bullying older boys. I suppose it was one of the reasons why it was decided to move me from the school at West Mersea to the Roman Catholic school of St Thomas More, Priory Street in Colchester.

The teachers were all Nuns from the order of The Sisters of Mercy, some of whom should have gone under the title. 'unmerciful sisters' There was one in particular, Sister Dominic, who taught needlework and took sadistic pleasure when she regularly rapped us over the knuckles with a ruler; her bushy eyebrows almost meeting in the middle with a frown of condemnation and her thin lips pursed, as though she had just sucked on a lemon, as we were made to 'unpick that shoddy work'. On the other hand, Sister Anthony, the head teacher, was among my favourites. Calling me to her office one day, she asked if I had been baptized; I didn't know. She went on to say that if I wanted to join the other girls in taking First Holy Communion, then I would have to show evidence in the form of a Certificate of Baptism. Neither of my parents was in the least bit interested in religion and I was dismayed when the answer to my question was "No".

"Don't you be worrying yourself, we'll soon put that right," her gentle Irish accent endeavouring to reassure me when she saw how upset I was.

"I'll arrange it with Father O'Donnal. Is your mummy

able to come one morning next week?"

"No, they told me that if that's what I wanted to do I would have to do it on my own as they both have to work and can't afford to take time off."

She looked sad when she told me that I would need a signed note saying that they were in agreement to my Baptism and First Holy Communion Ceremony.

It was a lonely affair. Sister Anthony asked two dinner ladies to act as witnesses and she held my hand whilst Father O'Donnal, after saying a few prayers, made the sign of the cross on my forehead with holy water.

"There now, your soul is a white as snow. You must be very good and not be committing any sins." She said as we walked from the church. I felt so happy and couldn't wait for next week. "You'll be needing a white dress and veil."

"When do you think I'm going to have time to get these things?" my mother said that evening when I told her what I was going to need, "and where do you think the money is coming from may I ask?"

"She'll only need a new dress Gwenny," my father told her, "I'm sure your Johnny will manage for a couple of hours while you take her shopping," there was a sarcastic tone in his voice, .but the look of anger in his eyes softened as he lead me upstairs. Pulling a parcel from the cupboard of the tallboy that stood in their bedroom, he un-wrapped the tiny, delicate garments and laid them out on the bed. Handing me the fine lace shawl, he told me the story of how the complete Christening Layette had been a present from the young actress Edith Evans.

Edith Evans heard of my father's birth from Roberto, my grandfather, who worked as a chef at Monaco's Italian restaurant, where she and a group of her theatrical friends regularly enjoyed an after-show supper. Heavily pregnant, my grandmother Lydia often sat in the entrance lounge waiting for Roberto to finish his shift. Miss Evans spotted her one evening and guessing who she was, invited her to join them, along with other regular customers, all waiting to be serenaded by

Roberto, who, having finished his kitchen duties, climbed the stairs to the minstrel gallery where he sang arias from popular Italian operas.

The church hall rang with the excited voices of mothers pulling up white socks and giving last minute adjustments to dresses and veils. It didn't occur to me that my mummy wasn't there to help me. I felt proud as I had Sister Anthony paying me special attention.

"Nobody will have such a beautiful veil, God Bless you child," she said putting in the final hairclip.

The church was full and as I walked up the isle hand in hand with my friend Eileen Reidy, a lady reached out to touch my veil. In my innocence, I wished that I had a new one like all the other girls

First Holy Communion.

The Christening Layette has remained in my possession since the death of my father. I now realize what a privilege it was to wear the beautiful lace shawl that was also worn by my father as a baby, when he received his special blessing over a hundred years ago.

I was a devout little Roman Catholic and regularly went to confession before attending the Sunday morning Mass which was held in the bar of the British Legion Hall as there was no Roman Catholic Church in Mersea. The only incense accompaniment was the stale smell of cigarettes and the lingering odour of Saturday night's beer. I was alone in my religious pursuits, as would usually prove to be the case with the majority of notable events that took place throughout my life.

With both parents being only children, my brother and I knew of no other relatives in this country For some unknown reason, my father never kept in contact with his mother's side of the family The only Italian family member that was known to us was my father's Cousin Giachino Barbonaglia. I first met his mother, Zia (Aunt) Margherita - after whom I was named - and the remaining family when I was to accompany my father to Italy in 1971 where we were to attend the funeral of Giachino, whose unexpectedly sudden death at the age of sixty, was caused by a severe brain haemorrhage – a condition commonly suffered mainly by the male members of the family.

Due to an airport strike in England, our journey took longer than was anticipated. We arrived a day too late to attend the funeral.

Drastic changes took place when we finally moved into 19 Windsor Road. I recall standing alone in the spacious kitchen and jumping up and down with the excited realization that I was now into double figures; ten years old no less. And then feeling very alone; mum, dad and Dick were all at work. The postman had been and gone, there were no cards just a brown envelope addressed to Mr F G Oppezzo. I was still quite in awe of the spacious newness as I went from room to room. The carpet and furniture that had once looked resplendent in Nannie's front room, now looked rather drab and old fashioned in the bright sunlight shining through the curtain less, picture window of the sitting room. I opened the piano lid and perched on the piano stool, just able to reach the floor with my toes. The notes rang out discordantly as I touched the keys, endeavouring to pick out the tune to 'Happy Birthday'. I so wanted to be able to play.

"Happy Birthday to me," I sang, running up the bare wooden staircase, "happy birthday to me," I continued to sing as I opened the door to mum and dad's bedroom. The springs of the iron bedstead creaked as I jumped onto the lumpy mattress. Peering through the iron work at the foot of the bed and looking at my reflection in the mirror of the dressing table, also having once belonged to Nannie, I tearfully ended my song, "happy birthday dear Rita, happy birthday to you." Wiping my tears on my sleeve, I walked into the box room; a small bed stood against the wall where I had lined up my collection of dolls; Teddy lay on my pillow waiting for bedtime. The rest of my toys were still in cardboard boxes, there being nowhere else to put them. An orange box, covered with a cloth, acted as a bedside table on which stood an alabaster statue of Jesus, given to me by Sister Anthony, in commemoration of my First Holy Communion. There also stood three small luminous statues of Jesus, Mary and Joseph purchased from the convent. After school each week I called at the side door and handed over my shilling – two week's pocket money - and was rewarded with one of the statues wrapped in tissue paper. I soon had the full set and went on to save a further shilling for a small wooden Rosary.

I had never had a bedroom of my own, always having to share with my brother, who also now had his own room. The first few nights I found it difficult to sleep and trying hard not to wake him, I slid in beside him, he grumpily told me to clear off back to my own room. One night I did manage to creep in without disturbing him and wrapped in my eiderdown, slept on the floor beside his bed.

"What the hell are you doing down there?" he was

angry as he nearly stepped on me in the morning. "If you don't stop being so daft I'm gonna tell dad."

"But I'm frightened."

"What of?"

"The dark."

"You've always slept in the dark."

"Yes but you were always there with me."

Dad must have overheard our conversation because from then on I had the little oil filled nightlight, also having belonged to Nannie, giving a reassuringly warm glow from where it stood on my makeshift beside table. But I was still a bit scared and either my brother or dad had to look under my bed each night before I agreed to get into it.

One evening Dick was out with his pals and mum and dad had been invited to visit Bob and Frances Brewis who lived next door.

"You'll be fine" dad said as he tucked me in, "we'll only be next door and teddy will look after you" He must have seen the unspoken look of anxiety on my face. "I'll leave the landing light on."

I heard the back door slam shut and my mother's laughter as they walked down the path. The house was suddenly quiet; I had never been alone at night before. Teddy had never been squeezed so tightly as I imagined a burglar creeping up the stairs.

"I've got my pet lion here," I said letting out a loud growl, "grrr, he'll eat you if you come in my room." Letting out a few more growls, I must have fallen asleep. I was awoken by footsteps on the stairs, suddenly remembering that I was alone, I let out another loud growl and then a frightened yelp as the shadow of a figure, cast by the light on the landing, loomed as my bedroom door swung open. I pulled the covers up over my head and clung to teddy. "Where are mum and dad?" My big brother once again comes to my rescue.

It was Saturday and mum was at work; she worked half day on Saturdays. We had just sat down for breakfast when the clatter of the letterbox signalled the arrival of the morning post. "Go and get that love, it's probably only a bill," dad said, lifting the eggs from the steaming saucepan. "First eggs from our own hens, yer mum'll have to have hers when she gets home from work later." I loved boiled eggs; dad always drew a smiley face on mine and cut my bread into 'dippy soldiers'.

Having scanned the page of the letter, dad's light hearted mood changed "Nonno is ill." Taking the letter from him, my brother read it aloud.

" '.......I write to inform you that your father is very ill and as his landlord I cannot take responsibility for the necessary ongoing care of my tenant. I would be grateful if you could give this matter your immediate attention.' Jim Briggs hasn't written this, he can't read and write, he must have got someone else to do it," Dick said handing the letter back to dad, "what are you going to do?"

"We'll have to bring him here," dad said as we finished our breakfast, "you won't mind sharing with Nonno for a while will you son?"

"When are we going to get him?" my brother said, showing his approval of the idea.

Leaving a note for mum and armed with a flask of tea and jam sandwiches, we were soon London bound.

The front door of 69 Burton Road was opened just enough to show the dirty face of a small child. "Dad they're ere, shall I let em in?" The door then swung wide, revealing a dishevelled, short, fat, balding man; evidence of his breakfast smeared on his filthy vest.

"Out o the way you," he said pushing the just as dishevelled little girl to one side, "you'd better come in, scuse the mess, the wife aint been too well, you know ow it is."

"How did you know we were coming?" dad said, eying him up and down.

"Cos yer ol man said e thought you'd be ere today, it being the weekend an all."

As we walked into the cluttered hallway, the foul smell from the combination of cat's and human pee, along with rank fat, made Dick say that he and I would wait outside.

"No, I'll need your help with Nonno's things," Grabbing me by the hand, dad marched us past two more scruffy children and a barking dog, into where Nonno lay on his bed looking very frail. When he saw us he sat up and tried to smile.

"Federico,Grazie a Dio, you come. What we do? My feet they are bad."

"You're coming home with us," dad said as he began packing Nonno's meagre possessions into his heavy leather suitcase. "Let's get out of this hell-hole; Dick, go and find out where we can order a taxi."

"I would offer to elp yer mate, but I can't leave me cab," the taxi driver said as he summoned a porter.

Fumbling awkwardly into his pocket for his wallet, "Grazie per la vostra gentilezza," Nonno quietly said to the taxi driver, handing him a pound note, "is enough?" Refusing the offer of change, he handed more notes to my brother, "Ricardo, you go get tickets per il treno, your papa he look after me, get chioccolato per Margherita." Nonno refused to call any of us by our shortened names.

It was Dark when we arrived home. Nonno was exhausted and refusing the supper mum had prepared, he went straight up to where she had made up the spare bed in the room that he was to share with my brother. When I crept in to say goodnight, I was shocked to see Nonno giving himself an injection. "You be good girl and get me biscotti out of my case."

I was soon to learn that my grandfather suffered from sugar diabetes – whatever that meant - brought on, my father said, by the shock of a bomb dropping on the side of his house during the London Blitz in 1940.

I asked dad if that was why there was always a funny smell in Nonno's bedroom. "No," he said with a smile, "that's your brother's cheesy feet."

I knew my brother had really smelly feet, but this smell was different. It wasn't until I found mum changing the dressings on Nonno's poorly feet, as she always did when she came home from work each evening, I realised what the smell was. Three of his toes on one foot were black and all the toes on his other foot were very red and swollen; looking much like the chilblains dad and I suffered from during the winter.

"Is ok, your Madre she do a good job," he must have seen the frightened look on my face, "they soon get betters." They didn't, they just got worse over the next few weeks. At the time it simply didn't occur to me that my beloved Nonno would not be with us for much longer.

The time that he did spend with us was very precious to me. I was perhaps too young to appreciate his previously infrequent, short visits, however, now that he was living with us, I spent many happy hours listening as he recounted stories of his past, especially during the time when I was ill in bed with the mumps, when he told me how he had met and fallen in love with my grandmother, Lydia. He usually fell asleep mid sentence and would wake up with a start. "I no asleep, I just rest the eyes." With a little persuasion, the story continued. "Where I get to," ending with his favourite expression "that is the question?"

Feeling unwell one afternoon, he asked me not to go back out to play; if only I had known what was going to happen I wouldn't have been so stubborn. I came in to find him laying on his bedroom floor covered in his own vomit. The smell was dreadful. He had cooked soused herring for his lunch. Fish was his favourite food. It was never a part of his family diet when he was growing up in Vercelli, it being too far inland for the transportation of fresh seafood.

"You go get bucket of hot water, we get this clean up before your Papa he come home."
Looking back I think he was rather frightened of upsetting his short-tempered son. "You bring disinfectant."
I had to help him onto the bed where he sat shakily giving me instructions. I suppose I felt guilty for leaving him and didn't

mind doing what I could to help him. Using a garden trowel that I found in the shed, I scraped up the partly digested fish and wrapped it in newspaper. It took several buckets of disinfectant laden water in the vain attempt of cleaning up the rug that covered the lino floor. I did my best, but when dad arrived home from work, he took it up the garden to be burnt. Having persuaded Nonno to get into bed, he then cycled down to the nearest phone box outside 'The Fountain Hotel', where he phoned the doctor.

Waiting in my bedroom I heard Dr Jones telling Nonno that he must be admitted into hospital immediately and something about 'septi mia' and 'ganger green'. Later when I asked dad who was ganger green, he smiled as he told me that it was the name given to a man with smelly feet, and not to worry my silly little head about such matters.

That evening an ambulance arrived to take my Nonno to Black Notley Hospital, where the shock of having to have his leg amputated was to prove too much for him. I overheard dad, when he returned, one evening, from visiting Nonno, saying that it was all to do with 'septi mia'. I wanted to ask who *she* was, but seeing how worried dad looked, thought better of it. Nonno died two weeks later.

It being the first funeral I had attended, I was traumatized by the thought of my beloved Nonno in that box being lowered into a deep hole in the ground and subsequently suffered recurring bad dreams. No matter how dad tried to explain that he was no longer in his body and his soul had gone to heaven, I couldn't think of his body being separate from his soul and to my immature mind my Nonno was in that box in the ground. I soon learned not to ask any more questions after mum warning me that it was upsetting dad.

It wasn't long after the death of Nonno, that mum decided to leave home, taking me with her. Dad's mood swings were worsening, he was becoming more suspicious and the rows were a daily occurrence. He regularly pleaded with her to give up working with 'that bloody Johnny'.

I remember on one occasion, it was before Nonno's death, being in bed one night when I was awoken by a loud crash.

"I'll bloody kill you, you bitch." dad shouted as he chased mum up the stairs. I had never heard him so angry; looking back I think he must have been drinking.

"Federico," I heard Nonno's voice on the landing "don't be silly, you go to bed."

"Go to bed yourself and mind your own business," dad growled back.

I was terrified and hearing me whimpering he came into my room.

"What's the matter little un?" The light from the landing dimly lit his red face close to mine, his breath smelt, as he peered at me through the gloom.

"You're not really going to kill mummy are you?" I shielded my face with teddy.

"Course not love," he said picking up my statue of Jesus, "look I swear on this that I won't hurt a hair on her head." With that he snapped the head off the statue. This made me hate him, or should I say what he had become.

We stayed with Dawn, one of mum's friends from work. She and her husband, who was a blind piano tuner, were so kind. I was dismayed when a week later mum said that we had to return home. I think dad must have felt my resentment towards him. I didn't want to leave the lovely kind people; I didn't want to wake up to the sound of my father's angry voice. The rows continued as I knew they would, until one day, when I returned home from school, I found a note on the kitchen table; it was from mum saying that she had now gone for good. I ran through the house calling out for her but somehow knew that there would be no reply.

THE DECISION

I was upstairs, wrapped in a world of sweet make believe, surrounded by a dollies tea party, when her voice pulled me swiftly back to reality. I began to tremble with anticipation and as I cautiously crept down the stairs, the voices became louder; distress hung on the air like a huge black cloud. My legs wobbled and my fingertips tingled; my breath came in quivering gulps as I fought back stinging tears. I felt as though icy water was pouring into my belly making me feel sick. These feelings were not new to me; fear had become a well-known visitor and was never welcome. What was I afraid of this time? Those were the well-controlled, soft tones of my mother's voice. I was afraid *for* her, not *of* her. I was afraid of the out-burst her visit would cause. I was, for her sake, afraid of my father's violent temper.

I pushed the kitchen door open far enough to see my mother standing beside a tall well-dressed gentleman. They were talking about 'clerk of court' and 'here to make sure there was no trouble' and 'just wanting to collect belongings'. I pushed the door open further and hearing my attempt to muffle a sob, my father's care-warn face turned towards me; I backed away feeling sure that he would shout at me. I was wrong, he just turned back to my mother and began to plead with her, begging her not to go; telling her that things would be different, he would change; he loved her and couldn't, wouldn't, live without her. I had never seen my mother so resolute; she appeared taller and more upright, her dark hair shone like ebony, framing her unsmiling face. She looked beautiful; her dark eyes shone the message 'At last I am free, I am my own woman'.

The stranger turned to me on hearing my stifled whimpers. I was confused by the strangeness of this scene. I couldn't recognize anybody. They *all* seemed like strangers now. Who was this man from whom I had expected the usual red-faced shouting; this seemingly broken man with nothing more to say than feeble pleas for forgiveness? Where was daddy, I needed him to rescue me from the stranger's hand now clasping mine. Something about 'sitting in the car', and 'waiting for mummy' and 'don't cry', his strength over powering my timid weakness, I watched my father crumble as I allowed myself to be led away.

The smell of the leather seats jumped out at me as I was guided into the back of the stranger's big black car. The seat squeaked with luxurious comfort as if in an attempt to pacify my trembling body. I sat as requested, quietly waiting whilst the stranger returned to the aid of my mother. I was intrigued with all the knobs and dials on the shiny wooden dashboard. As I wriggled from one side of my squeaking comfort zone to another, a leather briefcase caught my eye as it sat at the end of the seat holding on to its own secrets. My curiosity was soon quelled by the sound of the boot being opened along with my mother's voice as she helped the stranger with her few possessions. The car shook, as the heavy door was slammed shut. The stranger climbed into the driver's seat and leaned across as he opened the passenger door for my mother. Her perfume wafted in as she gathered her skirt around her. Once again there was the sound of a leathery welcome as she sat heavily down with a deep sigh of relief and closed the car door.

"I like your new skirt mummy".

"Yes my Johnny brought it for me," she seemed to smirk as she half turned to look over her shoulder at me, "and this jumper." The skirt was maroon with tiny white polka dots and the polo neck jumper was 'dusty pink' as she called it. "He has brought me so many nice things," she continued, "and I've got *two* new skirts and *two* new jumpers". I was impressed, so impressed that the memory of that polka dot skirt is still vividly with me.

The stranger turned and looking at me with a gentle smile, as though wanting to quickly move things along, said, "Your mummy wants you to know that you can come with her today if you want to." I remember thinking how handsome he was, with sparkling blue eyes and how his thick wavy hair shone like gold. Then I thought of Uncle John, he had blue eyes too but his were close together and looked small in comparison with his big nose, and *his* blond hair was always greasy and lank.

I craned my neck to look towards the house and saw my brother looking over at the car as he leaned his bike against the fence. He looked very serious as he turned and went indoors. I wanted to call him back. I needed my big brother; he would know what to do, he always did.

"Well?" my mother said, "what do you want to do? You know that if you come with me it will have to be now and you do realize that you will not see your brother or father again. You either come with me now or stay with them and if you stay, you won't see me again. It really is up to you." There was no evident sign of emotion on her face or in her voice. Her lovely brown eyes, which she always enhanced with a little 'Betty Lou' brown eye shadow, were looking straight at me and as much as I searched, I could find no help coming forth. Her full-lipped mouth, moist with well-applied pink lipstick matching her jumper, remained closed to any words of comfort or guidance.

I started to cry and asked to be let out of the car as I fought with the handle. Running indoors, I rushed past my brother and father and ran up to my bedroom in search of teddy.

I could hear my father's raised voice as my brother tried to calm him. Clutching teddy I stood by the landing window watching as the big black car pulled away. All I could think of was the 'pink polo neck jumper' and the 'polka dot skirt'. Dropping teddy, I ran down the stairs crying out that 'I wanted to go with mummy'. If only Daddy had reached out and held me in his arms, maybe I would have changed my mind, but he was so full of his own misery, he didn't see my utter dejection and loneliness. They seemed to turn their anger on me as my father shouted "Oh that's right you clear off too," and handing Dick a piece of paper he told him to go and phone the solicitor's office. It seemed no time at all before the big black car arrived and I was whisked away to join my mother. No teddy or dollies, only a few clothes were hurriedly packed into a carrier bag. "We'll bring your toys another day". My father called out as he shut the back door with a slam. Dick was nowhere to be found.

Gwenny wearing the polka dot skirt!

THE PRIOR SAGA CONTINUES

"See this," Ida said as she shook the local newspaper in my face, "yer old man took an overdose, pity it didn't kill im."

I grabbed the paper from her and read the first few lines of the article, '*Local man, Fredrick Oppezzo tries to end his life by taking an overdose of Aspirin, after his wife left him for another man.*'

The bus pulled up in Monkwick Avenue on the Monkwick council housing estate.

"Come on, don't trail behind," she said as she hobbled off the bus, "what you looking so miserable about, you're better of away from im."

"But he's my dad."

"Well if you feel like that you should av bloody well stayed with im cos yer mother don't want yer you've always been a bloody nuisance."

The two weeks duration of our stay, felt more like two years. I could never please this woman that I had never liked. I was frightened of her and felt very much in the way. My mother was totally besotted with 'her Johnny' and was oblivious to my extreme unhappiness. She and I shared the double bed with Ida who, each night made a point of peering into my face to see if I was asleep before heavily rolling in beside me. My feeble attempt of pretence didn't fool her.

"You get to sleep or there'll be trouble." She shouted, poking me in the back.

I didn't get a lot of sleep; by the time my mother crept into bed, Ida was lying on her back taking up most of the bed, snoring like a fat sow.

One evening there was a heavy knock on the front

door.

"I haven't come to cause any trouble; I just wanted to bring some of Rita's Toys."

It was my father. I was thrilled by what he said but didn't dare get out of bed for fear of Ida. It wasn't long before he started to shout threats and obscenities. I heard Uncle George's voice calmly telling dad to leave.

"I want to see my wife; I know she is in there. Where's that snivelling little coward, hiding behind the skirts of that cow of a mother as usual is he?"

"Come on Fred, let's go," another man's voice called dad away.

"You tell the little creep to watch his back," dad shouted as the front door slammed shut.

I lay there imagining Johnny hiding behind Ida, shaking in his silly carpet slippers. I wanted to get up and run out after my dad. Why didn't he ask to see me? Why didn't he take me with him? Why wasn't my brother there? Oh how I missed my lovely brother. What had either of us ever done to deserve never being allowed to see each other again? I felt so guilty about having left them on that horrible day; were they angry because I chose to go with mum? I was so confused at the time, and desperately unhappy.

"What you snivelling for?" Ida's voice broke through my sobs. "See what that bloody man is like, he's not worth your tears, he only came so that he could have another go; he doesn't care about you and your silly dolls," she said in her usual cutting way. "Now shut up that row and get to sleep."

"I hate you, I hate all of you. I wish I had stayed with my Dad."

Pushing her ugly, fat face close to mine, she hissed, "Yes, so do I."

The following morning, Ida begrudgingly tipped the contents of the carrier bag onto the kitchen floor. I was devastated to find that there no teddy amongst the assortment of non-favourite dolls and stuffed toys delivered by dad the previous night. Years later I learnt that he had given all my treasured possessions, including teddy, to Helen, my friend from next-door. If I had known this at the time, it would, almost certainly, have compounded what was becoming the saddest period of my childhood.

"Can't see what all the fuss is about," Ida said, taking pleasure in seeing my look of disappointment.

"It's only a load of old rubbish anyway," she said kicking one of the dolls. "Anyway, what do you need toys for? At your age I was out on the fields working for my keep, its time you started to earn yours. Go and hang the washing out, you spoilt little brat, I'm not here to wait hand and foot on you and that bloody mother of yours."

Ida succeeded in making our stay more unbearable by the day and after my mother also became the victim of her jealous ranting, rages, it wasn't long before our cases were packed and we were on the train heading for London and dear Aunty Jess. Two weeks passed before Johnny joined us, during which time mum found me a new school and herself a job working as a counter assistant at 'Liptons' in Streatham High Street.

"I don't know where you think the money is coming from," mum said with a heavy sigh, as we shopped for my school uniform. "You'll have to make do with one of everything and two pairs of socks." She resented having to spend money on clothes, especially for me.

Every evening we walked to the public phone box on Brixton Hill where we waited for a call from Johnny – Uncle John as I now grudgingly called him – and every evening mum cried.

"Why are you crying," I asked in all innocence, "I thought you would be happy now."

"Oh do shut up, how can I be happy without my Johnny?"

"But I'm here to keep you company."

She ignored me. I truly thought that once I had my mother to myself, life would be different. I tried so hard to please her. I too was lonely.

Tim and Beverly still rented the first floor flat, which meant us sharing the small scullery with Aunty and Mr Wilkins. I slept in the smallest of the two attic rooms at the top of the house and Mum slept in the other soon to be joined by Uncle John. It was alright in the summer months, but very scary in the winter when the wind howled eerily through the trapdoor in the wall of my room. Plucking up the courage one day, I pulled back the bolts and peered into the sooty blackness of the roof space, not wishing to delve into its spooky secrets, I quickly closed it again and was relieved to shoot the rusty bolts back into place; I never opened it again.

Dick Shepherd Secondary Modern School, Tulse Hill was a newly built girls-only school and had only been open for the past six months. Compared to what I had been used to, I found the sheer size of the modern building, with its multitude of classrooms on several floors and a huge assembly hall very daunting. It took me a lot of scary searches to find my way around. However, I was not the only new girl and soon became firm friends with a fellow classmate, Joanne (Jo) Betts. The standard of education was far in advance to what I was used to; I found the arithmetic very confusing and felt too shy to ask for help. Jo found it easy and sitting next to her, made it possible for me to copy her work. I came unstuck when the teacher, seeing what we were up to, made me move to another desk. Miss Snow, our pretty, young French teacher, realizing that I was six months behind the rest of the class, gave me extra tuition during her lunch break. My enthusiasm for learning a new language soon paid off, I soared to the top of the class as I did with English composition, science, needlework, art and domestic science. I was never good at sports and hockey was my worst nightmare. A very tall lanky girl, who for some reason was nicknamed 'Stickles', made a point of hitting my ankles with her stick during the tackles. When she wasn't doing that, she would stand behind us smaller girls and take great delight in hearing us squeal as she dug her fingertips into our shoulders.

The school backed on to Brockwell Park where Aunty

used to take me whilst I was staying on one of my visits. There was a miniature village in one part of the park where we always sat watching the antics of the squirrels as they played amongst the small buildings. Many frogs and large toads inhabited the picturesque ponds and came to a grizzly end if they were unfortunate enough to venture into the school grounds. 'Stickles' and her gang took delight in catching them and forcing air through a straw down their throats until they nearly burst before throwing them to the ground where they stamped on them. I often wonder what sort of adults such sadistic children became.

The combined drama classes were auditioning for 'Alice in Wonderland' and Jo and me, being the same height and build, were chosen to play 'Tweedledum' and 'Tweedledee'. We were dressed in our drama mistress's striped pyjamas with cushions stuffed up our tops. Rehearsals were held twice a week after school for six weeks before the performance. I was so excited and couldn't wait to tell mum.

"Will you come and see it? It really is very good; I just know you'll enjoy it." Her answer was a very definite "No".

"But all the parents are coming." I so wanted mum to be proud of me.

"Don't be silly, some of us have to work."

"But it's on in the evening."

"Uncle John will be too tired and I have to cook his tea."

The only consolation was that Jo had the same response from her mother and stepfather, whom she had the same dislike for as I had for Uncle John. We often found comfort in sharing our experiences.

One day we decided to run away. Once again my life had become unbearable. Ida had come to live with us after the untimely death of Uncle George. I remember how ill he was when we stayed with them for those dreadful two weeks. I thought the reason for his bed being in the sitting room was so as to make room for mum and me, but it was because his hacking cough kept Ida awake and after all, she did need her beauty sleep! I was not told of the reason for his death until one day at school we all had to have a skin test to see if we needed the Tuberculosis inoculation. They said that I didn't need it as I had a natural immunity which mum said was probably due to having been in close contact with uncle George. I thought he coughed because he smoked so much and I wondered if by me breathing in the smoke from his cigarettes it had in some way protected me from catching TB. "No," mum said with a wry smile, "he died of TB and by being subjected to the bacteria, you must have built up an immunity to the disease."

Blisters formed where Jo had the skin test, which meant that she had to have the inoculation. I just had a small lump come up and was relieved when an X-ray showed that I didn't need any treatment.

Uncle George died in the late spring and by the time we broke up from school, Tim and Beverly having now moved out, Ida moved in bringing her two cats and her bad temper with her. When mum and Johnny were at work, I was once again subjected to her irrational mood swings and bouts of violence. It got so bad one day that Grandma Flood, our elderly next-door neighbour, shouted, as she banged on the wall, "Leave that poor child alone."

Grandma and Grandpa Flood had lived next door for many years with their son and daughter-in-law, along with their granddaughter Wendy, who was a year younger than me. I didn't see much of Wendy as she was very ill. Looking back, I remember her being a very delicate, pale-faced little girl who seemed to spend most of her time in bed. On the rare occasions that I was invited to visit with her, she always wanted me to wind up her gramophone so that she could listen to her favourite record, 'The Teddy Bears Picnic' to which we endeavoured to sing along. Her bedroom window looked out over the back garden, where she sometimes waved to me from her bed. Grandpa Flood had made a special window box that hung from her bedroom window-sill. In the spring and summer it was filled with sweetly scented flowering plants and during the winter months he put out food to attract the birds which she so loved to watch. Whenever I visited, I would run up Nanny's garden and look up at Wendy's window in the hope of seeing her. On one such occasion, it was a lovely spring afternoon; I was surprised to see the curtains to all the widows of the house tightly closed. Aunty looked very sad as she told me that Wendy had died the previous day. Grandma flood told Aunty that a Robin had sat on the window box, "singing his little heart out for most of that day." I always remember Wendy whenever I hear 'The Teddy Bears Picnic'.

Now, four years later, Grandma Flood was hammering on the wall and Ida rudely shouted, "Mind yer own business yer nosey old cow." after which, she carried on shouting at me. I knew better than to bother Aunty when things became unbearable and mum and Johnny were so wrapped up in each-other, they seemed to be oblivious to it all. That's when Jo and I decided to run away.

There was a small brass pot in the kitchen where Uncle John kept all his loose change; I had no money of my own. Jo said that we would need a shilling for the bus fare to 'The Elephant and Castle' where her Granny lived. I took a sixpenny piece a thrupenny bit and three pennies; I thought these would be less noticeable than taking a shilling coin; I knew that it was stealing, but I was desperate to get away. I wrote a note saying that I was running away and for them not to worry as I was going to be happier where I was going. My heart pounded, I was frightened by the thought of Ida catching me in the act as I pushed the note through the letterbox.

Jo and I truly believed that her Granny would take us in.

"You can't stay ere me little darlins," she said as she dished up two plates of egg and chips, "you tuck in to that and I'll get Jo's uncle Bill to run yer both ome in his van when he gets ome from work."

I was terrified when I knocked on the door of number 22. Uncle John answered the door, mum stood behind him with her arms folded over her chest (her usual stance when she was displeased) with a resolute look on her face.

"And where do you think you've been miss?" he asked trying to put on a stern face.

"You'll have a police record now, they've been out looking for you yer little madam," Ida said, pushing him aside Before she could say anymore, he stepped forward and led me upstairs. "We'll handle this mother."

Having explained where I had been, I was then asked why. The floodgates opened as I tearfully told all.

"Why didn't you tell us all this before?" uncle John carried on questioning me whilst my mother went down to see Aunty. All I really wanted was a reassuring cuddle from my mummy; that's all I had ever wanted.

Lying in bed later that night after hearing the usual loud noises of their nightly, lovemaking, I then heard the two of them talking about Ida. Grandma Flood was mentioned; how she had spoken to Aunty about the way I was being shouted at each day and Ida's abusive comments when they complained.

"Perhaps things will settle down now," my mother tried to reassure him, "don't let's worry about it anymore darling." She was always good at pushing unpleasantness to the back of her mind.

Nothing changed.

"Right young lady," Uncle John said putting on his 'I'm in charge' voice, "you need to be kept busy," he said as he pinned a list to the kitchen door. "This is a roster of jobs you'll be expected to do before and after school. I want you to tick them off each day, is that clear?"

"But I won't get time in the mornings," I said as I studied the list of household cleaning chores, "and I have to do my homework after school."

"Then you'll have to get up earlier wont you and put off going out to play after tea for the time being, and you are to wash your own socks and knickers and wash and iron your school blouse at the weekends, your mother has got enough to do."

"Look what you're doing stupid child, you're getting blood all over the potatoes." Ida shouted as I tried to peel the potatoes ready for the evening meal.

"Get out of the way," she hissed snatching the peeler from me, "get on with your other jobs, see if you can mess them up."

I ran down to Aunty who put a plaster on my cut finger and wiped away my tears on her apron. I so wanted to tell her how I felt but knew that her loyalties to my mother meant that she would spill the beans and I would be in more trouble as I had been told not to worry Aunty with my silly problems.

THE LETTERS

It was three days following our attempt to run away, that Jo returned to school. She wasn't her usual cheerful self and when I questioned her about her return home, she just shrugged and said that she wanted to forget it. I knew that her stepfather was a violent man and her mother drank heavily, I also knew that she would tell all in her own good time.

"What about you," she asked, "did you get into trouble?"

"Not really, they just seemed to shrug it off."

"What are you going to do now; do you still want to go back to your dad? I would if I knew who mine was."

She had never mentioned her real father. I could see by the hurt look in her eyes that it was better not to question her.

"I don't even know if he wants me back." I replied with a heavy feeling in my stomach.

"Why don't you write to him, you must have his address?"

"How can I? If *they* found out there would be hell to pay?"

"Not if he sent his reply to my address," she said letting out a mischievous giggle.

"Wouldn't you get into trouble?" I didn't want her to take any risks.

"They're never up when the postman comes so they won't know will they."

Jo was so excited when she handed me the letter a few days later. There was no mistaking dad's artistic script on the envelope. My hands shook as I unfolded the pages, my tears of pure joy momentarily blurring my vision. I could almost hear my father's voice as I read the letter which was several pages long. It took a few exchanges of letters between us before I finally plucked up the courage to ask if he would have me back

Once again tears of anticipation and fear flowed freely as I heard my mother and Johnny coming up the stairs.

"What's the matter with you now child?" he said angrily switching on my bedroom light. "Me and your mother are having an early night, we have to get up for work in the morning."

"I want to go back to my dad." The words almost choked me as my throat tightened.

"What did you just say?"

"I want to go back to my dad," I screamed the words out this time.

"How do you know he wants you back?"

"Because he said so in his last letter," courage now released fear's vice-like grip as I waved my dad's recent letter at him.

"Letter what letter? You mean you have been writing to him? Why? How? No letters have arrived here," he said snatching the letter.

Oh God! What do I tell him? Jo has been so kind. "To a friend's house, he sent them to my friend's house." I realised after I had said it, I shouldn't have said '*my friend*.' He knew that Jo was the friend that I had run away with.

"Right madam, get up and get dressed right now, right this minute, we'll get this sorted out once and for all. You do realize how this is going to upset your mother, knowing that you have been in contact with that man."

"He's my dad and I want to be with him and my brother, your mother told me that you have never wanted me here anyway." All fear now replaced by hatred, hatred of him for taking away my mother, hatred of his mother for her spiteful cruelty and hatred of this airless, poky little attic room where my imagination was plagued by the descriptive sounds voiced by my mother as they had sex night after night.

"Get up, we're going to see what your friends parents think of all this. Where do they live" he aggressively asked as he studied the envelope. "We'll need this as evidence. Get up damn you."

The door was opened by a tall, unshaven, dishevelled looking man with a cigarette hanging from the corner of his cruel mouth.

"What the el do you want at this time of night?" We were not invited in.

Having apologised for the lateness – it was nine thirty – Johnny went on to explain why we were there, adding that I was nothing but a little liar.

"Give er a good iding mate thas my policy. It aint easy being a ruddy stepfather; a good beltin thas what I gives em." The door slammed shut and as we walked away I heard him shout, "Jo, you git darn ere na."

I now realized the terrible risk my poor friend had taken to help me. I also realized why she couldn't talk about it when she returned to school the previous time. I was so afraid for her and I felt that it was all my fault.

I was sent to school for the next few harrowing days whilst awaiting travelling instructions from my father; this time sent to number 22. Those days were even more unbearable because Jo never spoke to me again.

THE RETURN

My mother was nowhere to be seen and Ida had locked herself in her bedroom; Aunty stood at the front door waving as Uncle John led me down Fairmount Road. His clammy hand, with its bitten nails, gripped mine as we crossed Brixton Hill towards the bus stop. We never spoke during the entire journey to Liverpool Street Station where I was to catch my train.

"Cheerio then," he said handing my small case in through the open carriage door, which he then slammed shut and was gone.

The friendly sound of the whistle signalled the departure of the midday train bound for Colchester. The iron monster breathed the familiar smell of smoky steam, blowing away all my pent up emotions, replacing them with feelings of shear relief and excitement. The sound of the wheels clattering over the track, seemed to be saying, "You're going home, you're going home, you're going home," as my rescuing giant gathered speed.

At last, my train pulled into North Station where the recognizable figure of my dad stood on the steam filled platform. My legs seemed to turn to jelly and just wouldn't move as he ran, arms outstretched, towards me; the so longed for strong embrace lifted me off my feet. The smell of tobacco and 'Lifebouy' soap filled my nostrils with pure pleasure as his embrace tightened and his tears mingled with mine.

"Cor you aint alf grown love," he said now holding me at arm's length. "Come on let's get you home, Dick is really looking forward to seeing you."

My brother was no longer the lanky sixteen-year old that I had left behind almost two years ago. I was now looking into the lovely brown eyes (so like those of our mother) of a handsome young man.

"You're a man now," I said, standing on tiptoes as I reached up and threw my arms about his neck. "I have missed you so badly, have you missed me?"

"You haven't grown much," he said in his usual dismissive manner. "Want a cuppa?"

Any signs of emotion always embarrassed him, causing him to quickly change the subject.

"You look a bit formal love, is that your school uniform," dad asked, "don't you want to put a frock on? Let's see what you've got in here," he said lifting my small case onto a chair, "this'll do, is this all you've brought with you?" he said rummaging through my meagre possessions. "Where are the rest of your clothes, there isn't much here?"

I felt awkward as I admitted to having left behind a few things that I had grown out of, at which Dad sent a frowning look in Dick's direction as he asked him what time Hadley's closed?

Hadley's was the local family run ladies and gents outfitters and haberdashers in Mill Road. Mr Hadley and their son John, before he was conscripted into the army to do his national service, ran the men's outfitters and Mrs Hadley ran the Ladies section with a local girl, Jenny Mills. They sold everything from good quality clothing to curtaining and dress fabrics along with a large selection of haberdashery.

"I know you close early on Saturdays," dad said when he saw the surprised look on Mrs Hadley's plump, friendly face as she opened the side door, "but this is a bit of an emergency."

The last time I had seen her, I was with my mother when she was purchasing some wool.

"Its little Rita, my how you've grown. Come in dears," she said as she ushered dad and me through to the shop, "I'll be with you in a minute, I must just turn the spuds down."

The mouth-watering smell of roasting meat wafted through as she went into the kitchen.

"Now dears," she said taking off her apron and running her fingers through her thick mop of iron grey, wavy hair. "What can I do for you?"

Dad quickly explained that I had just returned home from spending almost two years up in London with my mother and her boyfriend. There was a fierce tone to his voice when he said the word 'boyfriend'.

"She's come back with nothing and needs fitting out with some pretty frocks and, well, you know what a growing girl needs," he said pointing to his chest.

I knew what he meant. I remember asking my mother for a bra when I first started to develop quite sizable breasts and was made to feel very self-conscious by the taunting remarks made by other girls. She told me that I wasn't ready for that type of thing.

Mrs Hadley was a good saleswoman and I went home armed with three new dresses, two for starting back at school in September and one for best; two pretty bras, knickers and white socks. I had never had such a lot of money spent on me and my feelings of guilt were dispelled when dad told me that Nonno had left 'a nice little nest egg' and how did I feel about a holiday in Paris.

West Mersea County Primary School hadn't changed, apart from the addition of a newly built classroom. I recognized most of the teachers with the exception of Mr Franklin who taught the top class in the new classroom and the headmaster, Mr Westcott. With me having been moved to St Thomas Moore school in Colchester when I was nine, it was strange to see all my friends, now three years older, were still there; it seemed as though I had never left.

As soon as he knew I was coming back and before my return to school in September, dad had my name included on his passport and booked the holiday in Paris with 'Blue Cars'

"Here y'are love," He said, handing me a five-pound note. "Get yourself some new shoes and something smart to travel in. Go into Colchester, there'll be more variety there."

Five pounds! I had never seen a five-pound note, apart from the old white ones dad discovered hidden behind an old picture of Nannie's. And now here I was, twelve years old and going shopping for clothes with a five pound note in my purse.

"I hent got that sort o change gal." The bus conductor was flummoxed when I handed him the five-pound note for my return fare. "What you a doin with all that money?"

"Going shopping for new clothes," I said proudly. "My dad is taking me to Paris."

"Well seein as though I know yer, you can pay me when you come back, but if the inspector gets on, make as though you can't find yer ticket, he hates bein held up."

Freeman Hardy & Willis in the High Street provided me with my first pair of fashionable slip on shoes at fourteen shillings and eleven pence. Wilsons Ladies Fashions fitted me out with a two piece suit at one pound four shillings and six pence and a pretty cotton blouse five shillings and eleven pence. After paying my return bus fare, I was able to hand dad two pounds thirteen shillings and ten pence change along with the receipts.

"Good girl, you can have the thirteen and ten to buy a nice handbag, I'm proud of you. Go and put your new things on, I want to see you all dolled up."

I felt so grown up as I paraded in front of dad and Dick.

We had no washing machine and I took pleasure in doing all the washing for my two hard-working men. The small mangle that I had so often watched my mother arduously using, was quite hard work, but I managed it and felt quite the little woman of the house as I hung it all out to dry. On wet days it was hung on the lines in the outhouse.

"Your brother and me have both decided to give you two and six a week pocket money for all the jobs you are doing," dad said as he put a half crown in my hand. "Come on boy, cough up."

It was to be my first flight when we boarded the 'Silver City' aircraft at Southend Airport bound for Le Touquet in France. The propellers slowly turned, as the heavily greased engines mounted on either wing, sprang into life. The noisy build up of speed down the runway, forcefully thrusting us back into our seats, was at the same time frightening and exhilarating, like nothing I had ever experienced before and then the stomach lurching thrill as we abruptly became airborne. Dad gripped my hand and gave me a broad reassuring grin as the plane banked steeply to one side, enabling a swiftly shrinking view of the runway and surrounding fields. Visibility was good and it wasn't long before we were over the sea with boats looking like insects on the surface of a garden pond.

"You enjoying it?" Dick shouted over the roar of the engines. "Not feeling sick are you?" letting out a laugh as he threw a sick bag over the back of my seat.

"We've got our own thanks," dad said throwing it back. "You're alright aren't you love?"

He could see by my broad grin that I was more than all right.

Landing at the small airport of Le Touquet, we boarded the coach bound for Paris. Dick and his friend Alfie, having made friends with the other two lads travelling with our party, sat at the back, where they proceeded to make plenty of noise, laughing and joking. The coach stopped at a café in a small town, en route to Paris, where dad and I, sitting outside at one of the small, ornate wrought iron tables, enjoyed a simple meal.

"Cheers love," he said raising his wine glass, "here's to a happy holiday," tapping his glass of red wine against my glass of lemonade, sparkling as though in answer.

The boys had gone in search of some beer to take with them on the coach. We were entertained for the rest of the journey as they all got into the holiday mood, singing and catcalling as we passed pretty girls.

Having arrived at Hotel L'Ermitage, Rue Lemarck, in

the region of Montmartre, situated a stones-throw from the Sacre Coeur, a rather austere, elderly lady showed us grumpily to our rooms. I had a small single room to myself and Dick and dad shared a large room with Alfie. The two Scottish boys, Keith and Steven – as I had now come to know them, were amused at having to share a room with a double bed. Each room had a washbasin and, what I was later to learn, a bidet.

"Dick thought it was for washing his feet in," dad laughingly told me when I questioned what it was. On further investigation, I learned what it was really for. The first time I put it to the test, I decided that I would rather wash my feet in it. Each room was equipped with a generous supply of clean white towels, the hand towels were stiff white linen and smelt of Lavender. A small bar of soap sat on the glass shelf over the washbasin along with a glass tumbler.

Opening the wooden shutters of the tall window that looked out over the street, the three white domes of the Sacre-Coeur, that Dad had pointed out on our arrival, loomed high in the evening sky; I felt that I could reach out and touch them. They reminded me of pictures of the Taj Mahal, which I had seen in Nannie's magazines, 'Mother India'.

"You've got the best view," dad said as he came in to my room. "We'll go there tomorrow. Come on love, we are all going down into Monmartre, I promised two friends of mine, Paris and Maurice, that I would look them up as soon as we arrived."

The evening turned out to be my first lesson in dealing with a very drunk father and not so sober brother. We met up with Paris, a rather scruffy Frenchman in his fifties and Maurice, a swarthy skinned Algerian of similar age, in a café just down the road from the famous 'Moulin Rouge'.

I suppose if I hadn't been so hungry for the thrill of being in such an exciting place with my dad and brother, I could have become quite bored by the endless evenings spent watching them all getting drunk in various seedy cafes and bars. One such evening, a very good looking young woman

smiled at me and as I returned the smile, dad, jumping up out of his seat, grabbed me by the hand and pulled me out on to the street, swiftly followed by Paris and Maurice. .

"You nearly caused a fight," dad said as I questioned him.

"But I only smiled at the pretty young lady."

"That was no lady, that was the big man's boyfriend," Maurice said as we walked swiftly down the road.

That was to be my first experience of seeing men dressed as women and of men being with other men in that way! Dad and his friends found it all really amusing; I just found it all very puzzling.

During the day dad and I visited a great many places of interest. We climbed the stairs to the first floor of the Eiffel Tower and then got the lift to the top where dad pointed out various famous buildings which we later visited. We sauntered along the Champs Elysees towards the Arc de Triomphe. Dad and I visited the Louvre where we looked at the famous portrait of the Mona Lisa and the beautiful marble statue of the Venus de Milo.

"You know this statue is hundreds of years old and became damaged whilst being moved from place to place many times," he told me when I asked what had happened to her arms; he then went on to tell me, "The Medici Venus in Italy is just as beautiful, and *she* still has arms. I'll take you to see her in Florence one day."

It wasn't long after our return from Paris, that dad met the woman who was to irreversibly change my relationship with my father.

Loneliness had driven him to have a short term affair with a married woman. Whilst changing the sheets on his bed, I came across a collection of letters tucked under his mattress. Curiosity getting the better of me, I read a few lines from what appeared to be a love letter; it was enough to tell me that dad had been and still was having an affair with the wife of one of our neighbours. I was rather shocked as I knew and liked the lady who shall remain anonymous. I tucked the letters back where I had found them and to my knowledge, nobody was any the wiser when it all came to an end.

The only occasions that I remember dad getting drunk, when we were children, were when there was drink in the house at Christmas, which always resulted in him becoming aggressive towards my mother, whose placidity only seemed to worsen the situation.

The potatoes were boiled to a pulp and the sausages were sitting in the congealing fat of the now cold frying pan. Dick staggered in through the back door; he went straight upstairs without even looking at me. I heard him banging about in his bedroom, it being above where I stood in the kitchen listening. An almighty crash had me rushing upstairs only to find him sprawled across his now collapsed bed, stark naked. It was seven thirty on Christmas Eve and dad still hadn't arrived home when there was a sudden knock on the back door; cautiously opening it I was surprised by the sight of dad being supported by a woman who was a stranger to me.

"Come on take this," she said as she held out a very large, very dead, very cold, featherless goose by the string round its feet.

"Don't be daft it won't hurt you," she said as dad slumped to the floor.

"Don't worry he aint dead just dead drunk," she said trying to haul him up. "I watched him get off the bus and stagger up the road," she said as I helped her to get dad into the 'old armchair'. "He must have fallen over the garden wall and was spark out, laying on the frozen lawn, with his goose beside him. If I hadn't followed him you'd have ended up with a frozen dad *and* goose for Christmas." She let out a high pitched cackle, showing her uneven, protruding teeth marked by badly applied bright red lipstick.

"Hello I'm Lil. Get the kettle on, he needs a good strong cup of coffee. Mind if I join you?" she said, not waiting for an answer she took a seat at the kitchen table. "Oh damn,

I've broken my bloody nail, scuse my french, you got a nail file?" Her long scarlet nails matched her lipstick.

This was the woman who, from then on, would gradually inveigle her way destructively into our lives.

Dick aged 19

Me and Dad disembarking at Le Touquet

THE STEPMOTHER

Lillian Williamson (Lil) lived with her husband Eric and ten year old son Danny in one of the first of the many new houses to be built on the Windsor Road Council Housing Estate. She had lived there for over a year before the house we eventually moved into was completed. Both she and her husband were motorcycle fanatics and were both owners of large motorcycles; hers with a sidecar. Dad was later to become the proud owner of a Triumph Tiger Cub and would spend a lot of time with Eric tuning, adjusting and generally getting covered in grease as they worked on the engines.

Lil was delighted by dad's presence and made this quite evident to her doting husband. We were regularly invited round in the evenings and for Sunday lunch. It became very obvious to me that there was something going on between her and my dad, especially when, having been out down the village with my mates, as I always did after tea, I was greeted by the cloying smell of her perfume as I went into the sitting room, where she and dad made no effort to hide what they had been up to. I had learnt a great deal about adult behaviour since I was a small child and was no longer shocked or surprised by the goings on that I was to bear witness to over the years. However, I did feel pangs of jealousy as I saw her sitting where I normally sat, cuddled up close to my father.

"What about Uncle Eric?" I asked as dad, later, made an attempt at justifying their 'little bit of a kiss and cuddle'.

"She doesn't love him, he's a bit of a bore," he said seeing my look of confusion. "She's in need of some excitement, you know how it is."

No I didn't know how it was. Uncle Eric, as I called him, was a shy, quiet gentle giant of a man; his large round balding head sat heavily on broad shoulders, seemingly leaving no room for a neck. He wore a broad leather belt beneath his fat belly so as to stop his trousers from falling over his hips and fleshless bottom. I felt sorry for him when, on many occasions, I saw and heard the unkind actions and comments Lil regularly aimed at him.

When I next saw her, she tried to justify herself by telling me the story of how she had first met Eric when she applied for the job of housekeeper to an elderly gentleman and his son. Her husband was a prisoner of war and she was living with her in laws at the time of the birth of her third child. It was obvious to them that the child could not possibly belong to their son and felt justified in telling her that whilst their son's two children could stay, she must take the baby and leave. Whilst telling the story she tried to convince me that Danny – her youngest son – did belong to her husband and that she had fallen pregnant whilst he was home on leave. Being very naïve and unworldly at the time I believed her and it wasn't until many years later that I realized how it would have been an impossibility for a prisoner of war to obtain leave. She went on to tell me how she found work in the kitchen of the local NAAFI, where she was able to take her baby. It was at that time that she saw the job for housekeeper advertised in the local newspaper.

"It was a small house in Bury St Edmonds where Eric lived with his aged father when he came out of the army," she went on to tell me.

I asked her where his mother was.

"Dead," she said with no further information on that particular subject. "Danny was two when the old man died and that was when Eric landed himself a job with 'Paxmans' in Colchester and asked me to marry him. I told him that I didn't love him, but Danny needed a dad so I accepted and that's when we moved to bloody Mersea," she said with a scowl.

"Don't you like Mersea?"

"No I don't, never have, never will."

And she never did.

Calling me in one afternoon as I passed her house on my way home from school, I was surprised to see her crying.

"We've had a row," she was shaking and her voice was shrill.

"You and Uncle Eric?" I asked.

"No not *him*, your dad and me."

I wanted to jump for joy.

"Tell him that I love him and can't live without him; you will won't you dear."

I had never heard her use a term of endearment aimed at me.

"I've always fancied your dad, ever since I first saw him over the gardens. I felt sorry for him when your mother left, but I was secretly glad really."

I wanted to smack her in her ugly mascara smudged eye; then she added insult to injury by calling out as I hastily made my way out of the door.

"Well after all, she was carrying on with that bloke on the bread round."

No I wouldn't give dad her message.

The next time I saw Lil she was standing at her gate waiting for me.

"You're late home from school today."

"Yes I got detention."

"We're all going on holiday together," she said ignoring what I had just said.

"Who?"

"We are, you and your dad and Eric, me and Danny."

"When?"

"When you and Danny break up from school, your dad is arranging it all."

"Where?"

Paris became a different place, a friendless place; dad was a different man; Dick wasn't there. I became babysitter to snotty nosed, forever winging, ten year old Danny, whilst

Eric, having had enough of Lil's bad temper and nagging, wandered off on his own after breakfast, leaving dad and Lil to spend most of the morning sitting outside various cafes drinking and smoking. After lunch, it fell upon me to keep Danny occupied playing cards in the bedroom that I unwillingly shared with him, whilst dad and Lil took '*a little nap*' supposedly in their own rooms. Eric usually reappeared in time to join us for supper after which time, having walked his stepson and me back to the hotel, he went to bed leaving me to my babysitting duties.

The monotony of the past few days was eased one evening when we had supper at a small café. We sat outside where tables and chairs surrounded a small dance-floor where people were dancing to the music being played by a six- piece jazz band. It was a warm evening and as the sun went down, strings of coloured lights came on, making me feel as though I were in a magic place.

"Danseras tu avec moi?" a rather scruffy youth asked; not waiting for an answer he took me by the hand and pulled me onto the crowded dance-floor. It was only when he gave me a sloppy mouthed kiss, stinking of garlic whilst leaning heavily on me for support, that it became obvious that he was very drunk. Dad was too caught up in conversation with Lil to notice my plight and becoming bored, Eric had taken Danny back to the hotel. I began to panic when all at once my drunken dance partner was hauled off by a young man, who, holding him by the collar, whilst saying something angrily in French, marched him out through the entrance. Before I knew it, my handsome young hero was back.

"Veuillez excuser cet homme, qu'il boit trop lourdement," he said placing a reassuring hand on my shoulder as he guided me back to my seat.

"We wondered where you were," Lil said, looking over the top of her glass. "Come on Fred let's dance. You can stay here and look after my handbag with your young man Rita," she said dragging my rather drunk dad reluctantly onto the dance-floor.

Jaques, my new friend, spoke very little English, but with the moderate amount of French that I had learnt at school' we succeed in holding a polite yet light-hearted conversation. I was embarrassed when dad and Lil joined us. Dad looked suspiciously at Jaques whilst a very tipsy and flirtatious Lil, attempting to speak with what she considered a French accent, fired pointless questions at him, none of which he remotely understood. At this point Jaques stood up and politely offering dad his hand, apologetically announced his departure, but not before asking for permission to take me to see Le Jardin des Tuileries the very next day. Dad was able to understand his request having spent time in France during the war. I instinctively knew what his answer would be as drink usually made him more amicable, so long as nothing was to upset him. "Bonne nuit mademoiselle," Jaques said as he bowed and kissed my hand. I hid my embarrassment.

I knew better than to show my disapproval of their antics as we made our way back to the hotel through the dimly lit streets. I walked on ahead so as to avoid becoming the brunt of dad's drink fuelled mood swing.

The next morning Lil endeavoured to buy my silence, by persuading dad to treat me to a new dress when we visited 'Bon Marche'. I had never seen such a huge store and found no difficulty in choosing a pretty dress to wear for my outing with Jaques.

"Your dad is paying for my dresses and things cos I haven't got enough money with me," she said as dad got out his wallet. "You won't mention it to Eric will you dear," she whispered as Eric and Danny walked sullenly towards us.

"Did you get your shorts Danny love?" He nodded as he shuffled off holding Eric's hand. Both would rather have gone to Clacton!

Hastily finishing a snack lunch, I left the rest of them as they tucked into the huge ice-cream sundaes which the Moulin Rouge restaurant was famous for. I quickly walked back to the hotel where I changed into my new frock and did the best that time allowed with my hair.

I was greeted by the smiling face of my new friend as I stepped out through the door of the hotel. The Taxi, my Brother's favourite make of car, the Citroen DS 19, arrived on time and Jaques stood holding the door open for me as I tried to contain my excitement. The leather seat issued a comforting welcome as my gentlemanly, seventeen year old friend lowered himself into the seat beside me. His golden hair shone with well-applied brilliantine; over his top lip was the shadow of the beginnings of a moustache; a broad smile of greeting revealed even, pearly white teeth and his pale blue eyes sparkled with pleasure. We spent two idyllic afternoons together; his gentlemanly behaviour towards me was impeccable and I felt quite the little lady. I was very sad when he broke the news that having been, conscripted into the French Army, he was due to leave within the next couple of days. He assured me that he would write, making me promise to do the same. We continued to correspond over the next eighteen months; his letters sometimes contained small Lilly of the Valley scented cards, which I proudly showed off to my friends at school. Finally, I was saddened when he wrote informing me of his engagement to be married. I sent my congratulations, after which I never heard from him again. The sweet memories will always remain with me especially when recalled by the perfume of Lilly of the Valley.

Subsequent to our return from Paris, the mild autumn stretched into November, with leaves still clinging to the trees, until unexpectedly icy high winds loosened their grip.

Eric was suffering from the aftermath of a bad dose of influenza when, following another row with Lil, he took to the road on his motorbike so as to yet again escape her sharp tongued nagging.

"Daft Bugger, he didn't even bother to put on his coat or helmet," Lil said as the ambulance pulled away. "They think he's got pneumonia."

"Do you want me to run you into Colchester?" dad offered.

"No, I'll ring the hospital later; can me and Danny stay

here the night" not waiting for an answer she went on to ask if I minded sharing my bed with him, "he's a bit upset by it all."

Eric died that Night.

Looking back, I think it was more than likely that he died of a broken heart.

Dad always had an afternoon nap on a Saturday afternoons and having not spent much time alone with him lately, I curled up on the sofa with his arms wrapped around me. This particular afternoon I had a strange pain in my tummy and was glad of the comfort as I soaked up his warmth and fell asleep. When I woke up the pain had worsened and when I went to the toilet I was alarmed by the blood stain in my knickers. I thought that I was going to die.

"Don't worry love," dad said when I told him why I was crying. "It's all part of growing up; after all you'll be fourteen in a few months time; go round and see Lil, she'll know what to do."

Handing me a packet of Dr White's sanitary towels and two safety pins, Lil told me to go to 'Hadley's' and buy a sanitary belt and a replacement for the half empty packet she had given me.

On another occasion dad and me were enjoying our Saturday afternoon nap when Lil's harsh voice broke into our slumbers.

"What the hell do you think you're doing," she bellowed, "it's bloody disgusting, she's too old for *cuddling up to daddy* now."

I disentangled myself from dad's arms and ran upstairs; I could hear their raised voices through my sobs. My father never cuddled me again.

As time went on his temper worsened and he became more aggressive towards me. Strangely it was as though she had awakened feelings of unfounded guilt that he suppressed by acts of physical violence. He became a changed man in my eyes.

He spent a lot more time at her house and with Dick

now courting I was alone most evenings, sometimes into the early hours.

My friend Susan Fahie's mother ran the bar at the Hall Barn Country Club where dances were held every Saturday evening. At thirteen we *were* actually too young to attend, however, Susan's mother turned a blind eye and a group of us spent most Saturday early evenings swinging to whatever the live band was playing, which was anything from ballroom to Rock n Roll. Susan who was a lot taller and looked a lot older than any of us, always went up to the bar where her mother would serve us Cherry B's made into long drinks by adding soda water; these would have to last all evening unless we got lucky, which I usually did when dad and Lil arrived or my brother with his chums.

"Do you girls want a Babycham?" my handsome brother asked, causing my pals to giggle flirtatiously.

"Come on kid let's dance." I loved it when Dick, knowing that I could jive as we regularly practiced at home, twirled me around so that I showed my knickers; one minute I was over his shoulder, the next minute through his legs and up the other side; I became the envy of all my pals.

When dad and Lil came to the dances, before Eric's death I was allowed to stay until the end, me being their alibi as I begrudgingly walked home with them. They were usually quite tipsy and the shortcut through the folly became frustratingly longer because of frequent stops accompanied by stifled giggles and whispers.

"Wait for us Rita," Lil called out as I ambled along ahead of them, "I can't go any faster in these heels, your dad has to help me."

I hated her tarty way of dressing. She always wore figure hugging pencil skirts just above her ugly knees, along with tight, cleavage revealing tops. Her thick, coarse, permed hair was styled into what was then fashionably known as a 'Bubble Cut' and to cover up the grey, she regularly dyed it jet-black. I often thought that she was trying to copy my mother who had silky, naturally black hair worn in a similar style.

"I think your dad fell for me because I reminded him of your mother," she once told me. She couldn't possibly have reminded him of my mother, who was beautiful and unlike Lil, her flawless olive skin didn't need makeup.

Life didn't get any easier; dad spent more time with Lil, Dick was happily involved in a serious relationship with Barbara, his future wife; I spent a lot more time alone in the house, apart from when my school friend Elizabeth found it necessary to stay the night when the weather was too bad for her to cycle home to where she lived with her foster parents in East Mersea.

When I tackled dad about going out so much, he flew into a rage.

"You're just jealous of Lil," he shouted.

"So what if I am, you're never at home when I need you," I shouted back.

He came towards me with his hand raised.

"Go on then hit me," I bellowed expecting the now familiar backhander across my cheek that I was becoming so accustomed to, made worse by the sting of the large silver ring, worn on his little finger, which Lil had bought him whilst we were in Paris. I found myself bravely confronting him; he just growled and walked away. It was the last time that he ever attempted to hit me.

My brother once said "No matter what dad does, we still can't help loving him." He was right.

Well he was all we had, apart from each other.

BEGUILED – DEFILED – REVILED

Doris Thompson had made a good job of styling my hair.

"The short style makes you look quite grown up Rita," she said brushing the loose hair from the back of my neck. "You've left school now haven't you?"

Feeling happy and proud, I paid her with the money that I earned doing my Saturday job, working for Mrs Hadley.

Standing outside Woodward's general shop, armed with a packet of 'Gold Leaf' cigarettes and a box of matches, I felt like the 'bees knees' with my new hairstyle and wearing the pencil skirt that I had made with the help of Mrs Johnson, the school sewing teacher, in readiness for the school leaving party.

A white Austin A40 drew up beside where I stood. "Hello Poppet, want a lift?"

The scent of Old Spice reached out to me as he reached across and opened the passenger door. I had often seen him driving past, but didn't know who he was.

"You're Dick Oppezzo's sister aren't you?" his cultured voice impressed me as I got into the car. I realised that he was a lot older than me and although he was showing signs of losing his hair, he was very good looking.

"Daddy is away in Paris with his girlfriend at the moment," I said endeavouring to impress him with my poor attempt at a posh accent.

"How long is he away for?"

"Ten days."

"What about your brother?"

"Oh he's never in now that he is going out with Barbara." The risk I was taking never occurred to me.

"Would you like to come out for a ride in the car tomorrow evening? We could go to East Mersea if you like."

I did like. I was beguiled by the overwhelming charm of Leslie Lester.

"Walk over to my workshop around seven thirty; you'll see my car there," he said as he dropped me at the end of the road.

The workshop - a large double garage - stood on a piece of overgrown land and was easily reached by cutting across the steep grass verge separating it from Windsor Road.

"Hello Poppet, you get in the car, I just have to lock up." There was that 'Old Spice' again. He looked so smart in a perfectly ironed white, short-sleeved shirt and a precise crease in his obviously expensive, dark beige slacks. I felt very self-conscious wearing the same skirt and blouse that I had worn the day before. I wondered if he knew that I had just left school.

"What a pity you haven't got a mummy to make you a nice new skirt for the school leaver's party," Mrs Vine sarcastically commented as she pinned up the hem of the blue needle cord skirt. "Do keep still dear," she said as my school friend looked down from where she stood on a chair.

Mrs Johnson was horrified when, at the next sewing class, I told her what had been said. "Well you will have a nice new skirt: you get the material and a zip and we will make it together.

Having borrowed five shillings from Lil, I bought a yard of blue tweed skirt material and a zip from Mrs Hadley who kindly threw in the matching cotton.

My new pencil skirt, which was completed in the two hour lesson, was the envy of all my friends. Not only do I have to thank Mrs Johnson for her patient guidance all those years ago, but also Mrs Vine; for it was her unkind comments which had the effect of inspiring me with what resulted in a lifelong love of dressmaking.

"Where do you work?" he asked as though reading my mind.

"I haven't got a proper job yet."

"What do you mean by a proper job?"

"Well I have a Saturday job at Hadley's and now that I have left school Mrs Hadley wants me to work on Wednesday mornings."

The fact that I was only fifteen didn't seem to worry him. I was too shy to ask him *his* age.

"Does your brother know about you coming out with me?"

"No, he thinks I am round my friend Diana's."

"Good, only he might think that I am a bit too old for you."

The sun was just starting to set when we arrived at the furthest point in East Mersea to be reached by car. He pulled up close to the gates that led down to the golf club. The redness of the sky reflected on the mirror like surface of the outgoing tide as the sun dropped down behind the horizon. I blushed as he reached across and began to undo my blouse. His kisses were hard against my naively, tightly pursed lips.

"Come on Poppet, relax, I'm not going to hurt you."

"I must go home now," I said as I nervously fumbled with the buttons on my blouse.

"Why? We've only just got here."

"Yes but I've just remembered, Dick is coming home early," I lied.

It was all happening too quickly; I just wanted to go home.

"Ok," he sighed as he started up the engine, "I haven't put you off have I? I would really like to see you again, how about tomorrow?"

I had been seeing him for a week when one evening he took me down a narrow lane leading off East Road.

"It's nice and quiet down here," he said as we passed the sewage works, "and you get a good view of the sea from here."

"Come on Poppet, let's get into the back."

His kisses seemed more urgent. I now felt that if I didn't

give in to his demands, he would lose interest in me. I had had enough of my father's increasingly violent temper; I wanted to get away and make a life of my own. Maybe this would prove to be my means of escape.

I painfully lost my innocence and prematurely grew up as the setting sun turned the clouds to a vivid scarlet. As Leslie got back into the driver' seat he trapped the flower head of a dandelion as he closed the car door; its petals fell to the floor as he started up the engine. For Some unknown reason, the sight of the petals being crushed beneath his feet made me want to cry.

"Once you let a man have you *in that way*," My brother once told me, "you will have to marry him, as no other man will want you." I believed him.

Knowing that neither my father, nor my brother were at home in the evenings, the sound of pebbles thrown at my bedroom window, usually after ten o-clock, meant my getting out of bed to open the back door to a rather intoxicated Leslie. He smelt different, not just of alcohol, but somehow different. I didn't dare let him come up to my bedroom as he requested, however, after half an hour, having taken what he wanted from me on the sitting room floor, he was gone. At least he did take precautions.

"The wife of one of the chaps I work with is a supervisor at Marks & Spencer in Colchester," Leslie told me whilst on one of his visits," "and they are looking for staff at the moment, why don't you go in and make some enquiries, "he said handing me a piece of paper with a woman's name on it. "He said to ask for that name when you go in."

I did and I got a job as a counter assistant, starting the following week. The weekly pay was three pounds fifteen shillings and after paying my bus fare and giving dad a pound towards my keep, I was able to save a small amount.

Mrs Hadley was sad when I told her about my new job.

"I only wish I could offer you full time work dear, but I couldn't afford to pay both you and Jenny and not only that," she said putting her arm around my shoulder, "it will do you good to get off the island and make new friends." She gave me a motherly kiss on the cheek as I tearfully left. In a way I was sorry to leave, I liked her; she had always been very kind to me.

A huge row developed when my brother tackled me about my relationship with Leslie

"What the hell do you think you're doing? He's nearly twice your age."

"Who told you?"

"Never mind who told me, he's been seen coming round here late at night when me and dad are out and you've been seen going about with him in his car."

"Well you're never here, nor is dad and I get lonely and he's kind to me," I shouted through my tears. "Does dad know?"

"No but I'll bloody well make sure he does if you carry on seeing him. Have you had sex with him?"

"So what if I have, that is none of your business."

He went to slap me and caught me painfully across my breast.

"Oh God, I didn't mean to hit you there, I meant to hit you on the arm, have I hurt you."

I couldn't understand the reason for his tearful concern; we had often had brother and sisterly scuffles. It all became clear when he told me that our grandmother Lydia had died of breast cancer supposedly caused, according to what dad had told him, by her brother punching her in the breast.

"You won't tell dad will you," he pleaded as I showed him the angry red hand mark, "you know what a temper he has."

Yes I did know and couldn't bear the thought of being the cause of any unnecessary upset between my father and brother.

I had, witnessed many of my father's violent outbursts aimed at my brother when I was a small girl. One such occasion springs to mind. We were living in Waterside at the time, I was six and he was twelve. It was

during the summer and having arrived home from school I was made to sit on the sea wall and watch as he and one of his friends decided to try out dad's new outboard motor. He didn't go out far as he knew that he had to keep an eye on me, but the reflection from the descending afternoon sun on the mirror like surface of the water made it difficult for me to see him. Suddenly there was a loud noise that he told me later, was the propeller hitting something hard beneath the surface of the outgoing tide. Securing our dinghy 'The 'Gwenirita' to the sea wall, Dick and his friend Sid carried the injured motor back to where it was kept in the lean-to shed beside the cottage.

"Listen, if it looks as though I'm going to get a thrashing for this, for God's sake start to cry," he pleaded as he lay the broken piece of the propeller on the kitchen table. It didn't need much to bring on my tears when I saw the colour rise in my father's face as Dick, shaking with fear, endeavoured to tell him what had happened. My tears, along with my mother's pleading, had no effect as dad, not waiting to listen to the full story, grabbed him by his clothing and threw my poor brother against the back door; the whole house seemed to shake with the force of the impact and as Dick collapsed to the floor, I ran upstairs in search of teddy with the continuing sound of my mother's pleading voice ringing in my ears.

"I did try," I whispered into the darkness as I heard the muffled sound of him crying into his pillow. He didn't answer.

My father's mood swings didn't improve and as time went on, for some unknown reason, I felt the need to contact my mother. I hadn't seen or heard from her for over two years and it was only through her solicitor, Mr Thompson of Thomson, Smith and Puxton, that I learned of their new address and how, having sold the house in Brixton, they now lived in Hadleigh, Essex where they had purchased a bungalow. After corresponding with my mother, Mr Thompson was able to pass on her telephone number.

My hand shook as I dialled the number from the telephone box outside the Fountain Hotel. I propped the door open with my foot, letting in the cool evening air and letting out the strong smell of urine and stale cigarette smoke.

The coins clattered into the black metal box as I pressed button A.

"Hello love," the dulcet sound of my mother's voice reached out to me. "Hello, are you there?"

A tight throated sob was the only sound I could make.

"Rita, is that you love?"

"Yes," the choking pent up emotions now loosening their grip.

My Money ran out and I had no more change. I rang again the next evening, making sure I had enough change this time. There were always tears as I told her the reasons for my unhappiness. "Well my dear you are growing up now and I am sure you will soon be finding a nice boyfriend, or have you already got one?" There was a hopeful tone to her question. "Has he got a car?" she asked when I told her about Leslie. "He could bring you to visit us for tea one Sunday; we would like to meet him. Give us a ring and let us know when you can make it."

On leaving the phone-box that particular evening, I was both surprised and delighted when I unexpectedly bumped into Ruthie; she was pushing an old pram with two toddlers sitting at either end. I had last seen her about three years .ago at one of the dances regularly held at the Hall Barn Country Club. In her teens she was very pretty and always attracted a great deal of attention from males of all ages. She was now, at the age of twenty two, a beautiful young woman. I heard that she had left the island, having got married and moved with her husband, who .was serving in the RAF, to Malta.

"Now young lady, I want a word with yeu," she said after telling me how she was now back on the island with her two small sons. "I hear that you've got yourself involved with that thar Lester bloke; well yeu wanna stop that lark or you'll end up like me, tied down to a man a lot older than yourself with kids to contend with," she said wiping the nose of the youngest of the two small boys

"Oh Ruthie I *have* missed you and so much has happened and you weren't there for me."

"Well I'm here now and I shall be keeping an eye on yer from now on." She seemed changed and hard. I didn't like the grown up Ruthie. Getting hurriedly on my bike, I called over my shoulder that I had left school now and I didn't need her telling me what to do. She shouted something as I quickly peddled away down towards the village where I hoped to meet up with my friends. Like most teenagers, I didn't want to listen to the advice given by grownups and that is how I now saw Ruthie, all grown up.

The first visit to see my mother and stepfather felt strange. I hadn't seen them in so long; they had both put on weight. Aunty was sat in an antiquated bath-chair out in the garden, she looked very frail and didn't open her eyes until I handed her a cup of tea. Her deafness seemed a lot worse.

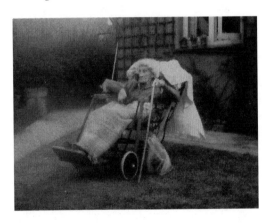

Johnny, attempting to impress Leslie with a pseudo posh accent - that is when my mother stopped chattering and allowed him to get a word in - told us of the instructions, left, by my Grandmother in her will, saying that Aunty Jess was to have a roof over her head for the duration of her life. She was now in her late eighties and being very frail, she needed constant care, a task that my mother was only too pleased to undertake. He went on to tell us how Ida was no longer living with them as she had become so objectionable following my departure, that he had found it necessary to evict her.

He never saw or spoke of his mother again.

My father and I once came across Ida whilst shopping in Elmo's, a small Colchester supermarket in Long Wire Street; she was on her knees scrubbing the shop floor. Mumbling some inaudible profanities, she glared at us as we walked over the area still wet from her efforts. I never did find out the details of how she had found accommodation back in Colchester.

My mother had always been talkative but was now even more so, hardly waiting for answers to the multitude of questions she fired at us both

"Such a gentleman, I like him," she said as I helped her with the tea tray, "and such endearing, brown, spaniel eyes; he's very handsome. I think Johnny likes him; they seem to be getting on well. "

I was embarrassed as Leslie, sitting on the edge of his chair, tried to get a word in as my mother fired questions his way.

"So you own your own business, isn't that wonderful Johnny and what a lovely car; Johnny has promised to teach me to drive. Will you teach Rita? Oh yes you're not old enough yet are you love." And on and on!

"Does she always go on like that," he said as we thankfully made our way back to Mersea.

PECULIARITIES OF LESLIE LESTER

To Leslie, everything had to be of the very best quality; goodness knows where that came from. Izzy, Leslie's' mother and Bert, his father, were just good old-fashioned country folk. Izzy was a humble and genuinely sincere practising Christian who regularly attended the local Methodist church and Albert was a quiet, gentle family man who loved his wife with all his being. He worked as a manager a local grocery store and was highly thought of by all who knew him. Neither of them drank and Bert's only vice was his pipe. The only transport they had ever owned was a bicycle each.

Bert was seriously injured with flying shrapnel during the final stages of the First World War. Izzy journeyed over to France to visit him where he was first taken to one of the military hospitals before being transferred nearer to home. This must have meant a great deal of courage on her part as she rarely left the island and when she did it was by bus to Colchester. They were both natives of Mersea Island although I believe others of their respective families did journey further afield. Francis, Bert's brother, immigrated to New Zealand where he was to remain for many years. (It was said at the time that he ran off with a local married woman whom he later married).

I first met Izzy and Bert when Leslie told them that he intended to marry me. They were distraught and tried very hard to put him off. Of course I now realise they wisely knew that at the tender age of fifteen, I was far too young and their son, who was approaching thirty, was far too old for me. They must have had many sleepless nights. Yet still they were kind and gentle, possibly in the hope that maybe time would eventually tell!!

Having had enough of my Dad's temper and unreasonable behaviour and after many tearful phone calls to my mother, I was relieved when she suggested that I go and stay with them for a while. I did and yet again it wasn't a good move. Life with her and Johnny, who were both still very much wrapped up in each other's company, was not what I had hoped for. With the bungalow only having two bedrooms, one of which was Auntie Jess's room; there really wasn't enough room for me. Whilst living out of a suitcase and having to sleep on an ancient camp-bed in the small sitting room, I never really felt at home, in fact I felt quite guilty for having invaded their lives. My one consolation was looking after Aunty, so as to allow my mother the time to accompany Johnny to various sales promotions, held in the large food stores, put on by 'Brazill's', the company for whom he now worked as sales promotion manager.

It wasn't long before I decided that the journey made by Leslie, each weekend, from Mersea to Hadleigh, near Southend, was too far for him to travel and that it would be easier if I agreed to his proposal of marriage sooner rather than later. If the truth be known, what I really wanted was to get out of my mother's hair and have a home of my own.

Leslie agreed to bring the wedding forward and the weekend of my sixteenth birthday he took me to a jeweller in Southend where he purchased an engagement ring.

"We are engaged" I announced to a delighted mother as I proudly proffered the solitaire diamond ring.

"That must have cost a bob or two" my stepfather said sneakily winking at my mother.

"Damn good quality diamond," Leslie said puffing up his chest as he always did when he boasted.

"When is the wedding?" my mother asked. There was almost a sense of urgency as she added "I expect you won't want to wait; the long journey won't be made any easier with the onslaught of winter."

I knew that all she really wanted was to hand me over

as soon as possible. I never felt welcome.

It became necessary for me to make the journey back to Mersea so as to obtain my father's permission before the wedding could legally take place.

The following weekend Leslie met me off the coach at Colchester bus station. I was extremely nervous, but need not have been as my father showed no interest in what I had to ask. Leslie felt it best if he waited outside in the car.

"You do what the hell you like," my father dismissively commented, "don't expect to see me or your brother come to the wedding. He's bloody furious with you going off like that and I'm not too happy either."

I was relieved when I realised that Dick was out.

"The Christening gown is upstairs if you need it," dad said sarcastically.

"Why should I need the Christening gown?" I was shocked, "I'm not pregnant."

I could see by the look on his face that he didn't believe me.

We were married in late September at the Thurrock registry office in Grays. I was driven there alone in a rather shabby limousine hired by Johnny from a Gypsy acquaintance of his, who, it was later revealed, was ripping him off for bogus repairs on his car.

I have very few memories of the ceremony, especially who, if anyone, gave me away.

The enduring memories of the reception, which took place at the bungalow, were the bowls of pickled onions; halved, hard boiled eggs surrounded by limp lettuce leaves and sliced tomatoes; Haslet (a sort of spicy Spam) sandwiches, along with thick slices of veal and ham pie; all provided by 'Brazill's Sausage and Pie Company'. I could tell by the disgruntled look on Leslie's face, that none if it matched up to his expectations of the occasion

There was of course the absence of Izzy and Bert, however Leslie's brother Gerald came with his new wife Sylvia, with her loud, coarse laugh and strong west-country accent. It amused Leslie when he saw the disapproving look sent in her direction by my mother. Also attending were Basil Underwood and his beautiful blond wife Jean who were great friends with Leslie. Jean was dressed in a stylish black suit and wore a fox fur round her slim elegant shoulders. My mother later informed me that the suit was 'Barathea no less'! Coming, as they did, from wealthy families, the entire affair must have thoroughly amused them both. The whole event made me feel totally inadequate and self-conscious. Leslie had paid for everything, including my dress. I was married in white even though it was a registry office ceremony.

We spent our honeymoon in the Lake District and on the way there we stopped at a local pub for supper. It was all so new to me and I was extremely nervous. The last time I had been away from home was with dad and Lil when we all went on holiday to Paris. Leslie ordered Steak and Chips and *bloody peas*! I chased those peas around my plate as I tried desperately to scoop them onto my fork.

"No, no poppet, the correct way is to turn your fork over and press them onto it like this," he expertly demonstrated with a sardonic smile as I looked on with growing embarrassment.

During that time away I was very conscious of the fact that I hadn't got the kind of clothes enabling me to 'dress for dinner' and was crestfallen as I gazed around the opulent dining-room of The Royal Hotel in Keswick, where we stayed for the first couple of nights. It was full of well dressed people all of whom, I imagined in my naivety, must have been staring at me. I dreaded each time we had to enter that dining room and I was relieved when we left to find less pompous surroundings.

Leslie had a peculiar manner which at times I found quite frightening. We were visiting Grasmere where we stood looking into the black waters of the 'Screes'. He seemed to take great delight in describing how there was a shear drop down the side of the mountain into the murky depths of the black water and how it just kept on going.

"If anyone was to fall in there, no one would ever find

the body as the water is so deep," there was a macabre teasing tone to his voice. "Anyway who would think to look?"

It was strange how he seemed to instil fear. As he stood behind me, I found myself wondering if he was going to push me over the side of the mountain. I had never experienced fear of this nature before, however this was an emotion that became more prevalent over the next few years.

As we drove away, parked on the side of the track against the backdrop of the scene that had so frightened me, was a shabby old caravan and to add to the drama, peering through the grimy window, lit only by a candle, was an aged grim face staring out at us; it was hard to see if the face was male or female. In the fading light of dusk, an autumn mist was beginning to descend, adding a kind of eeriness to the late September evening and I remember praying that the engine of the Austin A40 would not fail to get us away from there, post haste.

Going to bed with my new husband did not prove to be the romantic experience I had expected. He never showed any tenderness towards me. Every touch of his hands signalled his lustful desire for my inexperienced young body. It was the first time that anyone, apart that is from family when I was a small girl, had seen me completely naked. He couldn't understand why I insisted on putting my nightdress back on before going to sleep.

I so yearned for love. I had never really experienced unconditional love, especially from my parents and brother. There always seemed to be a hidden reason for their touch which usually resulted in an unexpected outcome. Both my grandparents were non-tactile. Nonno, my dad's father and Nannie, my mum's mother, were both wrapped up in their own thoughts and feelings and were very unapproachable. I don't ever remember them giving me a cuddle or being invited to sit on either of their laps. I suppose in a way it was easier for me to accept the way Leslie was and yet there was always something missing; I couldn't identify what it was. It meant that I was always searching, looking for that certain something in everyone who entered my small world and would continue to do so for many years; causing me to make a great many wrong decisions, choosing to take the wrong paths and yet doing so has been a huge learning process for which I can only be grateful.

As I look back on those times, I realise that Leslie never really learnt how to love for the right reasons. He, as was so with my parents and grandparents, was so wrapped up in himself; it was as though he had tunnel vision or was blinkered and could only see and feel what he wanted or needed to at the time.

I was too young to fully appreciate the true beauty of the lakes and mountains of Cumbria and after a few days all I wanted was to return home and start a new life of my own.

The long journey home was made easier by a one night stopover in Cambridgeshire where we stayed in a rather shabby hotel in St Neots. The water heater over a non-too clean bath made strange popping noises as barely warm water gurgled its way out of the heavily lime-scaled tap. I was doubtful about using one of the scruffy bath towels which sat in an untidy pile on a chair; however I was left with no choice.

On our return, it was necessary for us to stay with Leslie's parents, (Mum and Dad as I now called them) until we were able to find a place of our own.

Mum was a sweet country woman and dad was a gentle quiet man. They were devoted to each other. I can still see them sitting together on the sofa in their comfortable homely lounge. Dad always sat very close to his wife with one of his strong arms encircling her small frame; with his large hand dangling over her shoulder, resting on her ample breast. They were not a bit self-conscious and neither was I, thinking how lovely it was to be in the company of such genuinely loving and contented people.

Leslie and his brother Gerald must have had an idyllic childhood. One never heard raised voices in his parent's house and the mouth-watering aroma of Mum's home baking always seemed to permeate the spotlessly neat rooms.

There was always order and harmony. On Mondays, the whole day seemed to be taken up with the task of washing. I still remember the damp smell that hung on the air as the old fashioned 'copper' bubbled away in the outhouse; the fire beneath fed with wood from various sources Linen steeping in the boiling soapy water was periodically prodded and stirred around by the 'copper stick'. The wooden rollers of the ancient mangle, showing the wear and tear of years of use, creaking and grumbling as the rinsing water (having been made blue by a small muslin 'blue bag' swished through it so as to add the illusion of extra whiteness) squeezed from the heavy linen sheets, ran into a galvanised bath. Most of all I remember dear Mum, hardly pausing for breath, whilst bustling around like a busy little bumble-bee. The weather always seemed to be fine, which of course it wasn't. The pristine washing blowing out on a good breeze like the sails of a great sailing vessel bound for far off lands. Goodness knows where all the washing came from. I do know however, that the linen sheets on the beds always felt fresh and cool against your skin and whilst taking a bath, in preparation for bed, the clothes you had just removed somehow miraculously disappeared. Mum lived to care for those around her. It always caused great amusement to the family, when after the days washing was completed, the kitchen floor, which was red quarry tiles, would be thoroughly scrubbed, using the water from the copper, then covered with cardboard (which Dad used to bring back from the store for this purpose) this was then covered with a layer of newspaper so as to keep the cardboard clean!

It's wonderful how the influence of some folk can imprint only sweet memories on an impressionable young mind.

One thing I will always hold dear in my memory of Mum was her generosity; always bringing or sending little gifts. When she visited anyone; she never went empty handed. Gifts ranged from produce harvested from a very productive garden, to clothing or 'handy' items thoughtfully chosen from a church jumble sale or bazaar. All gifts were meticulously wrapped in tissue paper or a brown paper bag (all bags, wrappings, string and elastic bands were religiously saved for this purpose) and then having been tied up with string, the parcel was then placed in another bag and secured with an elastic band.

Mum was small framed and quite chubby, whereas Dad was tall and lean and also very handsome. I always pictured him in a deerstalker hat and flowing cape, magnifying glass in hand following in the trail of a murder suspect; there being a strong resemblance to Douglas Wilmer, actor of stage and screen, best known for his role of Sherlock Holmes

Winter and summer, rain or shine, they both rode their bicycles everywhere. Dad, with cycle-clips securing his trousers away from the well maintained and greased chain, his long legs sticking out either side of the bike and his feet looking too large for the pedals, ambled along beside his wife, whose short legs had to go round twice as fast so as to keep up the pace. On the front of her bike was a large basket filled with goodies for some fortunate or needy person.

During my stressful period, both before and after the birth of Jeanette, they were so kind and gave me a great deal of support; I think they loved me a little. They had always wanted a daughter. I seem to remember the mention of a miscarriage of a little girl before the birth of Leslie. I can never imagine how two such devout people could have raised such (in my eyes) a monster; I suppose they made the mistake of spoiling him until Gerald, came along five or six years later.

Leslie once had occasion to tell me that as a child he didn't like anyone using anything that belongs to him, once they had he usually threw it away, no longer wanting it. I was to witness this many times whilst married to him. I once made the mistake of using his 'Parker' fountain pen, apparently a present from an old flame; he raised the roof and after telling me how it was such a 'damn good quality expensive pen,' warned me never to touch it again, in fact never to go into the writing bureau without first asking permission. His need to imprint his possessions must have been what first attracted him to me. After all I was very young and most importantly a virgin. To him I was an unsullied possession. Thinking about it now, I realise how contradictory his life was. Not wishing to have anything to do with used goods did not deter him from having an ongoing affair with a divorcee before, during and after his time with me.

Leslie was fastidious to the letter and made a point of telling me "Damn good quality these Daks," holding up a new pair of trousers; to me they were just like any other trousers. The shirts had to be different too; 'sea island cotton' no less! All I knew was that they were a bloody nightmare to iron especially for an inexperienced sixteen year old who merely wanted to please her lord and master by getting it right

Gin and tonic was one of his 'poisons', 'It's a clean drink' he told me as I sat looking at a row of assorted barely touched drinks in front of me; hoping to God, as I sampled this 'clean drink', that I would like it. Screwing up my face, alas the answer was a very decisive 'No'; yet another one to add the assortment. It embarrassed me to sit in the local pub whilst he tried in vain to get me to have a 'grown up drink for once.' "Babycham and Cherry 'B' is for kids," he told me reproachfully

They were about the strongest alcoholic drinks I had experienced, except that is, for one dreadful New Years Eve.

I was about fourteen and we, me and my girlfriends, had been enjoying ourselves at a local hop. Margaret, who was a bit older than the rest of us, suggested that we all go back to her house to see in the New Year as her mother and father were out. I knew I didn't have to worry about my dad or, my brother, as they were well out of it at the dance so they wouldn't have known if I had arrived home or not. Anyway dad would have been staying with Lil and Dick would have gone on to party most of the night, which meant I would have been alone at home anyway. Margaret raided her father's drinks cupboard and I was handed a tumbler almost full of a very sweet, orange flavoured drink which I later

*learnt was a liqueur called 'Cointreau'. Thinking it was Gin and
Orange, I enjoyed it and asked for another, after which I was very ill!
When her parents returned home they were quite amused and didn't seem
to mind that we were drinking their drinks. I was put into Margaret's
bed where she cuddled me all night (I thought I was going to die) I
suppose that's why I gagged each time I tasted strong alcohol thereafter
and it was a long time before I could even touch 'Babycham'.*

Leslie spoke with a deliberate tone of voice, giving him
an air of authority no matter the subject he was holding court
over. My accent had become that of a typical teenager, trying
to be one of the gang, since returning to Mersea. (Gwenny
would have been appalled!). He often picked me up on my
poor grammar and the way I spoke; laughing at my childish
conversation caused me to feel humiliated, especially in front
of his posh drinking pals. His expectations of me were too
high, wanting me to be a woman with the innocence of a
child.

Being extremely materialistic, when he bought a present
it had to be and always was, 'Damned good quality that
poppet,' having to outdo the next man at all times; especially
my brother who, coincidentally, had also become very
conscious of material wealth and possessions.

"See what your brother thinks of that then," his chest
swelling with pride as he stuck out his chin and guffawed
gruffly (his attempt at laughing).

My first Christmas present was a 'Roberts' radio

"You can't get better than that you know poppet, last
for years that will."

*And it has, I still have it after so many years and it still works,
but alas it gathers dust up in the loft as it won't tune to FM.*

The dreadful sheepskin coat he insisted on buying for the
next Christmas was very expensive, very heavy and too big

"It's too big and heavy." I protested as I eyed an elegant
Ocelot Cat fur coat hanging limply on the plastic shoulders of a
stony faced mannequin, standing in the window of 'Sachs &
Brendlor', the furriers in Head Street, Colchester.

"You'll grow into it and there will be plenty of room for extra jumpers when it gets really cold."

I didn't have a choice. I was never to have a choice.

A good housekeeping diary was also to be a regular 'must have' each year.

"Help you keep account of the money you spend." Money? What money? Every penny of the meagre housekeeping I was allowed to handle had to be accounted for. I used to get so worried if I couldn't make it last; reminding me of the pound a week my dad used to give me to buy the week's bread and meat; I got just as worried about that. At least it resulted in my continued thriftiness throughout my life, which I suppose can't be a bad thing.

Leslie rarely laughed and when he did it was almost as though he were holding back, not wanting to show his inner feelings to the outside world; or maybe he was just afraid to let go of his emotions. He was always so immovable in his outlook, having to always be right and would dismiss as nonsense any other points of view. It was his philosophy that Oswald Mosley and to a certain extent Hitler, were both on the right track. He was a strong racist and believed in the perfect race. I used to wonder if there had been a history of foreign blood in his family as he was really quite dark haired and easily bronzed but never burnt by exposure to the sun; that and the Latin look of his most endearingly large, dark brown eyes (my mother always referred to him as 'spaniel eyes'). He appeared to be physically rigid, causing him turn his whole body whilst turning his head, as though there was no flexibility in his neck. If only one could have found the key to the imprisoned heart and release the timid soul that dwelt therein. I was too young, too frightened and too insecure to even begin to understand him.

I am sure at some stage in his life he must have read the Karma Sutra because he always wanted to experiment during sex; one would have needed to be a contortionist to carry out some of his more bizarre wishes. In those days not a lot was spoken about the finer details of the sexual act. As teenagers we used to giggle about things which we thought we knew about and made up what we didn't know. One would have expected my lack of experience and embarrassment to have frustrated him and yet sometimes it appeared to excite him. He found my being quite shocked amusing. I can't have been a very stimulating partner in that way but then again, he was so wrapped up his own small world, I doubt if he was even aware of me as a person at times. I might just as well have been a blow up plastic doll. Occasionally he would get quite carried away, especially after too much alcohol, when he became quite rough, causing me injuries. Doctor Dorothy, having known me since I was a small girl, showed great concern over my plight, whilst at the same time offering a sympathetic ear. She also kept records!

Having been living with Mum and Dad since coming back off honeymoon, it was quite a relief when we moved into the rented flat which I managed to find through the local estate agent.

'The 'Nothest' stands at the end of a row of very old cottages at the furthest habitable point of Coast Road where it then joins the sea-wall and the marshes leading to 'The Strood'. I knew and loved this area, it being only a stones-throw away from 'Waterside', the house we lived in as children. Our flat was quite a modern addition to the 'Nothe'. It consisted of a very large room which, I later learned, was originally designed to serve as a dance studio for the owner's daughter Jenny, who eventually went on to become a 'Bluebell Girl'.

The room was later divided so as to provide a sitting room, bedroom and good sized bathroom. It was very cold in the winter with only a small open fireplace in the lounge area, which was hardly any help at all due to most of the heat rising into the high ceiling and more especially because of my lack of knowledge about fire lighting. Many a frustrated tear was shed as the blackened newspaper and kindling breathed its last few coils of smoke before dying completely; after which the whole messy lot had to be hauled out and the entire procedure started all over again. Although Leslie's trade was as a carpenter and joiner, he never once thought of bringing home off-cuts for kindling. I either had to collect driftwood or depend on Bert bringing chopped up apple boxes from the store.

A large bay window took up one end of the lounge giving a marvellous view of the estuary and the spectacular big sky sunsets. However the blustery north easterly winds across the marshes rattled at the curtain-less bay window during the colder months of that year when, having stayed in bed for as long as I could and after having finished the housework, I then spent most afternoons and early evenings huddled in an eiderdown and blanket.

A door led through from the main part of the cottage, where Mr and Mrs Lane resided, into the small kitchen where I often stood listening to the sounds of a luncheon or dinner party taking place. When Jenny came home on a break from the theatre, there was always a party. The chink of glasses and the clatter of plates along with the sound of happy, laughing voices made me feel very envious and lonely.

Mr Lane was a professional illustrator and cartoon artist and mostly now worked from home. He appeared to be unwell most of the time and found difficulty in walking any further than a short stroll around the garden. I only ever saw him on the odd occasion when he was sitting out in the front garden with a cigarette in one hand and a glass of amber coloured liquid in the other. He gave the impression that he drank and smoked too much; however, I discovered that he was a likeable gentleman.

Mrs Lane was a very sweet lady who impressed me with her cultured accent and gentle manner. She was always very complimentary about the way I had cleaned up and looked after the flat, as it was in a filthy condition when we first moved in, especially the kitchen.

I spent a lot of cold lonely hours in that flat. Standing - in the large bay window, shivering with the relentless cold, I would look out towards 'The Ray'; tears of forlorn emptiness streaming down my cheeks whilst I listened to the distant sound of the riggings jangling against the masts of the sailing vessels moored against the 'Dabchicks' Sailing Club where once stood the boat sheds of Admiral Bill Wyatt

It was that same old sea dog who saved my life all those years ago, when as a small girl of four, I had decided to don my father's ex-army 'May West' life jacket and wade out for a swim. Having forgotten to tie up the straps, the life jacket floated up over my head as I sank into the briny depths.

"Yer silly little bugger yer could have drowned "he said hauling me up by the straps of my hand knitted swimming costume coughing and gagging. Dangling like a string puppet, I was carried back and dumped on the door step as he hammered on the door of 'Waterside'

"Yer nearly lost er this time missus" he called back as he strode away from my very surprised grandmother who was on one of her rare visits from where she lived in London. She was supposedly looking after me whilst my mother was at work!

Admiral Bill Wyatt

Being too immature to enjoy the beautiful views of the setting sun glinting on the outgoing tide, I was filled with longing for the return of the days when as children we used to row out to 'Ray Island in our small dingy 'The Gwenirita' and spend a carefree weekend camping with our dad; a place where it always seemed to be summer and where we were always happy. Now standing in the draughty bay-window watching storm clouds gather as galloping white horses, whipped up by the strong wind, raced over the grey-green waves of the incoming tide, another memory sprang to mind

We were returning from one of our regular trips to 'The Ray' when the wind got up and storm clouds began ominously gathering overhead. Dad, hell-bent on getting my brother and me back to the safety of the sea wall,' struggled at the oars as our small craft bobbed about as though made of paper. Large crewless boats, tugging at their moorings, came menacingly near. Dad and Dick could both swim, but I had yet to learn and even if I had been able, my feeble efforts would have proved useless against the swell of the storm charged sea. When we finally reached dry land, the storm broke with such violence that I remember dad – who wasn't a religious man - letting out a great sigh of relief as he offered up a prayer of gratitude. I had such confidence and felt great pride in my strong, handsome daddy; I never felt afraid of anything or anyone when he was around. It wasn't long after that terrifying event, that dad decided to invest in a second-hand out-board motor.

What was I doing here? It's entirely my fault; I should never have married him. I should never have got married at all; I'm only sixteen. Where are all my friends? Since leaving school, Gloria was now working for Lenny Pullen, a local grocer, as his delivery girl. Quiet, shy Helen, whose father knew no sexual bounds and whose mother was totally besotted with her 'Bobby dear', was now off in search of boys and the Beatles. Little Pat whose fanatically house-proud mother drove her gentle unassuming father to an early grave and was to be the cause of her only daughter prematurely leaving home. The Conway boys whose pretty mother

Bubbles, being innocent of the knowledge that smoking may cause cancer, left their broken-hearted father a widower to bring up two teenage boys alone. And I thought I had troubles!

How I filled those long lonely days and most evenings, I cannot remember. Writing to my mother filled a small space. During the winter months I mostly wore gloves, making writing a bit difficult. I busied myself with the daily tasks of cleaning the flat and doing the washing, wringing it out by hand as I had no modern appliances, not even a mangle. The only place for a linen line, which I strung between a tree and a rickety piece of fence, was on the north end of the building and my fingers froze as I struggled against the fierce north-easterly winds cutting across the marshes.

We only had one set of sheets and I felt very ashamed when bad weather meant that I couldn't wash and dry them the same day. I felt even more ashamed when I had to ask Leslie's mother if she could spare any old sheets. The next time she visited, she brought a parcel wrapped in brown paper and tied up with string and as I unwrapped the beautifully laundered and patched sheet she mistook my tears of gratitude, thinking they were due to disappointment until I explained. Then wrapping one of my dirty sheets in the brown paper and tying it up with the string, she took it home with her to be lovingly laundered. Saving all paper bags, rubber bands and string for reuse, she was the original recycler, nothing was ever wasted and when plastic bags became popular, she was in her element. I had never experienced such genuine, thoughtful kindness.

Looking back I now realise how seriously I took on the burden of housewifely duties. I was twelve when I returned to Mersea and took pride in doing what seemed to come naturally; looking after my two favourite men, my father and my brother who both gave me two shillings and sixpence a week pocket money in payment of my efforts. Since my marriage, I continued to carry out, what I still considered to be my duty, in the best way that I knew how.

Leslie, who had been spoilt up to the age of going on thirty, by his mother's constant attention, was now expecting 'Poppet' at the tender age of sixteen, to do the same with the added bonus of sex on demand.

Mum and Dad cycled down to visit with me each week and always brought goodies which Mum carried in the basket on the front of her cycle. It would either be a pot of home-made Jam or lovely apples picked from their numerous fruit trees and stored in the summerhouse throughout the winter. There were also various root vegetables along with onions and leeks, cleaned and wrapped neatly in newspaper.

"Buy some shin of beef or oxtail and make a nice warming srew for Leslie's supper, he'll love that," Mum advised. She was a real-life Fairy Godmother and I grew to love them both dearly.

Endeavouring to repay her kindness, I attempted to make Mum a summer frock. I *had* made one or two skirts and blouses for myself, but never a frock and for someone else. I owned an old hand driven 'Singer' sewing machine that had once belonged to Lydia, my father's mother; it worked very well. The frock was a great success and being very proud of it she wore it for church and special occasions. Although they were not hard up, Mum never spent a lot on herself, however, she gained a great deal of enjoyment out of performing little kindnesses towards others.

A FALL FROM GRACE

It was now January and Leslie's birthday. I had been shopping up the village, which meant walking a mile there and a mile back, so as to buy his favourite, rump steak and the ingredients to make a sponge cake, which I had now become very proficient at since dear Hilda had shown me how. Having started to prepare the meal I realised that I had forgotten the mushrooms to go with the steak. Luckily there was a small general store opposite the causeway. The mushrooms were a bit past it but I was able to buy them at a cheaper price, which was a relief as I was nearly out of money.

As I left the shop I bumped into David, one of my old school pals. We had a bit of a chat about old times and caught up on the gossip; he told me he was working on the trawlers. It seemed longer than eighteen months since we left school at the age of fifteen. I was so pleased to see a familiar face and someone of my own age. I asked him if he would like a cup of tea; he collected his bicycle and we walked back to the flat.

As children we were all very close. Our families moved into the newly built council houses in Windsor Road in 1953. It was a great experience living in a modern three-bedroom house with a proper bathroom. Dad was delighted with his large garden and outhouse.

Along with David and his sister Susan there was Gloria; Geoffrey and his older sister Sylvia; the Conway brothers David and Steven; little Pat, and Helen who were a bit younger than us. The Sibleys were never allowed out to mix with us as their mother always acted as though she were a cut above the rest of us. I felt rather sorry for Pat Sibley, who was the same age as me, and I tried to befriend her but she was a very nervous, shy girl and used to get badly taunted by the others at school. We were a regular troupe; to call us a gang would be too harsh. We were innocents enjoying being together. When the sun shone we climbed the huge haystacks or played our favourite game of 'Rounders' in the field at the back of the houses, or hopscotch drawn out on the pavements. When it rained there was David and Susan's dad's shed where we occupied ourselves playing indoor games. One morning we awoke to find deep snow, so deep that there was no school that day and we played snowballs until our fingers were numb and our cheeks as red as cherries.

Then suddenly we were teenagers and everything changed. We made new friends from the village and our playground was further away down in the shopping area where we would hang around trying to look older than our years, spluttering and coughing over a first 'ciggy' and where some of the older boys showed off their motorbikes. We would all crowd into Brassy Mussett's, one of the small general stores in the High Street. Brassy would get very flustered as we teased and confused him. He was one of the old characters of the island and folk were amused by the eccentric way he always bit into a coin to see if it were genuine. The dimly lit shop always smelt of the paraffin lamps and rotting vegetables and the shelves were packed to the ceiling with ancient as well as new stock. He would allow us to buy five Weights or Woodbines that we used to call 'coffin nails' but it was still all very innocent.

David left his bicycle leaning against the low wall which ran along the full length of the cottages. Although it felt a bit strange now that I was a married woman, we soon found ourselves laughing and joking and enjoying each other's company. The time flew and as I walked with him to the front door, for some unaccountable reason, I didn't want him to go. It was as though I was watching my youth leave with him and it hurt and I cried; he seemed to feel my hurt and instinctively put his arms around me. It felt good. Just then Leslie's image appeared through the glass of the front door, seeing what was happening he literally sprang into the hall grabbed poor David and threw him out. I don't know if he did, but I could swear that I remembered him growling. He was furious, as one would expect a newly married man to be. I stood there frightened, very confused and rather embarrassed.

Then the ordeal began

"What the hell have you been up to?" his eyes were aflame with anger. I, with trembling voice, told him the truth. He marched me into the bedroom where he closely examined the bed. I was then ordered to take off my knickers, which he grabbed out of my hand; these were then closely examined as he held them up to his nose; I was rather bemused to see him sniff them.

Slamming the door behind him he left and came back half an hour later with my stepmother Lil. She was quite sympathetic and tried to calm the situation. Why he needed to bring her into it I will never know. I had never been able to get close to her; I suppose in reality I was jealous of her relationship with my father, that, along with her hostile attitude towards me, I looked on her as a bit of a threat.

Feeling utterly dejected and alone, I realised that life was not going to be easy; the imagined fairy tale romance was now turning into a horror story and I was trapped within its pages.

The story would have to go on as there was no other way and nowhere else to run to. He was not going to be that handsome prince on a white charger rescuing me from the Cinderella syndrome; he was the self-opinionated older man in a white A40 who wanted his child bride to tow the line and play the role he had expertly written for her.

The birthday tea I had planned was never eaten. Leslie, having taken Lil home, did not return until very late. I went to bed and cried myself into a fitful sleep; being awakened by a cold body, smelling of alcohol, getting into my warm refuge. He showed his need for me and although I was sickened by his lustful kisses smelling strongly of alcohol; I hoped that he had forgiven my fall from grace.

The Next Move

We stayed at The Nothest for approximately nine months until one blissful early summer evening, Hilda invited me round to tell me the good news that the dreadful tenant, Mrs Marsh - who had occupied my beloved 'Waterside' for the past two years, had been given her marching orders by Bernard due to considerable rent arrears. Would we like it?

"It will need a good clean," Hilda chuckled as she released herself from my tearful embrace, "that awful woman did nothing around the house except smoke and drink tea and my dear" she continued in her 'attempt at being posh' voice "she never seemed to cook anything other than chips and was always fighting with that good for nothing man she called her husband". She went on to say how the whole house would need re-decorating and that Bernard would be only too pleased to pay for the materials. I was so excited I could hardly wait to move in.

The facilities in 'Waterside' had improved a little since previously living there as a child. There was now running cold water in the kitchen with a very antiquated electric water heater which provided hot water to the rather battered sink, both of which Bernard had probably acquired from one of the council houses being modernised by Colchester Borough Council, for whom he worked. Although a very kind hearted chap, Bernard was rather parsimonious and being the landlord of several other rather neglected old properties inherited from his father, he never missed an opportunity to salvage discarded building materials, which was obvious by the over full out-buildings which in the past had been stables and storage for his father's horses and carrier's cart That was during the days when Bobby Cudmore and Mr Rudlin were the main carriers of goods and postage to and from Colchester.

Having established a reasonable rent and with the agreement that Bernard would replace the old water heater and fund the materials for the badly needed redecoration, we moved in. Luckily it was a sparsely furnished let and the only items we had to move from the flat were our clothes and the few bits and pieces of household goods that I had managed to collect for my 'bottom drawer'.

Once again I found myself cleaning someone else's filth; however none of that mattered now that I was back under the roof of my beloved 'Waterside'. Standing on the well worn, wooden, staircase and breathing in the musty scent of the old ships timbers, with their tar like smell, brought many childhood memories flooding back. I wasn't going to mind being alone here as I felt as though the very spirit of the house wrapped me in its warm embrace. As I scrubbed and polished the ancient oak floorboards that had had many high tides wash over them, the memory of one particularly high spring tide came back to me as though it had only happened the week before.

The winter of 1947/48 was extremely severe and when the thaw finally started in the early spring, the rapidly melting snow on the land and the huge blocks of frozen seawater floating like so much flotsam and jetsam, caused the spring tides to rise higher than usual. Mum had just finished work at Mrs Passadora's house in Firs Road, where she worked as a cleaner. I was in my little seat on the back of her bicycle as we sailed down towards The Yacht Club. She was whistling one of the popular tunes of the time as she always did when she felt good. The tide was over Coast Road as she cycled on through the freezing water. As we approached the cottage, she had to pull up sharp; the deepening tide was well over the road by 'The Old Victory' and swirling up The Lane. Bernard Cudmore's elder brother Jack was wading through the glistening water towards us

"Y-y-yer wont g-g-get through m-m-missus" he stuttered " yer house is u-u-under water." He was well known for his stuttering drawl

and the more agitated he become, his impediment worsened. I can see him now, standing in the deepening water in his thigh boots; a greasy old flat cap worn at a jaunty angle, covering his balding head; the typical navy blue seaman's jumper tucked into the heavy tweed trousers being held up by a wide leather belt, accentuating his ample girth. He liked his beer.

"I'll hev t c-c-carry yer across if y-y-yer wonna git in," he said with the slow, drawl of the local accent, making it even more frustrating whilst waiting for the words to form in his almost toothless mouth with a damp dog-end wobbling, on his bottom lip.

I stood patiently watching as this stout, rosy-faced fisherman waded through the water, cradling my dainty mother in his arms; seaweed and debris swirled around them as he made for an area where the rising tide had not yet reached. It seemed like an eternity as I nervously awaited my turn; I knew dear old Jack, he had been a part of my life since I could remember. He used to bring us fish and sometimes there would be winkles which he taught me to poke out with a pin.

"C-c-come you on little un," he chuckled as he swept me up onto his shoulders, "don't you be a g-g-gittin all upset, ol Jack'll look a-a-arter yer." The strong smell of stale sweat and tobacco wafted over me as he waded over to where my mother was standing looking very worried and handing him the key to 'Waterside', she asked him to try to find her Wellington boots.

"H-h high tide int afore one th-thirty gel, as got another hour t to flow a-as yit" he stuttered over his now very spittle soaked dog-end still clinging to his bottom lip. "Yer hed better g-g git out what yer can, I'll g-gi yer and missus." he said as he sat me on the kitchen table. "I've p-p put yer bike round the b-back, int narthen wus un ol salt w-w-water fer the rust n rot." He loved to make up little quotes which he emphasised in the local dialect.

As the icy water came over the top of mum's boots, she let out a little shocked gasp, but knowing that there were still items to be saved and fearful of my father's temper when he saw a lot of his hard work ruined, she valiantly carried on

"We had better turn the electric of Jack dear" she said through her tears as the water rose over the legs of the 'Belling' cooker.

I began to cry when I saw my lovely dolls house, which stood on the floor,

163

nearly submerged under the cruel water. The brick effect paper was beginning to float off and as Jack waded towards it, the surge of water caused the tiny furniture, expertly made by my father, to spill out of the open front. He had taken great pride and spent many evenings, whilst I was in bed, making it all as a surprise for Christmas; it even had battery-powered lights.

"That'll d-d-dry out little un, don't y -y-you goo a cryin," he said lifting it onto the dining room table and patting the sodden paper back into place. Reaching into the icy water, he made an attempt at retrieving some of the floating pieces of tiny furniture.

Opening the door of the water filled sideboard, Mum let out a cry of despair.

"Oh no, not Fred's camera," this being the proverbial 'last straw' and as she watched the corrosive water dripping from the much-prized piece of equipment, poor Gwenny broke down and wept.

"Sh-sh- she'll soon be on the turn now missus," Jack being a confirmed bachelor, didn't know how to deal with women's emotions.

"Fred'll likely be hom s-s-soon , I'll sh-sh-shove orf now."

Jack Cudmore

We were all devastated after the flood and not long after the event, Mum went down with pneumonia. Dad, who, along with Len Harvey, did odd jobs around the village and so was able to take time off work so as to care for her, I can remember following him everywhere like a lost puppy. Dick was of course at school and his way of helping was by looking after me in the evenings when, after first putting me to bed, he always read to me. He was going on ten years old and took his responsibilities very seriously.

Gwenny was a strong girl and Dad, armed with meat bones from the local butcher and a few root vegetables, gave strength to her speedy recovery with the aid of his lovely home-made soups and stews. She was soon up and about again and helping to get the house back to normal.

The very high tides usually occur around midday or midnight at which time, as children, we were regularly awakened by the voices of the Coast Guards as they warned of imminent flood tides and to the sounds of furniture being put up on bricks and rolled up rugs being laid on the stairs. It was always more frightening at night and when the murky water crept in under the floorboards, the rats could be heard scrabbling and scratching their way through the myriad of their under floor tunnels.

My brother and I shared a room and having been awakened by all the activity downstairs, would lie there listening to the muffled voices of helpful neighbours who had 'just popped in to lend a hand'. We always fell asleep, as the evening usually stretched into the early hours, midst plenty of chatter and many cups of tea, or, when funds were good, the odd glass or two of ale. The tide had probably only lapped at the doorstep and then crept away without anyone even noticing.

Leslie was kept very busy with new contract work and along with other building construction contractors, was involved at the particular time, with the renovations being carried out on the Hall Barn Country Club. Local builders, such as Glen Cock, Peter Farthing and Ronnie Fisher were amongst those offering sub-contract work to local up-and-coming young tradesmen. My brother, having served his time as an apprentice, was now a qualified electrician, and worked alongside Leslie and most of the others who, up to this time, had been struggling to find work. New properties were springing up all over West Mersea, whilst the east side of the island, being mainly farmland, remained for the most part, unchanged.

When the newly re-furbished Hall Barn finally re-opened for business, I often found myself sitting alone at a table, with a drink in front of me which by law, I was too young to consume; Leslie sat up at the bar with his cronies, all being a great deal older than me and with whom I had nothing in common. The women appeared to me, to be dressed up to the nines and looked very glamorous; whereas 'Poppet' in her rather outmoded and shabby attire, sat feeling very out of place and lonely. Every so often, my bleary eyed husband would push a glass my way, containing yet another concoction, which was, to my inexperienced taste buds, foul; gin and tonic, whisky and dry ginger, brandy, all of which, having tentatively sipped, I screwed up my face and either splutter and cough or shudder; causing great amusement to those sitting at the bar. 'Babycham' or 'Cherry B' was about as alcoholic as I could tolerate in those far off days;

"Drinks for kids." he chortled, "have a proper drink for God's sake girl," pushing another noxious glassful my way. "I can't damn well keep wasting money if you're not going to drink anything I give you," he called out from amongst his cronies sitting at the bar, initiating sniggers from the other wives as they swilled themselves into, what seemed to me, drunken stupidity and ignorance.

I sat enviously watching as my friends filed past the bar door, their full skirts with multiple layers of tulle swishing and rustling as they made their way back into the club dance hall, where they were enjoying an evening of 'Rock'n'Roll'. The music from the live band issued forth as the swing doors opened and closed. Sometimes, making a detour as I ostensibly made my way to the toilets, I pushed the hall door open ajar and took a peep at them all jiving, showing off their stocking tops, having so much fun as they were swung round by various handsome *young* lads. I usually met up with one or two of the girls as they re-applied their makeup and plumped up their bouffant hair dos.

"Why don't you come and have a dance?" one of them asked, looking at my forlorn reflection in the mirror.

"Leslie won't like it."

"Aw Bugger him. What's happened to you Rita? You used to be the liveliest of us all."

"I'm married now."

"So!"

"Well I just can't, he would get mad. "

"What the bloody hell did you marry *him* for? He's old and going bald, what the hell did you see in him?"

I wanted to say 'security, my own home and an escape from, what had become a lonely existence and … well… I think I love him.'. My mother had her new life with Johnny, Dad now had Lil, and Dick had since married Barbara. I had to try to make a life for myself.

My social life – if it were to be called that – was narrowed down to once a week, on a Saturday night. Leslie, having had a belly full of drink at the club, arrived home for his - by then - dried up lunch and, would then suggest 'having a nap' before which he would lustily show his need for the use of my body before falling into a snoring, deep sleep.

I so looked forward to going out and spent the early evening trying to make myself look pretty, with my meagre supply of make-up and the only, rather drab clothes that I possessed. It wouldn't have occurred to him that a young woman needed new clothes or other little extras to make her feel good and I never had the nerve to ask. My friend Helen, being taller than me, would bring me her cast-offs that she had grown out of. Then out came Nanny's sewing machine to aid my endeavours to refashion them. She also used to let me have the make-up she had tired of.

Time seemed to slow down as I sat clock watching; I

had been ready for two hours or more; getting increasingly frustrated with my fruitless efforts to wake him. When finally he emerged, it was almost too late to bother going out and it would usually be past ten when we walked into the club. Looking back, I don't think he really wanted to take me out; I suppose, when the initial buzz of having a young girl on his arm wore off, my inexperience in the art of socialising, embarrassed him somewhat.

The usual group were sitting at the bar and their suggestive looks accompanied by snide remarks, made me feel ill at ease. Had I been more mature, I would have taken it all in my stride, but my youthful insecurity did me no favours. The only saving grace of the short outing was usually when Leslie invited some of the group back to 'Waterside' for biscuits and cheese and where, of course, the drinking would continue. At least I was on home ground, where I played the part of an accommodating little wife and dare I say – tongue in cheek – with more confidence. Each week I tried to impress with the inclusion of little extras, such as olives or various chutneys. In those days the selection of 'nibbles' was very limited, as was my housekeeping allowance, especially when shopping locally.

With all the energy I put into decorating, scrubbing and polishing, time still crept by at a snail's pace as loneliness and frustration engulfed me. Then I discovered the thrill of shopping. Each week I called into 'Chatters' (one of the two hardware stores in the village - the other being 'Digby's') where you could purchase anything from a pound of nails to a wheelbarrow. The scent of pure beeswax polish along paint and paraffin oil added to the magic of what was to become my Aladdin's cave full of treasures. The lovely green 'Denby' earthenware cups and saucers were carefully wrapped in brown paper and placed in my shopping basket as I proudly handed over the money; having managed to save a few shillings a week from my meagre housekeeping allowance. I continued in this way until I finally had the full set - my pride and joy.

Dennis Chatters ran a television repairs and rental service from the shop. Leslie had agreed to take out a year's rental agreement and it was whilst taking delivery of the set and me being alone in the house, Dennis thought he saw the opportunity to steal a kiss; he had always innocently flirted with me whilst serving me in the shop, but this time it was not so innocent and I soon told him where to go. After that event, I had very little trouble getting items reserved – I think he was worried that I would tell his mother, whom I seem to remember, also worked in the shop.

Having been married at such a young age, I think it was expected that I was a girl who 'put it about' or was 'willing'. I was, as were most teenagers of that era, very immature and shy; I really didn't know how to handle embarrassing situations and hated any form of confrontation. There was no one to teach me the subtleties of the growing up process and the hard knocks of life's experiences continued to be doled out for many years to come; the perpetrators were to be my greatest teachers.

As promised, Bernard paid for the pretty rosebud wallpaper and palest, pink paint, along with decorating materials, all of which I purchased from Chatters. It wasn't going to be an easy task as the bedroom walls and ceilings were, not only very uneven, but there were also several oddly shaped beams running from ceiling to floor on each wall.

Hilda, who loved decorating, kindly gave me a hand; we had such fun. We shared many happy times together over the years, more especially when we first lived in the cottage as children. During her first marriage, Hilda lost a baby and nearly her own life, due to an ectopic pregnancy. It was to become a double tragedy when her husband died of a fatal heart attack a few weeks later. Her marriage to Bernard was good, but she, rightly so, considered herself a cut above with high ideals. Bernard was a hardworking, country lad, with very little ambition. They met and married during the war. Bernard's war effort was serving part-time in the Home Guard; whilst Hilda always used to say how she enjoyed her war effort, serving as an ambulance driver. It was always said that she was quite a bit older than Bernard and by the end of the war; any thoughts of having children were soon forgotten.

Working space in the bedroom was limited and this meant moving furniture away from the walls; as we moved the wardrobe, something fell off the top; to my embarrassment, it was three, knotted, used condoms, which must have been thrown up there by Leslie. After my initial shock and embarrassment, Hilda and I went into paroxysms of hysterical laughter and knocked over the bucket of wallpaper paste, the sight of which made us laugh even more. I never spoke to him of the find and didn't have the courage to ask the reason for the unusual site of disposal for these personal items.

The room was finally finished and I, having never attempted anything so complicated before, was very proud of my efforts. Dear Hilda gave me a pretty pair of curtains to add the finishing touch. That evening, on his return home from work, Leslie managed a grunt of approval as his eyes strayed towards the top of the wardrobe.

A PLEA FOR INDEPENDENCE

A year had passed since my marriage and I was beginning to spread my wings, or should I say, there were bumps where wings might eventually form. I acquired a job at a local, up-market grocery store; I say upmarket because 'Dixons' and 'Whitings' catered for the more discerning customers who required – to quote Hilda – 'That little something different dear'.

"Oo yes dear, Repton attends our Whist Drives regular you know. I always get the very best cheese from him; he's got a very good *delicate essence* department." She always gave a little sniff and a toss of her well-groomed hair, whilst in her 'posh voice' mode. Hilda had the edge on the proverbial 'Mrs Malaprop' when it came to getting her words mixed up. She was totally unaware of the amusement that her little transgressions of speech caused over the years.

I was very excited; Mr Dixon seemed to be such a pleasant gentleman. He told me how delighted he would be in giving me the relevant training and how I would make a very presentable shop assistant. My disappointment came when, having excitedly told Leslie my news, he said " Huh! You are not working there, so forget it."

"Why?"

"Because I said so, that's why. My friend Jan says he is a dirty old man because he flirts with all the women."

"So what! Most men like to have a little flirt with a pretty woman, there needn't be any harm in it and he happens to be a thorough gentleman," I rebelliously said as he glared at me.

It wasn't until many years later that I found out the real reason for his irrational disapproval. Not only was the so named woman a party to illicit liaisons, but was also prone to spreading malicious gossip about those who showed no interest in her; she was also one of Leslie's, old flames. She took pleasure in telling me that their relationship continued after he had married me. I learned of this whilst inadvertently running into her in a local pub many years later. I was also to learn that she was a fantasist and liked nothing better than to cause trouble by spreading untrue rumours.

Having not taken that particular job, I did, however, find a job that suited his lord and master. My mother in law told me to go and see her friend Miss Phillips who owned a small haberdashery shop called 'The Spinning Wheel'. She had known me since I was a baby, when my mother used to regularly shop there for her knitting and sewing needs.

My first memory of Miss Phillips was when I was around the age of three and mum had pushed my rickety old pushchair inside the dimly lit shop, out of the cold. The over loaded counter looked as high as a house from where I sat and then I saw her, this large bespectacled lady peering out from what seemed like a mountain of packets of wool and rolls of cloth. Her chubby face beamed as her outstretched hand clutching a huge bag of broken biscuits came towards me. From then on we were firm friends as there were always treats of one sort or another whenever we visited the shop; the best being her legendary brittle treacle toffee which she broke into small pieces with a silver toffee hammer.

With increasing age and her propensity to be rather obese, the arthritis in Miss Phillips feet and legs worsened; making it increasingly difficult for her to stand for any great length of time and she was only too pleased to offer me a job.

I had gained some experience in this particular type of retail trade, whilst still at school, working on Saturdays for Mrs Hadley who, along with her husband and son John, ran the Ladies and Gents Outfitters in Mill Lane.

I cycled from Waterside to 'The Spinning Wheel' five mornings a week. The conditions were extremely cramped as it was only a very small shop and over the years, Miss Phillips had accumulated a vast stock, some of which was stored in a spider and mouse infested lock up shed at the back. The branches of a large Medlar tree overhung the roof and the apple-like fruit which dropped in the autumn, made the path to the shed a bit precarious. When she was able, Miss Phillips used to gather up and sell bags of the fruit outside the shop. I never knew what they were until I worked there and certainly wouldn't have known that the fruit had to be almost rotten before it was palatable.

I spent a very happy six months working at the shop, until finally one day Miss Phillips told me that she really couldn't continue living alone and had decided to sell up and move in with a friend down in Sussex.

Once again I found myself lonely and bored. Not only did I not have the money, it just didn't occur to me to get on the bus to Colchester. Digs would visit once in a while and Gloria would break the monotony with a bit of local gossip as she delivered the groceries once a week.

The weekly excursion to 'The Hall Barn' was becoming increasingly dull; with the same familiar faces, the inane conversations that gradually declined into slurring incomprehensibility and the build up of frustration as I sat watching the laughing faces of my friends as they now passed me by without a second glance. Then one evening I was joined by a chap whose wife spent most of the evening playing on the fruit machines. They appeared to be quite an odd match as a couple, as she was tall and rather overweight, in comparison to his lack of height and skinny build. They made me think of Jack Sprat and wife, especially when he told me that his wife always cooked him boiled bacon and butterbeans when he came home from the sea. I used to imagine her eating all the fat and feeding him the lean meat.

He was very friendly and reminded me of Kenny Ball, my favourite jazz-band leader –. Suddenly I was enjoying myself. We talked about music and he told me of his large collection of records. I soon found out that he was in the merchant navy and only came home once a fortnight. I was always disappointed when he wasn't there. Then one evening he suggested that he could phone me if I were to be in phone-box at the end of Victory Road at an appointed time. I knew that what I was doing was wrong but I was desperate for a little unconditional kindness. We agreed to meet a couple of times, when he took me for an afternoon ride in his car. The first time, we just chatted and laughed a lot. The second time we kissed and cuddled and I cried a lot; I suppose it was just shear relief that he made no other demands on me. Finally he invited me to visit him at their cottage as his wife was going on holiday with her sister for a week and he would be there alone. Foolishly, I agreed. I was extremely nervous when I arrived and he appeared to be the same. After a rather restrained cuddle, there was a fumbled attempt at making love, but it never happened as he was unable to get excited and I was just plain terrified. We agreed to meet by 'The Yacht Club' the next day and having had a very restless night struggling with my guilty conscience, I decided to tell him that I didn't want to see him again. As it happened, he also felt the same and we parted, to my great relief, on amicable terms. This all took place the spring before my eighteenth birthday. Like any silly teenager, I unwisely shared my experience with an old school friend, who was on one of her rare visits. I was glad to unburden my guilt and we giggled and made light of it all.

Summer that year was lovely and I spent a lot of delightful week-day afternoons sitting on Hilda's small patch of lawn at the back of their cottage. At weekends I often helped her serve teas to the many holiday makers visiting the island. If it rained, tea was then served in one of the two beach-huts, set up at the side of the cottage with the sole purpose of Hilda running her 'summertime venture'.

"Well dear it does help me run my little car," she proudly said pointing to the 'Wolsey Hornet' parked in readiness for transporting her to the weekly whist drives.

We both had pet budgerigars that we taught to speak and if the weather was fine on a Monday afternoon, Hilda invited Mrs Thomas and Ida Farmen, two elderly ladies, who, only living a short distance up The Lane, also brought their pet budgies. The cages were placed side by side on the lawn, causing a great deal of bouncing on perches and garbled conversing (birds not ladies!) to take place, in fact a most enjoyable time was had by all attending the tea party.

Hilda was skilled at making the most deliciously light sponge cakes, I often wondered if it had anything to do with the ash from the cigarette she always had in her mouth whilst beating up the mixture.

"Well dear, it's the only time I enjoy a cigarette and I'm always careful not to let the ash fall into the mixture," she said, leaning over an ashtray as she expertly flicked the ash off the end of her 'Players' with her index finger. She also made all her own Jam which was served along with the thinly sliced brown or white bread and butter. No ready sliced bread for Hilda. First spreading a thin layer of butter over the surface of the bread, the large square loaf was then held firmly as she dexterously sliced towards her apron covered chest. It always amazed me how quickly a large plate of bread and butter was produced, after which it would then be covered with a damp tea towel and put aside until needed.

It was now approaching the end of December and winter was well and truly taking a cold grip, with sharp frosty mornings and the occasional flurry of snow causing my chilblained toes to swell and itch, but that paled into insignificance when Doctor Dorothy Howes told me the exciting news that I was pregnant.

"How the hell did that happen?" Leslie asked angrily. I was crestfallen. I really don't know how I expected him to react. Babies were never mentioned, apart from when his Brother Gerald's wife gave birth to their son Rodney around the time when Leslie and I got married two years previously. He obviously had no desire to start a family of his own. That evening he went out as usual but came home much later, smelling of perfume.

I was not invited to join him when he went to see in the New Year at the Hall Barn. I didn't feel like going anyway. With feelings of extreme nausea I went to bed and fell sound asleep, oblivious to the entrance of 1963.

The weather turned extremely cold and so did Leslie's moods; he hardly spoke to me; I found myself shaking, not just from the cold, more the anticipation of his arrival home each evening. I just couldn't take any more and finally I begged him to speak to me and tell me what was wrong.

"How do I know that is mine?" he shouted, pointing to my, as yet, flat belly. "I always take precautions."

I knew exactly when I conceived; my periods had been late that month and I had told him what I thought was true, that I couldn't fall pregnant at that time of the month and so he didn't wear a condom.

"You had an affair with that Carlton bloke, is it still going on?" he said, ignoring what I had just told him.

Ice cold shock and fear made me strongly deny the accusation. There could have only been one source of this information; there was only one person with whom I had shared my guilty secret.

"Your so called friend let your 'cat out of the bag' so you had better come clean girl."

Evidently he had met up with my friend at the Club on New Year's Eve, when she is supposed to have told him all that I had told her. This thoughtless act was to have the most profound effect on my life for many years to come.

I continued with the denial until he finally broke my resolve by telling me that if I told him the whole story, we could then forget all about it. This statement brought back the memory of my stepfather saying exactly those words as I, aged eleven stood in front of him – accused.

Leslie's dark stare seemed to penetrate my head as I broke down and poured out the truth. He didn't believe me and even worse, he said that the child I was carrying was not his. He accused me of still carrying on the affair. I was horrified, having told him truthfully that it had all happened eight months ago, during which time nothing of that nature had taken place. In my naivety I thought it would all now be over - how wrong I was – it was just the beginning.

"Right, get your things together; I'm taking you back to your mother." His eyes burned as he pushed me towards the stairs. "Hurry up, I haven't got all night."

My mother and Stepfather had moved from Hadleigh into a more spacious bungalow in Rayleigh, near Southend, so we were about to embark on what was for me, a harrowing journey. The nausea, I was constantly suffering from, was worsened by the waves of anticipation and fear in my stomach. Leslie explained our sudden visit as we stood on the doorstep. My stepfather's eyes narrowed and my mother gave me one of her usual looks of disapproval as she turned and walked back into the house.

"You had better come in, we don't want the whole neighbourhood to know our business," my stepfather said, standing back, allowing us to pass through the hall and into the warm sitting room. He took up his usual interrogational stance, with his back to the fire, feet apart, arms folded in front of his flabby chest, with that oh so familiar self-righteous look on his face.

"Well, what have you got to say for yourself? Are you going to tell the truth?" Memories of that same question flooded back.

Whilst rummaging through my schoolbag, supposedly looking for a pencil, he, my stepfather, had found some torn up pieces of paper. For reasons best known to himself, he had spread the pieces out on a tray and fitted them together like a jigsaw puzzle, which he then covered with a folded newspaper. When I came home from playing with my friends, I was commanded to stand in front of where he was sitting with the tray on his lap.

"Did you do this?" he demanded, whilst removing the newspaper and trying to imitate a 'stern father' look.

Realising the jigsaw was a picture that my friends and I had giggled over as we drew a naked man and woman, or should I say our interpretation of the same; with the male private parts looking more like a small cannon, whilst the female had two circles with dots in the middle for breasts and a fuzzy triangle representing her nether region. "No," says I feeling very embarrassed.

"Don't you lie to me young lady." he said as we were joined by my mother, putting on her 'disgusted' look.

Each evening, the tray was presented and the same question was fired at me.

"If you don't own up we'll get a hand-writing expert on the case" he threatened "and if I find out you have been telling lies, you'll go in a home."

Although very frightened, I was still too embarrassed to own up. Until finally after about two weeks of, what would now be classed as mental cruelty, he threatened my bicycle.

"If you don't tell the truth, I'll get rid of your bike, however, if you tell us the truth now, we'll forget all about it," he appeared to smirk as his slimy thick lipped mouth spat out the words.

That, for me, was the final straw; my bike was my only means of escape. I did own up and the cause of two weeks of hell was thrown in the bin and that was that – for them - my scars remained.

I now found myself feeling just as I did then, very small, very alone and very frightened. The armchair I was sitting in seemed to become huge as I shrank into it, wishing it would swallow me up completely

"Well," my stepfather said, puffing himself up with self importance – even his large nose looked bigger and his eyes looked even closer together, "I would just dump her in the river on your way home boy, she's not welcome here, little tart that's all she is."

That was rich, coming from a man who had tried it on with me when I was fifteen; a man whose, full on the mouth, wet kisses, made me want to spit his saliva back in his face. The man who regularly fornicated with my mother in the back of the bread van, whilst she was still living at home

178

with my father all those years ago; this man and this woman who gave me my first lessons in telling lies when I was five years old,

"Don't tell Daddy that Uncle John (as he was known to me then) held Mummy's hand." "Don't tell Daddy that I kissed your Mummy" "Don't tell Daddy that you had to stay in the van whilst we went for a little walk." Hypocrites!

"Don't ever darken our door again."

My mother said nothing as he slammed the door.

The drive back to Mersea was terrifying and proved to be the beginning of the worst period of my entire life – at the time I felt that I deserved it.

I confessed all to Izzy and Bert, as they found it hard to understand why their son was constantly in a foul mood and why he didn't take me to visit with them anymore. I had so much love and respect for these dear folk that I felt the need to tell them everything. Of course, they were very shocked and yet very sympathetic and kind; they were true to their Christian faith and very soon had me joining them at the Methodist Chapel for the Sunday services.

The terrible treatment began when Leslie, refusing to speak to me, just sat in the armchair opposite and glared at me. My feeling of abject guilt grew so much that I felt as though I were being swallowed up by it all. The nausea became so severe that I went off my food and instead of gaining, as was expected, I lost weight and became very lethargic. I wanted to die.

It was one of the coldest winters known since records began, even the sea froze, making it possible to walk to the opposite side of the estuary .Huge slabs of ice washed up on the shore, giving the whole scene an arctic appearance; the hard freeze continued into early spring.

Waterside was very cold as there was only a small electric heater mounted on the kitchen wall and a very inefficient, solid fuel Parkray stove, in the sitting room that gave out the most noxious fumes every time the doors were opened for refuelling. I had to re-light the beast in the morning as it refused to stay alight overnight; I never had enough kindling wood and now even the driftwood was covered by the ice. My father in law brought bundles of neatly chopped wood when he visited or Hilda often gave me some of hers. Some days, when I was just too cold to go and fetch a bucket of coke from the ice covered pile, round the back by the privies, I just whiled away the time sitting in the kitchen with only the mean heat from the electric heater, a mug of hot chocolate to keep out the cold and 'Benny' my dear little feathered pal's relentless chatter along with the radio keeping me company. I tried to stay in bed for as long as I could in the mornings, but the intense cold usually crept in under the blankets and nibble at my toes through the woolly socks – knitted and given to me by dear Izzy.

Every morning I had to empty the night time toilet bucket, which was mainly used by Leslie - having had quite a few pints of beer the night before. The privy toilet pan then had to be flushed; by a bucket of water collected from the standpipe tap which I had to defrost each morning. One morning I slipped on the icy path and the contents of the bucket stained the surrounding frozen surface of the snow which remained yellow for weeks.

During the hard winters, when we were children, especially 1947, I remember my mother having to take enough water indoors so as to de-ice the tap each morning. I was fascinated by the ice sculptures caused by someone not turning the tap off properly the night before.

"Aw the bloody water ont come out, goo an fetch yer mother gel."Nelly frequently squawked as she kicked at the frozen pipe; she never remembered to have enough water indoors.

"If my Charlie wor here, he'd piss on the bloody thing." She knew how to wind my mother up.

"Nelly dear you really must try to remember to collect your spare water the day before." she chastised as she poured the hot water from the

steaming kettle over the tap.

"Thank yer missus, want some o this ere bacci ? as good ol shag," she said knowing my mother didn't smoke, but she always offered. On one occasion, she came out of her cottage with two very grey looking pastry 'things'.

"Thank you Nelly dear, how kind of you," knowing that they hadn't got an electric supply to their cottage, she went on to ask how she had cooked them. "Do you have a nice range in the cottage?"

"Aw no, I does all me baking in the oil stove o course," she said giving my mother a very serious stare. "I spose you got one them thar new fangled lectric things; we hint got lectric, anyways thar hint nothen as cooks like my ol oil stove."

Later my mother having relayed the tale to my father, amid the laughter, he said; "Well what do you expect, daft old bat probably doesn't know how to keep the wicks cleaned."
The 'pastry things' were reverently carried back to our cottage where they were instantly thrown in the bin.

My cooking skills in those days weren't very good, but I tried very hard to please him with what I thought he liked. Having finished his supper Leslie sat sulkily staring at the flames from the burning off-cuts he had brought home from work. At one stage the tarred up chimney leading up from the stove glowed red and began to roar, I was frightened that the chimney had caught fire; it pleased him to watch my mounting fear. He would suddenly jump up out of his chair and grab the poker as he glared at me. I felt my stomach lurch and wondered if this might cause me to miscarry. On other occasions, he just sat banging the arm of his chair or tapping his foot, which he also did whilst we were in bed; to this day, I cannot stand it when a hand is brought down heavily on the bed. One evening he brought out a small revolver that he kept in the locked drawer of his writing desk

"Do you know what 'Russian Roulette' is?" he asked whilst spinning the chamber and aiming it at me as he pulled the trigger. I didn't know at the time that the single bullet, he took great pleasure in showing me, was only a blank.

Sex became very degrading and when at its worst, he told me, "That's all the likes of you is good for." When he did take my body, the act was very cold and loveless and usually very rough. In my naivety, I thought that by doing everything to please him, it would eventually endear him towards me.

I truly believe that I was going through a nervous breakdown, which probably started when my mother left home all those years ago. The torment that I now endured compounded the years of mental cruelty dealt by my stepfather, his mother Ida and to a certain degree, my own mother. My father, now living with Lil, the dreaded stepmother, used to tell me "You've made your bed, now lie on it." My brother who was now living his own life, married to Barbara, wasn't interested in my problems; I'm not sure I ever shared that much information with him, and there was no one else.

I was so full of guilt, thinking that I had brought it all on myself; I tried so hard to please Leslie but it never worked – he despised me. He once told me that as a child, if anyone else played with his toys, he destroyed them or threw them away.

For those long months, my only saving grace was my dear friend Hilda. Most days during the week, having finished my daily tasks, I went round to have coffee with her; some days, when the weather got warmer, I invited her to have a light lunch with me; however during the severe weather I was glad to sit and chat with her in the warmth of her cosy kitchen whilst she pottered about and fussed over me.

I heard all about how, when she and Bernard were first married, they moved in with Bert – Bernard's father (also known as Bobby) and his sister Annie, who in those days, ran the small shop adjoining the house. Hilda told me that as it was wartime her war effort was spent as an ambulance driver, transporting the very sick from the island into the Essex County Hospital in Colchester.

"I first learned to drive before the war," she proudly told me, "which enabled me to volunteer to become an ambulance driver

I enjoyed listening to her wartime experiences and remember being shocked when she stated, "I enjoyed my war dear."

The Cudmore family had been a very prosperous in days gone by. Bert, having inherited the family carrier business, was well known for the speed at which he drove his horse and cart through the village and into Colchester each day, transporting the mail and other goods. Hilda told me about the time he thought he saw a ghost cross from one side of the 'Strood' – the road that passed over the mudflats, joining Mersea Island to the mainland - to the other. The horse must have seen it too because it reared up, throwing poor Bert off the cart and being injured he had to sit and wait until he was eventually rescued by the next horse and rider to pass by. It has always been said that many ghostly appearances have been witnessed over the years; especially a Roman Centurion seen crossing the 'Strood'. Up until then Bert had never believed in them.

"He did after that," she told me "because it appeared out of nowhere from one side of the road and disappeared on the other and with the tide being out, there was nothing but mudflats on either side."

Hilda was a constant friend and companion without whom I don't think I would have sustained my sanity. She enjoyed my youthful curiosity and we whiled away many happy hours, during that cold winter, together with our Budgies enjoying their freedom as they flew around her snug kitchen.

Hilda Cudmore in her younger days

Looking back, I now realise what a strain it must have been, listening to all my fears and anxieties day after day. She was more than a friend, she took on the role of mother and I truly loved and trusted her. Some evenings when I called into the tiny shop for my favourite ice-cream lolly, I would craftily creep into her small sitting-room and just sit quietly soaking up her company; she was usually sitting with her feet up on her leather 'Pooffe' enjoying a navel orange and watching one of her favourite soap operas; the latest one being Coronation Street. The small black and white television had a magnifying devise strapped over the screen which was supposed to enlarge the picture.

"My Bernard keeps promising me one of those new fangled sets, but ooh, he does take his time making decisions you know dear, especially when it means spending money," and with this she let out her 'smokers cough' laugh.

I remember Bobby watching football, his favourite programme, on Saturday afternoons, on that same television when, as a small girl, I used to visit with him. Hilda was usually off to a Whist Drive at the British Legion Hall. Looking like a film star, with her dark curls framing her pretty, meticulously made-up face and her fox fur clinging to the padded shoulders of her stylish black coat, she bustled out of the door, leaving the sweet aroma of 'Evening in Paris' mingled with cigarette smoke hanging in the air. .

"Your tea is on the table Bobby dear, don't let little Rita stay too long."
I loved nothing more than to spend a chilly winter's afternoon in the snug kitchen with Bobby.

"Sit yourself down child, I can't see me footie." he grumbled as he weaved from side to side. I was up on my toes in front of him, trying to imitate the ballerina I so wanted to be.

"Goo an fetch my tea little un." Hilda always left him thinly cut brown bread and butter with a hunk of cheese, covered over with a damp tea towel.

"Here yar little un," he always held out little morsels of cheese on the end of his knife. "Don't you goo a telling har that I hint eaten them thar crusts," pushing the plate of crusts towards me his eyes twinkled as he added "any old how, there good fer yer teeth." I remember thinking as he shone his almost toothless grin at me that he couldn't have eaten his crusts when he was a little boy.

On Christmas eve dear old Bobby, used to open the shop door and jangle the bell which I was able to hear from my bedroom window – a plan cooked up by him and dad - making me believe it was Father Christmas on his rounds.
The little shop did a good trade in those days, until the increasing popularity of the motorcar, led to folk travelling further afield for their shopping needs. I think that Hilda was secretly glad of the fall in trade as years went by; she had worked hard all her married life; looking after Bernard and his aging relatives in the cramped and archaic environment; taking over the shop when Annie became too frail. She then went on to provide refreshments in the two beach huts, when first Annie and then Bobby died.

It was now late July and the weather was hot and humid. I was feeling very heavy and weary; my ankles were swollen and Doctor Dorothy was concerned that I might be suffering from the early stages of toxaemia, which would then lead to an early admission into Colchester Maternity Hospital so as to be prematurely induced (whatever that entailed).

Leslie was still convinced that the child that I was soon to give birth to was not his and when the time came for me to go into the maternity hospital – albeit a false alarm – he just dropped me at the door and left.

A cold-eyed Chinese nurse led me into a small, two-bedded room.

"You still get pains?" she said sharply as she wrote down my details.

"You have bath, then I shave you."

I was shaking with fear as she scraped at my pubic hair. The old fashioned safety razor she used, had teeth surrounding the blade and she was very heavy handed as the teeth dug into my flesh, leaving deep scratches, some of which bled. I was too afraid to complain. She had either used the same blade to chip off some of her own sharp edges or just didn't like pregnant English women. I spent an uncomfortable, restless night and it being decided the next morning that I wasn't in labour, I was sent home.

I walked from Lexden Road, through the town to the Bus station in St. John Street before I realised that I had no money with me. I knew all the Mersea bus drivers and conductors and luckily Bill Green, Hilda's brother in law was driving the next bus out and agreed to loan me the money for my fare.

On reaching my destination, I was dismayed when I discovered that this particular bus only went as far as the bus station, which meant having to take the long walk down Coast Road. By the time I reached home, the insides of my thighs were red raw and I was suffering from a severe bout of cystitis.

"Hello in there, I saw you arrive back Come round when you're finished dear and I'll make you a nice refreshing cuppa whilst you tell me all about it."

Hilda's voice sent waves of comfort through the door of the privy as I sat passing a burning pee.

Dear Hilda.

THE BIRTH OF MY FIRST CHILD

Another week had passed before Doctor Dorothy decided that due to my raised blood pressure and very swollen ankles, I would have to be induced straight away. I returned to Colchester Maternity Hospital on the morning of 3rd August, having yet again been dropped at the door by a very stern faced husband. I was scared but too excited to feel lonely.

The induction process began with a glass containing caster oil suspended between two layers of orange squash

"No don't just sip at it, you're not supposed to enjoy it," my first meeting with Sister Smith, "take it down in one go and it won't taste so bad" she said as I gagged on the vile mixture. Next came the indignity of an enema. The very tall and masculine figure of Sister Smith strode up to my bed pushing a trolley laden with what turned out to be, instruments of torture.

"Now young lady, turn onto your left side," she ordered, swishing the curtains round my bed.

"Have you had an enema before? You must relax," she did not wait for a reply as she lifted a length of rubber tubing from the trolley and inserted one end into my rectum; I must have let out a little gasp of pain as it scraped past my haemorrhoid; she heaved an impatient sigh as she removed the tube and applied a jelly like substance to the end of the tube, before attempting to re-insert it.

"I told you to relax young lady, the more you tighten up, the more it will hurt."

As I watched her pick up a large jug of what turned out to be warm soapy water, I plucked up the courage to ask "Are you going to use all that?" to which she replied sarcastically "Well what do you suggest I do with it?" I know what I wanted to say but didn't have the courage.

The sensation of the warm liquid entering my body felt very uncomfortable and as it bubbled and gurgled, I wondered if I could do as ordered and 'hold it in for as long as possible.' I soon found myself – having only just made it – sitting in the loo wondering if the pain I was experiencing was my baby on its way or my innards dropping out; in a way, it was the later. I kept telling myself that every woman has to go through this sort of thing before becoming a mother. It helped a bit.

Feeling like a cast off sock I climbed back on the bed for the next stage, which was to be a nurse approaching with another trolley conveying more instruments of torture.

After making several painful attempts at trying to find a vein, the kind soul apologetically handed the task over to another, more experienced nurse who also had difficulty before finally succeeding to insert an intravenous cannula into my now much bruised arm. She then went on to fit the relevant tubing and drip bottle which was then hung on a stand beside my bed and I awaited the premature onset of labour. I will always wonder, had it been left a few more days, would my child have chosen her own birthday; or maybe shared my 19th birthday on the 11th, who knows?

By mid afternoon, whilst taking a nap, I was awoken by a bizarre feeling; I thought I was peeing the bed. I rang for a nurse as I could not easily get out of bed without pulling out my drip. Now, standing beside the bed, I was embarrassed by the increasing pool of water at my feet.

"Don't worry about the mess," the nurse said with a reassuring grin, "your waters have broken and you are now in labour."

By early evening, my contractions were beginning to show a regular pattern as the pain worsened. It was visiting time and I felt rather shy about letting out any sounds.
I had no visitors.

With the visitors now gone and what started as a subdued whimper, gradually increased to a moan and an irate Sister Smith, shortly to go off duty, impatiently told me to "Stop that silly noise, you'll frighten the others." Unable to carry out her orders, I was marched down to the toilet, with her carrying the drip bottle and made to sit on the cold, hard seat of the toilet; she hung the drip bottle on the toilet chain above my head and called back as she left, "You sit there till they're ready for you. Goodnight"

I don't know why, but the song "Kiss me goodnight Sergeant Major" sprang to mind. My fertile imagination then went into overdrive as I looked up at the swinging bottle; what if my baby is born down the toilet, it may drown. Oh God the pain.

What in fact *was* only five minutes, felt more like an hour before I was rescued from my throne room by two student nurses, who, supporting me on either side, walked me down to the delivery room, which seemed miles away as I struggled to walk, feeling as though I had a football stuck in my rectum. Arriving in the clinical, brightly lit room, I was told to climb onto the delivery table – with its hard surface feeling more like a sacrificial alter – and to keep quiet. Moments later, another nurse arrived carrying a covered kidney dish.

"Just a little prick." She whispered as she painfully jabbed a needle into my thigh. I thought about another 'little prick' who played an unwilling part in getting me into this situation.

"What is it?" I asked as she massaged my now tender thigh.

"Pethedine, Sister Smith got it written up for you; it should help to ease the pain." With that, she turned out the lights and was gone.

Alone in the semi-darkness I lay whimpering like a motherless puppy. As the drug took effect, I swooned in and out of a dreamlike state; sounds filtered in and out, as did thoughts, thoughts of my mother, where was she now when I most needed her?, at a time when all I really wanted were some reassuring words whilst offering a friendly hand to hold. Pain broke through my revelry; the space between contractions was closing in. Suddenly, lights came on in a triumphant blaze as the room filled with the chatter from the people now milling around me.

Without being told what was about to take place, my legs were lifted and supported by the two student nurses, standing once again, on either side of me. At first I felt embarrassed to be showing my most private parts to complete strangers. I then found myself looking into the badly made up face of a middle-aged nurse whose hard mouth looked as though she had been called away whilst in the middle of eating a jam sandwich. Words issued forth from the 'smudge.

"Only push when we tell you to dear."
My back felt as though it were splitting down the middle, like a log does when hit with an axe.

"Breathe deeply when we tell you dear," the smudge said as she handed me a hissing mask.
A wonderful swoon came over me once again as I gasped the gas into my lungs, followed by the screaming voice of pain breaking through my reverie in ever increasing intensity. The surrounding voices seemed to mingle together as the words "Push now dear." broke through the web of sounds being spun by all those strange beings. I was being crushed in the jaws of the 'smudge'. Oh God the pain.
"Push, don't go to sleep." Sleep! Where was sleep?
I kept drifting out and then dragged back by the sound of that voice that could only ever have learnt the words 'push dear'

It was never ending until finally, *wanting* it all to end; I grasped the backs of my elevated legs and pushed for all I was worth. My eyes bulged as though they were going to explode from their sockets – a momentary thought – could eyeballs explode?

I was relieved to feel a correcting finger pressed against my rectum, holding in my one and only haemorrhoid, maybe avoiding yet another threatened explosion.

The mask was over my face again as I gasped and swooned.

"Nice, deep breaths now," a voice from the painful end called, "this little cut will hurt a bit" - understatement of the evening.

I hurtled through a deep, black tunnel of extreme pain, which seemed to carry me for miles, until I finally emerged into the light. Relief came whooshing forward with a kind of uncurling sensation as my new infant entered into the brightly lit world of hustle and bustle. A cry, not my cry this time; landed like the first butterfly of spring, gently but full of life, on my eager ears.

The smudge smiled a big jammy smile as she cooed, "You have a lovely little girl dear."

Looking into the face of my newborn child, hot tears of joy and relief streamed down my cheeks. Her crumpled little face was covered in my blood and her dark hair was matted and stuck to her tiny scalp, she was here, she was beautiful and she was mine

Jeanette aged 4 months

JEANETTE ALISON LYDIA

I had not heard from my mother since that dreadful evening when their front door was firmly closed by my irate stepfather.

I was so lonely and gained great comfort from my baby as she drank her fill from my full breasts. I pleaded with the nurses to leave her with me as she was also *my* only visitor, apart that is, from the one visit from her father who, when asked if he would like to see his new daughter, refused whilst making a hasty exit. Judging by the attitude from the nursing staff, I think the general consensus was that I was an unmarried mother, as I never had any visits from my side of the family; it was as though I didn't really exist.

I remember my mother telling me how she used to hide me under the covers when she had finished feeding me, hoping that the nurses would forget to take me back to the nursery. She said that I was her only visitor as it was too far for Nanny or Auntie to risk the train journey from London. The ship's radio officer passed on the news of my birth, transmitted over the ships radio in the middle of the English Channel, to my father, saying 'mother and baby daughter, both doing well.'

She hadn't got a name, my new baby daughter.

"What are you going to call the little dear?"Izzy said as she held her new granddaughter against her ample bosom whilst rocking back and forth, from one carpet-slippered foot to the other.

Suggesting that we stay for a while, "so that you can catch up on your rest, and get used to things," she said as Leslie put down my case and left. Mum gave dad a worried look which was immediately reciprocated; it was as though they both knew what the future held for me.

What I really wanted was to go home with my baby. I knew that I could manage; after all, before leaving the maternity hospital, I had been shown how to change her nappy and bath her safely. Breast-feeding came naturally to me; I had plenty of milk, in fact I had so much when it first came in that I gave my consent for the surplus to be used to feed the premature babies.

The name Jeanette came to me as I sat watching a film on the television one afternoon. Mum, who sat watching the Jeanette Macdonald and Nelson Eddy movie with me, said how she loved the name and how about calling my baby Jeanette. We also agreed on Alison, as it was Mum's second name and Lydia being my grandmother's name and my second name. Nobody argued with the choice and so it was to be.

During our stay with his parents, Leslie never looked at his daughter until one day I mentioned that she had the same shaped nails as his. A day or two later, I walked into the sitting room, to find him bent over her cot examining her hand. Seeing me, he grunted and strode out of the room. From then on his attitude towards Jeanette changed, I often found him sitting, staring at her as she lay sleeping.

After two weeks, we returned to 'Waterside'. I was so relieved to have my baby to myself and couldn't wait to show her to my dear friend Hilda. This is when the daunting realities of motherhood first dawned on me, along with the fact that I was now truly on my own. Although Hilda was only next door, she could not offer any helpful advice, as she had never had children of her own. But at least she was there for me.

Jeanette and I settled in well and our days flew by, taken up mostly with feeding time; she was so contented that she kept falling asleep before I could put her to the other breast.

"You must make sure she has ten minutes on one side and then after winding her, put her to the other breast," Miss Wharton, the local health visitor advised. I was so anxious to get it right, I followed her instructions to the letter, even if it meant sitting with a cup under the leaking breast whilst waiting for my infant to demand her second course. I produced so much milk that I could have fed multiple babies. When I awoke in the mornings, I found the towel I was laying on soaked through.

My baby thrived and grew and with the onset of winter, life got a lot harder. With only a 'Baby Burco' boiler, a mangle which had to be clamped onto the kitchen table and a , 'Flatley' clothes drier for use on wet days, the task of keeping the laundry in good order was not easy. I was able to stretch a clothesline from one end of the small kitchen to the other where I endeavoured to dry woollens and of course, his master's 'sea- island cotton' shirts – having already ruined one by over drying it in the 'Flatley'.

"Do you realise how much these cost?" he shouted, holding up the shirt with its never- to- be removed creases. "Don't you know these have to be ironed whilst still damp? You can't get anything right can you?"

I felt like throwing the damn thing on the floor and stamping on it; instead, after he had gone out, I dampened it and wrapped it in a clean towel before spending ages trying to iron out the creases. I was fraught with fear as, what appeared to be brown scorch marks appeared on the collar. Oh God, now what do I do. Izzy– she will know what to do. Hidden under the pram mattress, my transgression was transported the next day to a very sympathetic mother in law.

"Don't you worry dear, that'll all come out in the wash; scorched you say? No, you want to give the bottom of your iron a good clean." She was right. The next day she arrived with the pristine shirt wrapped in brown paper, inside a plastic bag. I gave her a huge hug and burst into tears of grateful relief.

'Waterside' was very draughty and any heat produced by the inefficient Parkray in the sitting room, was soon dispersed through the ill-fitting windows and doors. It brought back chilblained, childhood memories of being fascinated by the rippling floor rugs as the draught blew through the spaces between the floorboards. The strong westerly winds blew in through the ground level hole on the corner of the building, which was usually covered by a heavy slab of slate. This provided an outlet for the floodwaters that regularly flowed into the ancient earth footings of the house. Bernard told my father to leave the outlet open after a flood tide, so as to allow the area to dry out.

Leslie always put in an appearance for his evening meal and after a hurried wash and brush up, departed, leaving only the smell of 'Old Spice' hanging in the air. It was usually after midnight before he returned smelling of alcohol and another woman's perfume. Still carrying the heavy burden of guilt, I did not complain; never losing hope that one day he would realise how hard I was working on trying fulfil his every need, whilst at the same time caring for our growing child.

GORSE COTTAGE

One evening, having enjoyed a meal of spiced steak – a recipe I discovered in my new Oxo Cookbook – Leslie sat staring at me across the table; his look had its usual intimidating callousness; the dark brown irises of his large eyes appeared to be swallowed up by the black pupils, reminding me of the seemingly bottomless black water of the Screes in the Lake district, where we spent our honeymoon; when, whilst standing behind me, he whispered close to my ear "If a body was dumped in there, no one would ever find it." I was as frightened then just as now as he held my gaze; I wondered what new disclosure was about to be revealed to my tormented mind.

"We'll be moving soon, I've bought a bungalow."
I was doubly surprised; firstly, he was actually looking me straight in the face as he spoke and secondly, he had purchased a house for us; then came the slap in the face.

"Don't think I'm doing it for you, I'm not; it's for Mouse." This was to be his pet name for our daughter from now on, he liked giving his chosen title to his possessions. "You will be there just to look after her and keep house."
There was a long silent pause. I sat fighting back the tears as he aimed, what had now become, his customarily cold stare in my direction.

"Well, what have you got to say for yourself?" he suddenly broke the silence.
I could not adequately put into words my true feelings and just stared at the plate in front of me feeling sick.

"Oh well, if you're not going to give me an answer, I'm off out."

The engine of the Austin Mini revved violently as he

backed up and turned; the tires screeching disapproval as he sped away. I sat and sobbed, head in hands, elbows either side of my plate, watching as the tears dripped into the congealing juices of my half eaten meal. What should I have said? What could I say? No answers were forthcoming.

Relief finally came when I heard my baby crying in her cot upstairs. Wrapping the eiderdown round the two of us as I sat on the bed, I entered into the warm world of breast-feeding my hungry child. She made soft, snuffling sounds of enjoyment as she sucked the warm milk from my full breast. The pure pleasure touched my sad heart as she looked up at me with those big, brown eyes - so like her father's – only this was a warm look of contentment.

It was nearly Christmas and I wondered how I was going to manage to buy Jeanette a present. I had no money of my own; every penny of the housekeeping allowance had to be accounted for in that damnable 'Good Housekeeping Diary' he chose to equip me with every year.

"This section at the back is specially for keeping account of weekly expenditure" he told me the first Christmas we were together, "make sure you don't forget to write down everything you spend; damned good diary that."
I did forget and when it came time to show him my 'accounts', there were usually loads of discrepancies that I couldn't explain and that meant a row.

The following evening, feeling a little more cheerful, I cooked some fresh fish with chips and frozen peas. I always cooked fish on a Friday; I suppose it was a left over from my Roman Catholic schooling. He enjoyed his meal – at least I got one thing right – I was becoming quite a good cook and had good experience in frugality when it came to shopping; my father had made sure of that.

"We are going into Colchester tomorrow; I've already asked mother to look after Mouse. I want to get her a good quality teddy bear from that toyshop in Crouch Street. I want her to have one with movable joints and a good growler; she'll like that. They only have the best and I want it to last."

I had a teddy bear like that once; it was my brother's and was quite tatty by the time I inherited it. We had to operate on poor Ted; his growler hadn't worked for years and so my brother and I decided to perform major surgery to remove it. Dick knew how much I loved Ted and so as to impress his fiends he often teased me by punching him across the room; it always made me cry. I finally lost my beloved bear when I left to go to live with my mother.

It was a cold, crisp day; I was glad of the 'Damn good quality' sheepskin coat Leslie bought me the first Christmas we were married; that and the dreaded diary.

The name of the toy shop, the premises of which were bought by Laura Ashley many years ago, escapes my memory, however the memories I still can recall are those of the rows of stuffed animals and cuddly toys all peering down from the top shelves, along with a multitude of dolls ranging from lifelike baby dolls, who, when tipped closed their eyes and called out 'Mamma'; some black some white; bride dolls looking through the cellophane windows of their boxes; cute little girl and boy dolls dressed in gingham, looking as though they had just stepped off the set of Oklahoma.

Whilst standing awaiting the attention of an assistant, I recalled the time Dad had won me a beautiful Spanish Doll from one of the 'chance your luck' stalls at the Mersea Town Regatta fair, which was held in August every year. The day of the month depended on when the evening tide was at its lowest so as to allow the setting up of the firework display.

It was my eighth birthday a few days before and when the man behind the Tombola stall at the regatta fair, had finished haggling, my father's look of determination turned to elation as the irate stall-holder begrudgingly handed me my prize. Dad was only a little man, but not one to be argued with.

"I would like to look at that one please." Leslie's authoritarian voice broke through the reveries of my childhood. "Look," he said showing me the label on the bear's foot,

198

" 'Merrythought', one of the best." The bear let out e deep growl as he tipped it and moved its limbs. "We'll take this one." Looking at the price on the swing-ticket hanging from the bright red bow, round the bear's neck, I nearly fell through the floor. "Isn't that expensive?"

He ignored me as he got out his chequebook and Parker Pen.

As we walked back to the car, I felt the stiffness of the cardboard box , having been expertly wrapped in brown paper and, tied securely with string. I thought of the comfort this inanimate stuffed toy was going to bring to my little girl. She will become attached to her bear just as I had to mine; he will be her best friend and fellow confessor just as mine was; he will soak up the tears and not object to being cuddled too tightly when things get scary, that's what teddies are for. She will know his personality, especially when I tell her what Aunty Jess once told me when I was a little girl.

"The more love you give to your dollies and bears, the more life you put into them. Always believe in them and they will always be alive to you; it is your imagination that brings them to life."

Mum had cooked her usual Saturday roast which was always followed by a delicious brown skinned rice pudding which had been simmering all morning in a low oven, along with an apple pie, smelling of cloves and sweetened with brown sugar and made with the Bramleys picked in the late summer and stored in the summerhouse, along with other apples and root vegetables from the garden.

Jeanette was sound asleep on the double bed, usually reserved for guests. She looked so cosy and contented as she lay surrounded by pillows in case she woke up; being over four months old, she could now roll over and push herself with her chubby little legs.

"What do you think of this mother?" I heard Leslie's voice as I went down stairs. He hadn't waited for me.

Mum beamed her approval as she rolled up the string and placed it on the folded brown paper. "Look Dad, a good old fashioned Teddy-bear; that'll last her for years; yours is still up in the loft, she could have had that one, but then I expect you want her to have a new one," she quickly added as she saw the look of disapproval on her son's face. "You used to love that old bear, it's still in good condition, I thought about giving it to Rodney."

Dad looked worriedly at Mum and shook his head as he saw the scowl on his son's face as she mentioned his brother's three-year old son.

, I don't want any cheap rubbish," he said a few days later, "this is cash in this envelope so mind what you do with it."

"Huh, you don't give them anything of mine, leave it where it is."

"You *are* coming here for Christmas aren't you dear? Gerald and Sylvia are bringing little Rodney, he gets so excited now that he knows what Christmas is all about," Mum asked as I helped her carry in the plates of overcooked beef and great chunks of well-risen Yorkshire pudding. "Bring that jug of gravy Dad.

Leslie sat staring at his mother, his jaw bulging as he gritted his teeth, "You know I don't like that bloody woman."

"Now lad, you know that's your brother's wife and you know the pleasure your mother gets when she has the chance to cook for you all." Dad didn't say a lot, but this he said with a loving look at his wife.

"I don't want that boy touching Mouse's things and that bear was damned expensive."

Mum smiled at Dad, she instinctively knew that this was her son's way of accepting the invitation. I was relieved, as I did not want to experience a repeat of the previous year

Both being sound asleep, my daughter and I were oblivious to the entry of 1964.

The purchase of 'Gorse Cottage' all went through smoothly. It wasn't long before I was measuring up for the curtains.

"I want these curtains to be floor length, keep out the

draughts," Leslie said as we stood in the spacious sitting room.

"You can manage that can't you?" he must have picked up on my look of surprised anxiety. "I want them fully lined too," he added as he examined the curtain rails. "Huh! These won't be much good, they won't take the weight."

Oh God; yet another challenge, I thought, whilst trailing behind him and listening to my orders.

I had never made curtains before, let alone full length and lined.

The neglected and rather dilapidated prefabricated bungalow stood in at least two acres of land. To the right of the property was a rather overgrown orchard and to the left, a grass tennis court that was also in need of a hay cutter rather than a lawn mower. The back garden had a large area of lawn shaded on one side by a huge tree and on the other, by a variety of straggly shrubs. I was delighted to find a dear little rickety garden shed full of terracotta flowerpots and ancient, garden tools; evidence of the previous occupant having been a keen gardener. I wanted to run amuck around this enchanted garden and whoop with joy. I was so excited, I loved gardening; however Leslie's serious demeanour soon put paid to any extravagance of emotions on my part.

"This is the old cess pit," he said struggling to lift the concrete lid "they used to have to empty this before the main drains were installed and connected. " You could hide a body in there and no one would find it," he said as I peered into the cylindrical underground, concrete chamber. With the pretence of not having heard his sinister remark, I was relieved when he let the heavy lid fall back into place.

A ramshackle lean-too outhouse led to the back entrance of the sparse kitchen. The three bedrooms, all with doors leading off the sitting room, were quite cramped and the small metal-framed 'Crittall' windows didn't let in a lot of light.

"Those bloody trees will have to come down," he said, as though reading my mind as he walked in behind me. "I don't like fir trees, can't burn the wood on the fire, it spits like hell. Have to get that fire alight as soon as we can, the place feels damp. The chimney probably needs sweeping," he said setting light to a piece of old newspaper as he thrust it up the chimney. "Good draw there." The burning paper disappeared with a roar. I knew that given time, I could turn this sad little house into a cosy home.

"Get good quality material Why did he always have to sound so dictatorial when he spoke to me? I was no longer a child; I would be twenty in August.

Having dropped Jeanette off with her grandmother for the morning, I breathed a sigh of relief as I took my seat on the almost empty double-decker bus bound for Colchester. She had handed me a copy of 'The Peoples Friend' magazine to read on the half hour journey. Mr Pavey, the driver, waved at me as he pulled up at the bus stop.

It didn't seem like five years ago that his son Mick had taken me on the back of his motorbike when we had all decided to go off to Maldon for a picnic. Mick's sister Theresa went on the back of her boyfriend's bike and my friend Diana went with Roy Bloomfield who, at the time, had the biggest of all the motorbikes. In those days you didn't need to wear a helmet or leathers, and it was just a case of wrapping your arms tightly round the boy's waist whilst resting your head against his back and hanging on for dear life. At first I found it difficult to lean into the corners and was frequently chastised, but as my confidence grew, I was thrilled by the whole exhilarating experience. None of the boys showed off or took unnecessary risks and with less traffic on the roads, everything seemed to move at a slower pace.

The large Co-operative departmental store in Long Wyre Street had an excellent soft-furnishings and fittings department, with a vast range of 'good quality' fabrics. I was and always have been an impulsive buyer and knew exactly what I wanted as soon as I saw the bolt of midnight blue 'Moygashell' fabric with its ornate pattern of large golden urns. Having told the assistant how much I required; I went in search of material for my little girl's bedroom. The 'Magic Roundabout' fabric was exactly what I wanted and I bought enough to make the curtains and cot cover to match.

Watching the assistant place the cylinder containing the

receipt with my share number along with cash into the conveyance tube, I wondered how and where it all went. It was soon returned with my change and receipt. My purchases including reels of cotton and 'Rufflette' tape, were expertly parcelled up with stiff brown paper and tied up with string.

By the time I walked down 'Sheregate' steps, towards the St John Street bus park, my arms ached. I was glad to take my seat on the Eastern National 75a bus bound for West Mersea; the 75b didn't go down Coast Road, so I would have had a long walk with my heavy parcel.

I was home later than expected and as the bus passed the Church, I saw my mother in law's small, rotund figure pushing the pram towards Coast Road.

"Little dear has been asleep since eleven thirty, so I thought I would walk back before she woke up for her lunch; did you get what you wanted dear?" she asked as she fed Jeanette with Farley's Rusk and milk. "You make us both a nice cup of tea, you look all in dear."

My baby reached up to my face with her small, chubby fingered hand, making little grunts of satisfaction as she latched on to my painfully full breast.

"You are good to keep on breast feeding dear, I lost my milk after about a month of feeding Gerald. Leslie was such a greedy baby; I fed him a bit longer but I got an abscess and had to put him on the bottle, he didn't like that much, but I was so sore." she said as she sipped her tea.

I was tempted to say that he hadn't changed much.

"Have you ever made lined curtains before dear?" she asked as she folded the brown paper and rolled up the string.

"No, I've never made *curtains* before, but it can't be so difficult, can it?" I asked proudly holding up the heavy fabric.

"What lovely rich colours and good quality too; hope Leslie likes it?"

His grunt of approval was becoming the norm; I was getting used to the reticent manner of communication that had developed between us. I got more conversation from my pet budgerigar, Benny.

Jeanette snuggled cosily up to Teddy as I crept out of the bedroom.

Hearing the familiar sound of the Austin Mini engine becoming fainter as Leslie made his way towards whatever form of entertainment the evening had to offer. I could not wait to get started on my hitherto, daunting assignment.

"Give you Mummy big big kiss," Benny chirped, landing on my head as I finished off the washing up.

"Come on you little devil, time to go back in your cage, I've got work to do." I always had to jingle the bell on his favourite mirror that hung in his cage in the kitchen and he seemed to know it was back in cage time. It was strange really how much pleasure this little bundle of green feathers gave to both Leslie and me; lightening the atmosphere with his chatter and funny antics. I bought him as a very young bird, from the same supplier in Blue Row, where Hilda had bought hers. With her guidance I soon had him finger tamed and mimicking all the phrases we taught him. During the many hours I spent alone, before Jeanette was born he kept me company; he was my little friend.

Pushing the chairs back to make more floor space, I spread the material out and started to measure and cut. The lighting in the sitting room was quite poor both by day and night, but I had good eyesight and with God's help, I managed.

The hand driven 'Singer' sewing machine which had belonged to my father's mother Lydia, was very slow but it did a good job.

I remember as a little girl, sitting in the wooden lid, pretending it was a boat whilst my father who was expert at tailoring was probably altering his demob suit, which he did to fit my mother. He once clothed one of my dolls in a leather cowgirl outfit. When we eventually moved to 19 Windsor Road, the machine was stored in a cupboard under the stairs, unused and gathering dust. It was then given to me when I returned from London, having spent two years, living with my mother and stepfather. Dad, having overhauled and oiled the neglected moving parts, was only too pleased to see it in use again as I attempted to make my own clothes.

I treasured it and now it was helping me to make my very first pair of fully lined, long curtains.

By midnight I was getting very tired. I had nearly finished the *long* pair, which were the most difficult; I decided to take Mum's advice and leave the hems for hand sewing after the curtains had been hanging for awhile 'so as to allow them to drop dear.'

I put my new non-stick milk saucepan on the hotplate and was out to heat up some milk for the thermos flask, in case Jeanette woke for a feed in the night; I wanted to start weaning her off breast-feeding. In my weariness, I decided to go straight to bed. Jeanette slept right through the night. In the morning I was woken from a deep sleep by Leslie shaking me, "You've bloody well murdered your bird" For a shocking moment I thought he said "baby" "You left the milk pan on the stove, it's a miracle you didn't burn the bloody house down."

My horror turned to heartbreak when I realised that the fumes from the burnt pan and the heat from the hotplate must have choked poor Benny. I tried feebly to explain how exhausted I had been, but my words hit the slammed door

Hilda cried with me as I later told her what had happened

"Well dear, at least you and the baby are alright, it could have been worse, you could have burnt the house down."

I didn't really want to be reminded of that terrible fact.

"You look exhausted dear," Hilda said handing me a cup of coffee, "I don't see much of you these days, I know how busy you must be with the baby and everything.

I knew full well what she meant by 'and everything'. She knew how even more difficult my life had become over the past few months. "I shall miss you when you move, any idea when it will be?"

As soon as the contracts were signed, we told Hilda and Bernard the date of when we would finally be moving

"Give you time to get some new tenants Bernard, wouldn't want you to lose money on our account," Leslie said, trying to make a joke.

To thank them for all their kindness, I invited them to supper. Leslie actually stayed at home that evening; we all enjoyed a very pleasant time.

A few days later, I was hanging some washing out round the back of the cottages, when I heard Hilda telling her sister Maud all about the meal I had cooked for them. "Oh it was a lovely do; she cooked such a nice meal and do you know Maudie dear, she served all the vegetables up in latrines."

When I told Leslie the story, he laughed fit to burst. There had been so little laughter between us of late; the laughter was usually aimed *at* me not *with* me. I was happy to think that I had achieved what I hoped was a positive outcome, even if it was at the expense of another of Hilda's 'malapropisms'.

We moved into Gorse Cottage at the beginning of April; the weather was fine and warm for the time of year.

Jeanette sat watching from her pram as I struggled with the boxes and cases Leslie had left in the garage earlier that morning. Mum, having arrived earlier on her bicycle, bustled about in the kitchen as she unpacked pots and pans.

"I thought this would save you having to cook today," she said unpacking her basket; the delicious aroma of her home-made steak and kidney pie filled the kitchen.

"Leslie will be hungry when he gets home. Dad is coming round when he closes the shop, so as to lend a hand with putting up the bed."

The garden was full of birdsong

"Look at the little dear, she's going to love sitting out there, it won't be long before she will be trotting about." Mum was so proud of her little granddaughter.

The curtains were a success.

"You must let these hang for a while," she puffed as she handed me one of the heavy long curtains, "poor Christine didn't take my advice and now hers hang all unevenly, but she does try hard bless her." My sweet mother in law never had a harsh word to say about anyone. "You be careful on those steps dear."

"Why doesn't Leslie like Sylvia Mum?" I asked, "I would like to get to know her better, seeing as we live so close now."

Empress Avenue, where my brother and sister in law lived in their newly built bungalow, was only two roads away and could be reached by cutting through a rough footpath.

"I don't know dear," she didn't look at me as she answered.

"Come on let's get the kettle on, I'm sure you could do with a nice cup of tea, I know I could and I've brought some rock buns, I know Leslie is rather partial to them." Dear little lady, she always did her best for everyone. She was one of the few people that I knew who could be thought of as a true Christian.

"Now that Jeanette no longer needs to be breast fed, I will have more time in the morning and would very much like to attend the church up the village; do you think Leslie will mind looking after her for the morning?" A look of delight shone through those kind eyes as she nodded her approval.

"I'm sure he won't mind dear, I think it will do you good."

I went on to tell her how, as a child, I used to walk from where we lived in Windsor Road, to the British Legion in Barfield Road, so as to attend Sunday morning Mass which took place in the club room. I was ten at the time and since starting at the Roman Catholic school – St Thomas Moore in Priory Street, Colchester – I had become a very devout follower of the faith.

"Have you been confirmed?" she asked "You can only take communion when you have been confirmed."

"No, I had to be Baptised before I could take First Holy Communion. The Nuns had to ask two of the dinner ladies to witness the ceremony, as my parents could not be there; neither of them were in the least bit interested in religion anyway; they didn't come to my First Holy Communion either." Telling her this, made me realise just how *many* events I had faced alone whilst growing up. "I haven't been to Mass or confession for years; do you think God has forgiven me for the wrong I have done?"

"God forgives all those who are truly sorry," she said handing me a pair of faded curtains as we organised Jeanette's bedroom. "These will do for now dear, I expect you'll be making her those nice new ones soon; the little dear.

Jeanette settled into her own room surprisingly well and by the time we all sat down to supper, she was sound asleep.

It was Saturday and although I knew that he would probably be going out after supper, I planned to make Leslie a special meal. We now had a proper dining room table and chairs, also left by the previous occupants and Mum gave me some pretty table linen and two wooden candlesticks. I placed two candles and a small vase of flowers on the table and to my amazement he actually commented on how nice it all looked. I prayed that maybe now we could pick up on the threads of our marriage and be happy at last. It was a chilly evening and I lit a fire. With my lovely new curtains closed and the glow from the log fire crackling in the grate, I hoped this would take the chill off his feelings for me.

After a steak supper and a few glasses of wine, we sat watching as the tiny sparks glimmering in the sooty deposits at the back of the fire, resembled a procession of candle-bearing churchgoers on their way to midnight Mass; a description my father gave as we used to sit looking into the fire as children. I reached for Leslie's hand and he didn't pull away this time. We made love and I hoped he couldn't see my tears of pure happiness in the now fading light from the dying embers.

With Jeanette now having her own bedroom, I took great pleasure in making her bedroom curtains and cot cover, using the fabric decorated with the characters of Florence, the little girl; Dillon, the rather laid back hare; Zebedee, the Jack-in – box; Brian, the snail; Ermentrude, the cow and Doogle, the dog; all from her favourite television programme 'Magic Roundabout'. I cut out the characters from the spare fabric, using them as decoration for the plain walls.

As the nights drew in, and once I had put Jeanette to bed, I spent many happy evenings either sewing little clothes for her or knitting her pretty jumpers. It was all a great learning curve for me and it helped to fill the many lonely hours. I made a good start on the garden with helpful advice from my father in law. The store closed at lunchtime on Wednesdays and he used to pop over to give me a hand whilst Mum took Jeanette out in her pram.

Before I knew it, it was Christmas and I decided that even if I spent most of the time alone with my daughter, I was going to spend Christmas day at home.

The cottage was made a little easier to keep warm by the small solid fuel boiler in the kitchen, struggling to heat the radiators throughout the house. The open log fire in the sitting room, which I lit mid afternoon, made a good job of warming ones front, whilst sitting with a blanket around our shoulders. However, I loved the winter afternoons when Jeanette and I would snuggle up on the comfortable old Chesterton settee, left behind by the previous occupants, and watch various children's hour programs, in particular 'Magic Roundabout'. We always had biscuits with our hot drinks; me, with my cup of tea, Jeanette with her warm milk. It all felt so right.

I sometimes felt quite lonely and wished that I had made more friends with other mums; I don't know why, but it just didn't happen; until one afternoon I was working in the garden when a small boy appeared through the long grass of the Orchard; Jeanette was toddling about whilst I was raking up the leaves on the lawn.

"Hello, I'm Richard" a stockily built, dark haired little lad gave me a cheeky grin as he went on to say, " can I come and play in your garden with your little girl?" after which, a woman appeared, emerging from the same direction.

"Richard, where are you?" On seeing me, she apologised as she chased after her small son. We introduced ourselves and the friendship had begun. I seem to remember her name being Vera.

"I've got some friends coming over for coffee tomorrow morning, why don't you join us," she suggested.
Vera was a lot older than me; apparently Richard had been a late addition to her now grown-up family. He spent more time with me than his mother did. When not watching Wimbledon on the television, she spent a great deal of her time reading and drinking coffee and also smoking heavily. I don't remember

seeing a husband, whom she said he worked away.

Leslie made Jeanette a lovely swing, which he hung from the large overhanging branch of the oak tree. It was a square framed affair, which she could not fall out of. He was very clever when it came to carpentry; he also made her a little cart filled with wooden bricks, which she used to love to push around the garden when she was first learning to walk

Although things seemed to be on a much more even keel, there was still an undercurrent of aggression and mistrust and most of my evenings were spent alone. Leslie's possessive attitude towards Jeanette increased and it was as though she knew it; she was becoming a daddy's girl, following him about like a little puppy.

One day I had a brainwave; I loved to cook and decided to make bread and pies to sell to passers by – of which there weren't many - but I thought the word would soon spread. I still didn't have any money of my own and thought this would be a good way of earning some pocket money. Leslie seemed to like the idea and built some wooden racked shelving in the lean-to. I started in earnest; the bread was passable but not as good as my Cornish pasties and meat pies. I hadn't got a clue about pricing goods and after a short while found that for all the hard work, I wasn't really making any money. One good thing - for Christmas that year I was treated to a 'Kenwood Chef' food-mixer.

"Damned good quality, 'Kenwood'; let's see what your brother thinks of that!" he boasted.

The Kenwood certainly revolutionised my bread-making skills, but didn't however, make any difference to making any profit.

Finally after four months of mostly unrewarding hard work throughout the summer, I made the decision to end my little venture knowing that there would be fewer holiday makers passing the cottage with the onset of autumn.

"Huh! That didn't last long did it," Leslie's disparagingly remarked; leaving me with the feelings of disappointment and failure. "Fat lot of good me making those racks, oh well they'll come in handy in the garage."

He was now getting a great deal of work from local builders, as were most of the local tradesmen. The population of West Mersea was on the increase; with new properties springing up all over the main part of the island.

With his greatly increased wealth, Leslie now invested in a larger car, a second-hand Rover 3 Litre, which he was very proud of. On Sunday mornings, providing the weather was fine, it would get washed and waxed,

"You can help by polishing the seats with this 'Hide Food', it's especially for leather seats," he instructed when I returned from church that day. Sitting in the front seat, I could hardly see over the steering wheel, I wondered if I would ever learn to drive.

"Where do you ever go? You don't need to drive, I do all the driving," he said in answer to my question about driving lessons, "anyway, you've got your bike." – end of conversation.

He made another new addition to his collection of possessions, a 'Remington' typewriter that I was warned never to touch. "That is for my use only, not for messing about on, I need it for my business." I was rather hurt by this comment; I would love to have learned to type and had visions of helping him by typing up business letters. He ended up putting a lock on the door of the spare room, with the excuse that he didn't want nosy parkers like 'rent a mouth' – one of the derogatory names he awarded his sister in law, – sticking their noses into his business. I was also told not go poking around in the garage. "There are expensive tools and equipment in there so I'm keeping it locked."

Nearing the end of the summer, he struggled in with a heavy-duty wet suit and hanging it on the kitchen door, announced that he was going to start water ski lessons. I didn't even know that he could swim. During our courting days, he always sat on the sea wall where he watched me splashing about.
I used to swim a lot with my friends before I met him.

Each Sunday, having cleaned the car, he left the house as

soon as I returned from church at midday and I wouldn't see him again until early evening. Saturday's he always worked until lunch time and after a steak and chips lunch, followed by a quick wash and brush up, he was gone for the rest of the day. When he finally returned home, he was usually the worse for drink and demanded that we go to bed. Sex was becoming very rough and painful as he wanted me to perform in uncomfortable positions. On two occasions, I had had to seek the help of my Doctor after he had carelessly split the cleavage of my buttocks, with his rough handling, causing me great pain. He was not aware of my needs at all; I felt used and abused.

One afternoon, he was on his way out when he heard me ask Jeanette if she needed to use her potty; she refused and looking at me defiantly, peed on the floor. I lost my patience and telling her she was a naughty girl, I slapped her leg - she screamed and ran to her daddy.

"Don't you ever lay a finger on her again," he shouted. She leaned against his leg giving me that same look of defiance. I knew then that I was the outsider. Looking back I feel that I was in a very frail frame of mind; may even have been going through a nervous breakdown. I had had enough; I couldn't face a future of drudgery.

"What am I here?" I whispered through my tears of helplessness.

"I'll tell you what you are," he shouted, "you are here to do your duty, I told you not to expect anything else."

Running into our bedroom in a fit of exasperated temper, I pulled all his shirts out of wardrobe and throwing them in a heap on the floor, I stamped on them shouting, "This is what I think of your bloody 'sea-island cotton' shirts."

Leaving Jeanette in the kitchen, he ran into the room and grabbed me by the hair; throwing me on the bed, he snarled, "You worthless little bitch."

As is hands went round my throat, I thought 'this is the end, I'm going to die; he is finally going to kill me'; it also flashed through my mind that he would hide my body in the cess-pit and no one would ever find me. Letting go of my neck, he took a painful hold of my upper arms, shaking me violently as his lip curled, "You had better pull yourself together and go and look after Mouse. I want those shirts ironed and back on their hangers before I get back, do you hear me?" he shouted as he kicked at the pile of shirts.

Damn him, damn him, damn his bloody shirts. I didn't want to be there; I wanted to run away; I was tired of ceaselessly being blamed. The increase in physical violence now adding to the mental cruelty that I had endured for so long

Calling in to see my father and stepmother the next day was a mistake. Showing them the bruises to my neck and arms, I was dismayed when the only response I got was being told to go to the police. There had been a time when my father had said, "I'll kill him if he ever lays a finger on you." He was always full of empty words these days.

"You must have done something to upset him." Lil said smirking in my father's direction.

"That's their business," he said walking out of the kitchen. They didn't want to know.

Feeling confused and depressed, I decided to go and seek the advice of Dr Dorothy Howes. I showed her my bruises and explained how they came about. As she sat and listened, my words bubbled up from the pit of my stomach like verbal vomit. Looking straight into my eyes as she reached over the desk and took hold of my shaking hands, she said, "You cannot go on like this, you will end up having a breakdown. I can give you medication to help you to cope, but in the long term it will not solve your ongoing problems. Couldn't you go and stay with your mother …?" quickly realising what she had said, she immediately apologised; I, having previously told her about my last visit to my mother, when I had been barred from ever crossing their doorstep again.

Dr Dorothy had known the family since we had moved onto the island when I was a baby. She knew the traumas I had had to endure over the years. There was the time when at the age of thirteen, I was sexually assaulted in the front garden of Nineteen Windsor Road by a drunken

neighbour and how I had been scared to tell my father. My stepmother, who accompanied me to the surgery where I was diagnosed as having Thrush, went on to tell my father that I must have been messing around with boys as a thought I was pregnant. I had in fact asked her if you could get pregnant by a man putting his finger inside you if he had stuff on his hands. The ignorance of innocence can be so cruel at times.

Having always patiently listened to my anxieties and fears and now once again she listened as a doctor, but advised as a lifelong friend. "You know what ever I say is not going to change things or make them any better. I think your only hope is to leave him."

Looking back, though she never said as much, I think she knew more about Leslie than she was ethically allowed to say and no matter what I did, she must have known that he wasn't going to change. As I left she told me that she would be willing to write to social services if I needed to claim for financial support.

One afternoon, there was a knock at the back door and on opening it I was surprised to see a stranger smiling at me.

"Hello, I'm Molly Western, Tom's wife," I looked bemused as she continued; "my husband works with Les on the houses Ron Fisher is building down Empress Avenue." The penny dropped and I invited her in.

"Jim tells me you're supposed to be good at sewing." She said trying to cover her strong Romford accent. She was a heavily made up woman of around forty, with long, henna red hair that hung thickly about her shoulders. I was impressed by her colourful hippy style clothing.

"You've got it very snug here," she said waving her hand, each scarlet nailed finger bedecked with large gold rings. She reminded me of a gypsy.

"Les was telling Tom about the curtains you have made, can I take a look?" Without invitation, she walked into the sitting room and lifting the bottom of one of the *long* curtains she said, "Very nicely done."

I thought she couldn't have just come to admire the curtains;

then came the real reason for her visit

"I need some new curtains for my lounge, could you do them for me? I'll pay you."

Me, make somebody else's curtains? What would Leslie say?

"Your old man reckons you would be glad to do it," she said as if reading my thoughts, "come and have a look, you can bring her with you," she said pointing at Jeanette who had just toddled in from the garden. "Tomorrow afternoon then, say around three." not waiting for a reply she was gone.

The noxious odours of stale cigarette smoke and boiled cabbage nauseated me as I climbed the steps with my tape measure. West House in Empress Avenue had once been a fine home; probably owned by an influential member of the community. Sadly, it was now shabby, dirty and very untidy. Looking as though they might once have been a rich royal blue, the now faded, velour curtains hung dust laden as the afternoon sunlight struggled to obtain entry through the filthy windows.

"They were up when we moved in ten years ago," she said as I stretched up with my tape measure, trying not to breath in the vile stink and dust, "they've done well haven't they? They would probably dry clean alright, but I want a change."

They would probably fall to pieces, I thought.

"I really need some help in the house," she continued, "I'm always busy on the market and with four men and a teenage daughter to look after, I don't get much time to clean windows," she said as though, once again, reading my mind. She went on to tell me about her market stall where she sold women's clothing.

"I used to make the dresses and skirts myself," she said showing me into a very cramped sewing room. Hanging around the walls were multiple paper patterns on coat hangers. "I designed and cut out all this lot myself, but I no longer use them. Anymore; no time, you know how it is," she said showing me boxes of buttons and zips, cottons and various tapes. "Take what you want; none of this will get used now."

Rolls of fabric were stacked against the walls; in the centre of the room, standing at the end of a large table, was an aged, industrial Singer sewing machine. I was very excited and wished that I could have spent more time alone in what felt to me, like 'Aladdin's' cave.

I staggered home pushing my sleeping daughter in her pushchair whilst endeavouring to carry the two bulging carrier bags full of sewing goodies.

"Where the hell have you been?" Leslie scowled as I struggled in carrying my sleeping child.

The aroma of the beef casserole I had left in a low oven filled the kitchen as I added the previously made dumplings.

"These won't take long," I said as I went out to the garden to fetch in my bootie, before rather hesitantly telling him about my new acquaintance.

"Tom reckons his missus is loaded, so you get what you can out of her," I was surprised by his reaction

"Come into the market on Saturday," Molly said whilst standing back so as to admire her new curtains, "and you can choose a nice dress for yourself." The sun shone brightly on her upturned face, "You've made a good job of the windows," she said screwing up her eyes, " makes it a lot lighter in here; you can do the kitchen tomorrow, only thing is it will show up the dirty paintwork," she said with a chuckle, "still you can get that done too."

I put in a great deal of hard work at West House over the next two or three weeks and always with similar rewards; a length of fabric; a half finished dress and other assorted haberdashery items. Luckily the weather stayed relatively fine enabling Jeanette to play happily in the large unkempt garden. I was in and out, either hanging out huge amounts of washing or shaking out dust-laden rugs. Time just seemed to fly by and to be honest; I was enjoying the work and the companionship.

"You're not happy with him are you?" the question came out of the blue one afternoon as Molly poured us both a cup of tea, "I can tell, I can see it in your eyes."

Being in an extremely vulnerable state and with no one

else to confide in, I broke down into floods of uncontrollable tears whilst pouring out my soul to this calculating woman who, in my naivety, I thought I could trust.

"Why do you stay with him?" she asked looking straight into my tear filled eyes.

"Because I have nowhere else to go and besides, I have this one to think of," I answered as Jeanette struggled to get onto my lap. I think she must have picked up on my emotional state of mind.

"Well if you want my opinion," she said handing Jeanette a biscuit, "from what you have told me, as she grows up," nodding towards Jeanette, " she will learn to resent you, he'll spoil her more and more as time goes on and you will just end up a drudge, continually at their beck and call."

Oh God, was she right? Jeanette certainly seemed to favour her father, or so it seemed to me. Was I becoming paranoid; maybe things would improve and then his words came back to me like a punch in the guts, 'You are here to do your duty, I told you not to expect anything else.'

"You ought to find yourself a flat," she said invading my fear-fuelled thoughts, "and prove that you no longer need him."

"But I have no money," I thought of his suggestion about how I ought to 'get what you can out of her.'

"You can get money from the government once you can prove that you and your child have nothing to live on."
My mind was in turmoil as I made my way home that afternoon.

"Has she given you any money yet?" Leslie asked as I dished up the supper.

"No, but she has given me a lot of sewing things and she said that I could choose a new dress from her stall if I go into the market on Saturday."

"Huh! That bloody rubbish, you don't want anything off her stall, it's all cheap crap."

"But I do need new clothes." I protested

"That's your look out," he said, noisily scraping his chair back, "I'll be late tonight, I've got to see a bloke about some work. Good job one of us earns some money round here," were his parting words as he slammed the back door.

Now alone with only my thoughts as company, I sat out in the garden, a shawl wrapped round my shoulders, watching as one by one stars began to pepper the darkening sky. The exquisite perfume of the night scented flowers drifted on the gentle, breeze. A lone nightingale serenaded me and was soon joined by a chorus of croaking frogs and chirruping crickets, along with the occasional screech of the 'Little Owl'. The outside light over the back door lit up the ballet enacted by colourful, feathery moths unwittingly performing for an audience of swooping bats.

Losing myself in the realms of this delightful fantasy and feeling tears, not of sadness, but pure joy, rise up from somewhere deep inside me, I felt as though I wanted to spread my arms and embrace the night. Nothing and nobody would ever take *this* away from me; it was mine and now that I had found it - this feeling of euphoric bliss, this deeper faith in God - although I did not know it then - would remain with me for the rest of my life; pulling me up from the depths of despair and over the years, empowering me with the ability to learn from the harsh lessons life perpetually set before me.

The next day, whilst I made an attack on a huge pile of ironing, Molly made her usual hands-on-hips stance, "Well, have you decided what you are going to do yet?" I looked at Jeanette as she happily played with a cardboard box and some wooden spoons. "You've got a good mother in law, she'll have to look after her," she said, nodding towards my little girl.

"It's her birthday on Saturday and her Great Uncle Francis is over from New Zealand. I'm putting on a birthday tea party in the garden." I didn't look up from the ironing; I knew by her silence that she did not approve.

It was a gloriously sunny day with not a cloud in the sky. Dad was up the stepladder pegging an old sheet over the lowest branches of the tree. "That should give us enough shade and the sun will be going round a bit as the afternoon goes on," he said as he leaned the folded stepladder against the wall of the garage.

"I can't put it away, I don't know why he keeps the garage door locked, probably stashes all his money in there," he chuckled.

"Don't you carry that table on your own Dad," my mother in law called from the kitchen, "Leslie said he would do that when he gets home."

By the time he arrived home – after four pm – the table was laid, Uncle Francis and his wife had arrived and Jeanette was playing happily with her new friend Richard who had arrived with his big sister, Sally. And I was feeling very frustrated.

The party was a success and by the time Mum carried out the 'Magic Roundabout' sponge cake which I had proudly made, I began to relax and enjoy my daughters second birthday.

With the celebrations set to go on into the evening, Leslie brought some bottles of wine from the garage; this then prompted Frank to hand him the carrier bag he had brought with him. "Present for you boy, I know you're rather partial."

"Damned good whiskey that, thanks," he said holding up the bottle of amber coloured 'Bells Whiskey' to the fast fading light of the setting sun.

Mum and Dad decided to go home once Richard and Sally had gone and Jeanette was in bed. I busied myself clearing up in the kitchen. It was getting dark when I carried out a tray of coffee and biscuits and cheese. The lead-light hanging from the tree attracted a multitude of moths and the mosquitoes were becoming a nuisance. We sat chatting for a little longer and by the time Frank and Val unsteadily stood up to leave, the wine bottles were all empty and so was the whiskey bottle. Leslie offered them a lift, but they had the sense to refuse, saying that the walk would help to sober them up.

He sat out in the garden alone for a while and when he finally came into the kitchen, I was scared as he staggered towards me "Come on I want you in bed." His words were slurred but commanding.

"No." I startled myself with my resolute answer.

"What?" his bleary eyes widened with rage.

"No. You're drunk."

"That's the only way I want to be when I take you, now get to bed."

"I have had enough of your unkindness towards me."

"Huh! What are you going to do about it?" whisky drenched spittle hit my face as he jutted his head towards me.

"I'm leaving you." The sudden rush of adrenalin, made me shake from head to toe.

"Well well!" he scoffed, "you needn't think you'll be taking Mouse, I'll see you in hell first. Anyway you've got nowhere to go, no one wants you; your mother shut the door on you, your brother has his own life to live and your father couldn't give a damn about you, you know that."

"I'll soon find somewhere." I started to cry.

"Oh! And how are you going to pay, you've got nothing and you need not think you are getting anything out of me." He appeared to have sobered up a bit.

"I can get social security."

"Huh! Who put that into your head? I bet you've been talking to the Western witch."

"So what if I have? I need someone on my side, you said yourself, that there's nobody else to help me."

"She's bloody trouble that woman, you've been seeing too much of her lately, well that can stop."

"I'm not a child any longer, I'll be twenty one next week." That statement made me feel stronger – for a second or two!

"Well stop acting like a stupid kid for once and get to bed." I resisted as he pulled at my dress and as he fell backwards he landed heavily onto the sofa, where instead of trying to get up, he just laid his head back, closed his eyes and almost immediately, started to snore. I stood looking at him for a few minutes wondering what I ever saw in him. He looked even older than thirty-six; a dark shadow of stubble around his open mouth, showing the gaps from lost teeth; the top of his head now completely bald with a few remaining wisps of greying hair, usually pulled over from the side, now hanging over his closed eyes. I hated him. I really hated him, he who had taken away my youth, leaving me with nothing but sadness and despair. He was even robbing me of the love of my child.

Having lain on the bed fully clothed, I awoke the next morning from a fitful sleep.

Jeanette was wide awake as I lifted her from her cot and carrying her through the sitting room where I expected to see her daddy, where I had left him the night before, there was no sign of him and the car had gone.

I didn't go round to Molly's for the next few days, not wanting any more advice. I had already decided what I was going to do.

A week had passed and it was the day of my twenty-first birthday. Calling in to see Molly on the way up to see my father, I informed her that I had told Leslie I was leaving him as soon as I had found somewhere else to stay.

"You make sure you take everything that belongs to you. Don't forget things that he has bought you as presents, after all they all belong to you; even that sheepskin coat you told me about, if you don't like it, it will do for one of my boys for work." Her eyes looked at me greedily. "You can store whatever you like here, until you get somewhere permanent that is. Oh yes here you are," she said handing me a box of Black Magic chocolates, "Happy Birthday."

My father and Lil were sitting in the garden when I arrived. "Oh it's you," she said getting up, "glad you've decided to come round, I'll go and get your present."

Dad looked at me uneasily as he got up with a groan, "Do you want a cup of coffee, we've just had ours."

"Have you wished your daughter a Happy Birthday?" Lil asked, passing Dad on his way to the kitchen. She soon reappeared carrying a small, roughly wrapped parcel. "He'll be out in a minute, miserable old sod. If it wasn't for me you wouldn't be getting this," she said placing the small parcel on the garden table, "so think yourself lucky madam."

Neither of them had paid any attention to Jeanette who,

having just woken up, gave a little grizzle as she wriggled to get out of her pushchair.

"Well, aren't you going to open your present?" She asked grabbing the parcel off the table and glaring at Dad as he was about to put the tray down on it. "Fred, for God's sake watch what you're doing," she yelled at him. "Here, don't ever say we don't buy you anything." She always had a sarcastic tone to her voice whenever she spoke to me; making me feel as though she really did not want me there.

"Thank you; but first I must tell you that I have decided to leave Leslie." Neither of them looked in the least bit surprised.

"Where will you go?" Dad asked handing me a cup of strong coffee.

"I don't know yet, I have to find a flat or something."

"Well don't expect us to put you up, we haven't got the room," Lil put in hastily. "Oh and by the way your Dad and me got married last week," I was stunned and must have shown it as she quickly added, "we didn't tell anyone because we didn't want to make a big thing of it. My Danny gave me away; imagine that, my own son giving me away. Do you like my rings?" she said holding out her hand. "Your Dad wanted me to have a nice diamond engagement ring as well as the wedding ring." The five stone diamond ring glinted in the sunshine as she sat grinning at me, like the cat that's got the cream. "Aren't you going to congratulate us then?"

Looking at my Dad who had hardly said a word, I said that I hoped they would be very happy. Endeavouring to quickly change the subject, he said "You know they need staff where I work at the Red Lion."

"Yes but she would have to live in," Lil interrupted, "what about her?" she went on, pointing at Jeanette who was now peering into the fishpond. Taking her hand I sat her on my lap and Lil handed her a biscuit.

"What about Mrs Leslie, wouldn't she have her whilst you're at work? You could see her on your days off. When my Danny was a baby, I used to take him to work with me, I worked in the NAAFI in those days and it was damned hard work.

"He was a new born baby Lil and probably slept most of the time and it was war time, times were different then." Dad told her.

Jeanette had grabbed the parcel and was busily tearing off the paper, revealing a shell shaped box with the title 'Rosita Pearls' on the lid.

"I thought you would like those. Your Dad always says that pearls are bad luck, he reckons his mother used to say that the suffering the oyster had gone through whilst making the pearl, could only bring tears to the wearer. Well these aren't real pearls so it won't matter will it"

Walking down to the village, my mind was in a chaotic whirl of everyone's words of advice when I bumped into my old school friend, Susan Fahie.

"Watcher mate, how goes it?" she asked in her usual cheerful manner "Hello little un, my how you've grown." she said looking at Jeanette wriggling to get out of her pushchair. She went on to tell me about her twin boys, both born with deformities caused by her taking the drug 'Thalidamide' during the early stages of her pregnancy. "Jem is Ok but my other boy died after an accident." Her look of pain wordlessly told me that she really didn't want to talk about it

"Where are you living now?" I asked, quickly changing the subject, "I heard you had moved off the island."
She told me that her husband was working on one of the new motorways and it meant them all living on site in a caravan.

"He insists on us being with him, I bloody hate it; the noise; the dust turning to mud when it rains; being miles from anywhere; no one to talk to apart from a couple of the other wives, or whatever they are. The only highlight is when a couple of the blokes bring round a few beers and we have a bit of a party. How about you? Are you happier now that you've got your own place?"

I told her that things had worsened and that I was looking for temporary digs."

"That's no problem. Go and see my mum, there's plenty of room at 'Woodstock'. What are you doing now? I'm on my way back there now, come and have a chat with her."

Susan and I used to have a love hate relationship at school. It was quite an amusing sight when the arguments turned into a fight. She, with her long arms and legs, towered above me; but even though she was a head and shoulders taller than me, when she called me a little 'Wop', I got stuck in. She inherited her looks from her father who looked as though he might have had Indian blood running through his veins. He was certainly a very handsome man. Susan and her brothers all had lovely olive complexions and very dark brown hair and eyes. I took advantage of these facts during our skirmishes by calling her a bloody Wog. One day, after a 'fir lying' battle, goaded on by the rest of the girls, we were called into the headmaster Mr Westcott's office and told that if we wished to fight, carry on so that he could watch. We were both so embarrassed and having declined his request, we were never fought again; in fact we soon became firm friends.

We were greeted by a number of bedraggled white poodles yapping round our legs when we arrived at the rather grand three-storey house in St Peter's Road.

Mrs Fahie appeared at the back door wearing a pretty, silk housecoat which clung to her slim yet shapely figure like a second skin. Her peroxide blonde hair was dishevelled and the previous evening's, now smudged, makeup gave her a clown like appearance. She was a very beautiful woman and when dressed up in her finery, whilst working at the Hall Barn Country Club, she strongly resembled Joy Beverly of the Beverly Sisters.

"I'm glad you're back," she said looking desperately at Susan, "your dad had to take Jem for a walk, he was upsetting the dogs. Make me a cup of coffee darling; I'm parched. Hello Rita what are you doing here?" hardly drawing breath, "excuse the mess, can't get the staff. Not like it was in India, we had only to clap our hands and there they were. I do miss it all. Susan's daddy was in the diplomatic service out there you know; all my children were born in India.

At School, we all thought Susan made up the story and used to scoff when she spoke of having had servants.

The sun, as it shone into the kitchen, didn't improve the cluttered, shabby conditions.

"So this is Leslie's little Mouse he is always going on about. She has his lovely brown eyes," she said lighting up a cigarette.

"Let her out of the pushchair, I'm sure she would love to play with the doggies, wouldn't you pet?"
Looking around at all the dog turds littering the non-to-clean kitchen floor and garden, I told her that we weren't intending to stay and got straight to the point as I asked her if it were possible for me to rent a room. "It wouldn't be permanent," I explained, briefly telling her of my dilemma.

"I didn't think you would be capable of domesticating that one," she said, referring to Leslie. "He likes the good life too much. He has always struck me as being a bit of a loose cannon. Susan you watch little Mouse. Come on up, I'll show you what we've got."
The small back bedroom was sparsely furnished with a rather shabby divan bed and a small chest of drawers. "Will this do?" she said, pulling down the sash window with a bang. "Two pounds a week. No cooking or washing facilities and you'll have to supply your own linen."

"You'll need transport," said when I told her that I had found a room.

"Supposing he comes home whilst I am moving my things?" I asked.

"No problem, the boys on the market owe me a few favours; they'll give us a hand and if he does come home, he won't want to argue with the two I have in mind," she laughed but there was no mirth in her eyes, "they will need paying though, have you got any money?"
I must have looked shocked by the question. "No I suppose you haven't. Well I'll pay them and you will have to owe it to me."

I must have been so naïve in those days, or just a sucker. It really didn't occur to me that she in fact owed me. She had never paid me a penny for making her sitting room curtains or for all the work I had put into cleaning her house over the past few weeks.

"Don't forget to bring all the things you want me to store for you. In fact if you leave those bits on the van, the boys can drop them off here. You know, things like the sheepskin coat and any little treasures you won't need whilst you are on the move. I wouldn't leave anything like that where you will be staying."

"I'll have to take Jeanette's cot to Mrs Fahie's and our clothes and bed-linen. I have packed up a box with my Grandfather's silver service spoons and forks and my books that I won as prizes at school. There is also my grandmother's ebony hand mirror and her coral beads. My statue of Jesus is also in the box. You will look after them for me won't you? I haven't many treasures and I would hate to lose them."

With her assurance that all would be safe and I could pick them up once I was more settled, I decided to trust her.

"Right now that's all settled, we will plan it for Monday; that's the only day when they are not working the markets."

"What, this coming Monday?" I asked, as my insides knotted up.

"Of course; if you don't do it now, you'll never have the guts to do it at all."

I felt as though I wouldn't have any guts left by then, I felt sick with the fear of what was to come.

How I got through the following weekend, remains a mystery. I think I was like the proverbial rabbit caught in the headlights; numb with fear. I must have blanked certain episodes of that horrible time, out of my memory. It's strange how certain memories are crystal clear, as though it were only yesterday, but try as I might the only parts of that day I can still recall are seeing the two men, looking more like all in wrestlers, carrying my few possessions out to the van and then one of them taking out a light bulb and wrapping tin foil round the end before putting it back into the socket.

"That'll teach the bugger." He said winking at his mate.

Finding the key to the spare room where Leslie thought he had hidden it safely out of sight, at the back of the sideboard drawer, I let myself into his hallowed domain where the Remington Typewriter mocked me from where it proudly sat on his desk. Taking my heavy dressmaking scissors, I rammed the blades down between the keys with such force that I couldn't remove them.

"You should have used those scissors to cut the legs off his trousers girl," one of the men said laughingly as he peered through the open door.

With my heart pounding as though it were trying to escape through my ribcage, I gathered Jeanette up in my arms and not looking back, I ran out to the waiting vehicle.

My poor child must have felt very confused by all that was happening and by the time we found ourselves alone in the alien surroundings of the small dingy room, she was grizzling and asking for her daddy.

As I recall all these painful memories, I cannot believe how I could have acted with such thoughtlessness and stupidity. The only answer I can come up with is that I was in such a frail mental state, I must have convinced myself that anything was going to be better than staying in such an unhappy relationship. I obviously was not thinking about my child's feelings whilst committing such an utterly selfish act, for which I ended up subconsciously punishing myself, in one way or another, for many years to come. Feelings of guilt will remain with me for the rest of my life.

Social services paid the princely sum of two pounds that I immediately handed over to Mrs Fahie; other than that, I had no money and was dependent upon for our food, which was in payment for the large amount of housework she was now expecting me to do. I cannot recall how long it was that we stayed at 'Woodstock', I don't think it was a full week.

I found it increasingly painful witnessing my child's continuing displays of confused emotions. She was missing her father and familiar surroundings. I felt totally inadequate, knowing that I was never going to be able to offer her a settled life. I never possessed much self-confidence and what little self respect I might once have had, was now gone.

My father was about to get into his car as I called in to see him on my way to Molly's one morning. "Glad you've called in," he frowned at me, "you alright, you look terrible?" He went on to quickly tell me of the vacancy where he works at the Red Lion Hotel in Colchester. "The chambermaid is leaving and they need someone right away. It will mean living in" he said looking down at his rather fractious granddaughter, wriggling to get out of her pushchair.

With no money, no support from anyone and nobody to help me, I despaired.

At my wits end, I pushed Jeanette round to my mother in-law's house. She looked shocked when I said "You will have to look after her now, I don't know what else to do."

I quickly turned and walked away, Oh God I just walked away as my little girl called out "Mummy".

THE RED LION HOTEL

The Red Lion Hotel, owned by Trust House Hotels, stands proudly in the centre of Colchester High Street.

A pang of extreme nervousness hit my stomach as I walked through the ancient, gated archway into the covered court yard which once echoed to the sounds of horse drawn carriages. Passing what I thought must be the windows of the kitchen and hearing the voices of the chefs and the clatter of pots and pans, I wondered if Fred was in there slaving over a hot stove; I wanted to run to him for support.

The receptionist looked and sounded very efficient as she courteously answered the phone with a polished accent that immediately changed as she put the phone down.

"How can I help you?" there was that accent again, for my benefit this time. An attractive, well dressed blonde, looked me up and down as I stood at the window of the reception desk. Feeling very underdressed and shabby, I swallowed hard and almost in a whisper, asked to see Mr Lamb, the manager.

"Sorry?" she said, peering at me and reducing me to a quivering mess of insecurity. Clearing my throat, I repeated the request. "I'm here to see Mr Lamb."

"Have you an appointment? What name shall I say?"

"Mrs er Miss um Rita Oppezzo." I gibbered.

"Ah yes. Your father, Fred Oppezzo works in the kitchen doesn't he," she said with a supercilious smirk, "he said to expect you today. Are you after the chambermaid's job?"

I must have looked like a frightened rabbit, I certainly felt like one as I nodded my head.

"Take a seat in the tea lounge," she said, pointing a well-manicured finger over my shoulder, "I will let the manager know you are here."

I hardly had time to sit down, when a tall, good looking middle-age gentleman dressed in a morning suit, appeared in the doorway. His dark hair, greying at the temples, swept back revealing a high forehead; beneath which shone his sparkling blue eyes.

"I can see that you must be Fred's daughter, you are very like him," he said in a broad Scottish accent as he ushered me into a small, windowless side room, where a highly polished desk stood, littered with papers. "Do sit down," he said pointing to one of the two leather seated chairs as he seated himself in the one behind the desk, "you look as though you need a cup of tea, I know I do; hectic day. Hope you have come to help?"

The interview went well. I got the Job and following the hall porter as he carried my small case up the rather grand staircase, to what was to be my room; I began to feel a little easier in my mind.

"Hello. I'm Jim assistant manager." A plump, jolly face, framed with a mop of blond curly hair, appeared from the room two doors down from where the porter had deposited my case. Wearing a smart morning suit with white shirt and red tie; smiling broadly he proffered a hand as he stepped out onto the landing. "You'll be the new Chambermaid we're in need of," he said, vigorously shaking my hand. Before I could answer, an attractive young woman came out of the same room and without a word, dashed down the stairs whilst struggling to put her long auburn hair up into a ponytail.

"That's Jane, you'll be taking over from her tomorrow; she'll be leaving tomorrow," his lilting, Irish accent rang cordially on my ears, making me feel even less tense.

I had the rest of that day to myself. I needed time to settle in. The windowless room was small, yet comfortable. A badly ring marked bedside table stood beside the already made up single divan bed; a battered chest of drawers and small wardrobe almost completed what was to be my home for the next few weeks. Looking into the mirror above the small wash basin as I washed my hands, I was shocked to see how worn out I looked and having very few possessions to unpack, I decided to have a rest for an hour; turning out the light I groped my way to the bed. Four hours later I awoke with a start and for a few seconds, wondered where I was. Light seeped in under the badly fitting door and as I reached out for the light switch that hung on a rather threadbare cable over the head of the bed, there was a tap on the door followed by the voice of whom, I was to learn later, was the head hall porter, "Supper down in the staff room at six thirty."

Walking into the vast kitchen, I was glad to see the familiar face of my father as he smiled at me from under his tall, white, chef's hat, "You settled in alright? I told you you'd get the job." The tapping of steel on board as he skilfully chopped herbs, that and the aroma, brought back memories, tugging at my heart strings

I was momentarily taken back to the kitchen of number nineteen, Windsor Road. Dad was chopping herbs from the garden, in readiness for our evening meal. I was once again an innocent young girl of thirteen, standing by her dad, wanting to learn to cook like him.

"Can't talk now love, bit of a busy time coming up," he said handing me a plate of ham salad. "Hope you get on alright, I've told Antonia to look after you."

"One sirloin rare and one Lamb to go chef," a waiter called, grabbing my dad's attention; my dad, the professional; a side of him which I had never witnessed.

"You're new here aren't you?" one of the two women said as I joined them in the staff dining-room, "I'm Jean," she said patting the chair beside her, "this is Wendy," Wendy nodded and smiled as she blew a plume of smoke through well made up lips. "What do we call *you* then?" the question came when I realised that I hadn't introduced myself.

"Sorry. Um yes, it's Rita." I said feeling quite timid. It all felt alien to me, sitting in strange surroundings, talking to complete strangers. I found it hard to swallow as I picked at my food. Jean seemed to sense my uneasiness as she continued to talk about the bars that they both worked in.

"The Doubles bar is where I work and Wendy works in the Back bar. The squaddies like her cos she's young and pretty, I suit the old codgers that come into my bar for their double tots and being an oldie myself, I find the slower pace suits me better. Then there is May who usually works the Lion bar and we all take it in turns to help out in the cocktail bar up in the ballroom, when there's a function. Can you work the bar? You might find yourself being roped in." She said winking at Wendy.

Oh God. I thought, trying to put on a brave face; let me first get used to *being* here

Back in the solitude of my room, having cleaned my teeth and having had a wash, and, I put on my nightdress and climbed into bed. Leaving the light on for a while, I lay listening to the creak of the stairs as guests made their way to their rooms on the next floor; in a strange way, I found the sounds comforting.

My room, as I was to discover later, was over the entrance to the ballroom. Next-door was a small box room with a hatch that looked out over the vast expanse of dance floor; it may once have even been used as a projection room, but was now used for storage of bags of dirty linen awaiting collection. The room next to that was from where Mr Mac and the girl Janice had emerged earlier. At the end of the landing was the door to the linen room where I was to report at six thirty the following morning.

Sleep did not come easily. Images and voices flashed through my restless mind; the look of shock on poor dear Izzy's face as I turned to walk away; the haunting sound of my child calling for her mummy; Molly Western's wide mouthed grimace when I told her of my intention to work at the Red Lion; 'You won't last ten minutes in that trade, you haven't got the guts for it,' she said with her usual sarcasm; my mother's look of total disapproval as my stepfather slammed the door in my face; Leslie's darkly, penetrating eyes accusingly staring into mine. It was like watching soundless film clips; the only sound I heard in my head, was "Mummy"; a disconnected sound echoing out of the past; which continued reaching out with its tortuous grip round my heart for many years to come. The same sound I also made, all those years ago, when on returning home from school I found the note left by my mother, saying that she had gone for good this time.

I eventually cried myself into a fitful sleep.

The next thing I knew was the sound of the night porters voice as he knocked on my door "Wake up call Miss" and then the creak of the stairs as he made his way up to the next floor. The light was still on and looking at my watch, I saw that it was just before six. Twenty-five minutes later I stood by the linen room door, awaiting the arrival of the linen keeper; she was late and as I was soon to learn, she was always late.

"The bloody car wouldn't start," she said as she bustled past me "oh where's the keys," she uttered tensely, delving into her pockets and bulging handbag. "I never put them in the same place" she said, retrieving a large bunch of keys and a tissue with which she mopped her brow and dabbed at her nose. "Sorry! Hello, you'll be the new maid, I'm Janet Davies, linen keeper and general dogs body," she breathlessly said, running her fingers through her dark, bobbed hair. She was a short, chubby woman in her mid twenties. "Here's your uniform, you might have to alter it; they always come in too long. You *can* sew can't you?" Her eyes looked small as she closely scrutinised me through the thick lenses of her glasses.

"As soon as you have changed, hurry down to the 'still room' in the main kitchen; I've told Antonia, our other chambermaid, to meet you there. You will be working with her today; she'll show you how we like things done, hope you are a fast learner." Her attention was quickly drawn away by a bony faced unkempt youth sleepily stumbling into the small linen room; his tousled hair showing evidence of his lateness. "Late again Jem, here's your jacket and waiter's cloths, drop these chefs whites into the kitchen, there's a dear. Returning her bustling attention hastily back to me she said, ushering me out of the door "You'll have to tie your hair back. Oh and by the way, don't mind Nell, her bark is worse than her bite."

Who's Nell? I thought as I speedily changed into my almost floor length navy blue uniform.

The 'still room' where huge urns hissed and gurgled, was an area just inside the entrance to the main kitchen. Breakfast trays had been laid up in readiness and toast catapulted from a large electric toaster. Behind the servery stood an ugly, stout woman with straggly wisps of grey hair poking out from beneath a gingham mobcap.

"Got yer list of orders?" she demanded, holding out a buttery hand.

"Er no... er, what list?" No one had mentioned a list.

"Is ok, she wif me today," a rescuing voice came over my shoulder, "You wif me yes? You new maid yes?" Before I could answer, Antonia handed the grimacing Nell a list which, as I was to learn later, was obtained from reception every morning. She then grabbed two breakfast trays and handing one to me, she dashed out across the yard and in through the main entrance. Gingerly carrying the tray with both hands, I followed Antonia as she went at breakneck speed up the main staircase to the first floor. "This for Meester Mac." She said pointing towards the room that he had appeared from the previous day. "e sleep wif Jane." She clicked her tongue disapprovingly as we headed towards the next floor. "Just knock and leave tray. No hang about, we got lot of rooms today."

"Enter," a gruff, male voice called in answer to Antonia's knock.

"Good morning meester Jackson, here your tea and new maid and clean shoes," she said, nodding me into the dimly lit room as she picked up the pair of highly polished shoes from outside his door. I was rather taken aback by the spectacle of a tall semi-clad, elderly gentleman, stooping to look in the shaving mirror over the washbasin as he brushed his hair. A blue striped shirt came half way down his thighs and his bony knees stuck out above the suspenders holding up long black socks. I had never seen sock suspenders before.

"Mornin m-dears," he said looking at us through the mirror, "You're to be m-new maid are ye? Well don't look so scared, I won't bite y-know." He gave a throaty chuckle as we left.

"E nice man. If e like you, e leave good tip."

Antonia worked at one speed – fast. Not all the guests had tea served in their room, most went straight down to the dining room for breakfast.

"We done," she said as we delivered the final tray, "now we have break."

The staff dining room was off one end of the main kitchen and the guest dining room, with a view of the High Street was at the other end. As we entered the kitchen, a combination of mouth-watering aromas made me realise how hungry I was. Standing at the stillroom servery, I caught a whiff of freshly made coffee emanating from the large silver pot that Nell handed to the waiter, Jem. Her harsh voice interrupted my reverie as she handed me a huge, steaming teapot. "Ere you'd better take this in wiv yer, those greedy lot of buggers av probably finished the other pot." I would have given anything for a cup of that lovely coffee. Dad always made good coffee from freshly ground beans; however, strong, over-stewed tea it would have to be today.

Standing at the multi-gas ringed hob, feeding rashers of bacon into a huge frying pan, dad looked up and grinned at me as the bacon started to sizzle, " Alright?" he asked. I wanted to go and stand by him like I used to as a little girl, when he always handed me a crispy morsel, which I had to pass from hand to hand, blowing on my scorching fingers, whilst he prepared our evening meal.

The loud babble of conversation momentarily ceased as Antonia pushed me into the crowded staff room; feeling embarrassed as questioning eyes stared in my direction, I felt the urge to turn and run. An extraordinarily handsome face smiled at us, revealing a mouthful of even, white teeth as Antonia nudged me towards where her husband Carlo was sitting. The teapot was rapidly removed from my grip as we sat down to join the 'breakfast bash' which by now had resumed its noisy cacophony of mixed conversations and laughter.

A large plate of gone-cold toast stood in the middle of the table beside which, was a dish with several knives jutting greasily out of a mess of oily butter; a tablespoon stood stickily in the catering sized, lidless tin of Silver Shred marmalade and to complete the scene, two overflowing ashtrays spilled their contents onto the badly stained surface of the ancient wooden table.

"We got to be quick, got lot of work esta mañana. You no eat?" she said, blowing a column of smoke into the already smoke filled air. "You smoke?" she asked, pushing her 'Gold Leaf' cigarettes and box of Swan Vestas towards me; shaking my head I took a gulp of the bitter tasting, almost cold tea; I pulled a face."Que?, you no like tea? Is bloody orible; me, I like coffee, but mean bastardos no let us have. In España, coffee muy bien, no ere. I buy beans from shop in Head Street; prefer grind our own, mi esposo, Carlo," she said as she lovingly gazed at her husband, "he like very much my coffee sí?" He grinned his whiteness at her with a look of love in his huge brown eyes. "My Carlo he un camarero in restaurante, pero he no like."

As he shook his head, I began to wonder if he were mute.

"I go, goodnight," he said, pushing back his chair.

"Morning Carlo, no night, e no speak the English so good." He grinned at me and nodded; his black wavy hair flopping over one eye as he stood up; it surprised me to see how short he was, not much taller than my meagre five feet.

Antonia's features softened as she spoke of her new husband. "We marry two month ago and then come ere, no work in España," with that, she whisked me out through the steamy kitchen.

"Good luck love." dad called out as he dished up some poached eggs. Without the presence of my stepmother, my father seemed more like the man I used to know.

I *had* managed to grab a slice of toast during the break, but eyed the eggs, sitting on buttery rounds of hot toast, with mouth-watering envy. Dad always gave me poached eggs on thickly buttered toast, when I was unwell; that and toast fingers dipped in a drink made by crumbling an 'Oxo' cube into hot water.

"We strip beds now," Antonia called over her shoulder, mounting the stairs two at a time; an assortment of keys gangling from the chain pinned to her belt.

One sharp knock at the door before she strode in, proved the room to have been recently vacated. Each room had its own particular odour, some quite pleasant, some not so pleasant. Throwing the widows open and gasping in the fresh air - well as fresh as town air could be – she started to strip the crumpled bed linen ."You watch good, only one day you learn, you learn quick, yes? meester Jackson, e very restless sleeper, e go home, come back la proxima semana, how you say week soon."
Stuffing the dirty linen into one of the canvas bags as we went on to the next room, I was amazed at the speed at which she worked and wondered if I would be able to do likewise when left to my own devices. It wasn't long before we were hurling the full bags over the banister, to the landing below, narrowly missing Mr Mac as he emerged from Janice's room.

"B'Jasus Toni, you nearly got me that time," he laughed, shining an impish smile up at her, as she leaned over the banister with another bag poised at the ready. "You'll be needing to take better aim with that one," he called back, sauntering down the main stairs.

"E good man meester Mac, I like im."

The heavy piles of clean linen which we had collected from the linen room, were soon distributed round the rooms and as we made up the beds together, Antonia showed her expertise at making neatly folded corners at the foot of each bed. "You make good beds, yes?" she said showing me the difference between the front side of the sheet, being smooth and the back being rough. "Bottom sheet, she smooth face up and top sheet, she smooth face down; is good, yes?"

I had never considered the front and back of a sheet, nor a top and bottom; to me a sheet was a sheet, so long as it was clean – but now I know!

Opening the bedside cupboard she pulled out a white chamber pot and quickly covering it with a used hand towel, she handed it to me. "You empty pissy pot, yes?" she giggled as she saw the shocked look on my face. "You no empty pissy pot before?" I shook my head "Is no bueno when the shit she is in pot."

It then occurred to me that I had lied about never having emptied 'pissy pot'.

The privies were quite a distance round the back of 'Waterside' and during the dark winter nights, it was more convenient to use the lidded bucket that we kept in the back bedroom. Being pregnant, my need to 'spend a penny' in the middle of the night, was becoming more frequent. Leslie, on the other hand, also found a greater need due to the quantity of alcohol he consumed each evening. Every morning, I found myself, slipping and sliding on the ice covered snow, hoping I wouldn't spill the offensive contents of my bucket before reaching my destination and then the return journey to the cottage so as to refill the bucket used to flush the toilet. The standpipe tap remained frozen from December to March during the 1963/64 period of severe weather. Hilda allowed Nellie to take water from her tap in the kitchen.

By one thirty, with the washbasins and taps clean and sparkling, soaps replenished; tooth glasses washed and polished; freshly laundered towels neatly hanging from the rails and 'pissy pots' emptied, washed and dried and replaced in the cupboards; only the vacuuming and dusting was left to complete the servicing of the rooms after a well deserved lunch break.

There were a few new faces at the crowded table and the smoke filled staff room was abuzz with chatter and laughter as we walked in.

"Carlo, e no eat till e finish in the restaurant." Antonia said as she made a young pot-man move along so that we could sit together.

"Bloody Spanish," he muttered, "think they own the bloody place."

The look on Antonia's face turned to rage, as she swung round to face him, "cerdo ignorante de ingles" she hissed, spitting on her finger and running it cut-throat fashion, across her throat. She winked at me as we watched the pot-man pick up his plate and make a hasty exit.

"The food it no good, for you and me, but it ok. I like cook for my Carlo and me. You like cook? You same as you papa, e good cook yes? I bet e teach you good."
It was easier just to agree at this point.

The food was edible; mostly rehashed leftovers. I hoped the contents of the constantly simmering kitchen stockpot, that looked more like a witch's cauldron, with its assortment of peelings, bones and bobbing eggshells, hadn't been added to the stew we were now eating. When I asked dad about it later, he told me the eggshells helped to clarify the stock which was used in the process of making Demi-Glace, for the preparation of sauces and soups. "It's all quite sterile," he assured me. I will never forget the smell and sight of that huge, brimming pot, glistening with fat, bloop blooping its unappetising odour at you as you passed.

On our return to work, a chap carrying a huge bouquet of flowers, followed us as we climbed the stairs "Bouquet for Jane; they said at reception that her room was up here."

"We take." Antonia said snatching the flowers from the startled deliveryman. "I bet is from meester Mac, is her eighteen cumpleanos, how you say day of birth? She go tomorrow. Is romantic, no?"

Jane looked very much the worse for wear, with her lovely long hair all dishevelled and mascara smudged around her sleep filled eyes. The stale odour of alcohol and cigarette smoke wafted out as she threw open the door, wearing only a see-through, baby-doll nightdress.
Antonia clicked her tongue as the flowers were grabbed from her hand and the door slammed shut in her face "She no good that one," she hissed in a whisper, " she sleep with im and then go casarse boyfriend, poor Meester Mac, e no deserve."

My first day went very smoothly. Antonia told me not to worry if things didn't go right the next day, "I do lot of clangings when I first here," her pretty blue/grey eyes twinkled as she smiled at me.

"Clangers," I said correcting her "you dropped lots of clangers."

"Si, that too, you teach me the English and I elp you learn empty pissy-pots."

We both laughed and I knew that I had made a new friend.

I slept like a log that night; not having been used to such intensively hard work and not sleeping too well the previous night; I was exhausted. It would have been nice to have had the facilities to make a hot drink to take to bed, but being already in my nightdress, I decided against returning to the main kitchen. I also decided to treat myself to some equipment for my room, as soon as I had earned my first wage. It did occurred to me to ask dad if he had a spare kettle, then I thought of Lil's disapproval at giving me anything she didn't want me to have and decided to buy my own, together with a cup and saucer and even a tin of biscuits. I had the need for comfort. I wanted to make my room a haven; my own space.

However, before I had a chance to make my mark and become accustomed to the confines of my windowless room; I was moved to a larger room over the back bar, which, along with several other staff rooms, was reached by a narrow iron staircase. Although I was glad to now have a room with a window that I could open, the noise from the bar, especially at closing time, could be quite disquieting, whilst endeavouring to have an early night. Soldiers, stationed at Colchester Garrison, as it was then known, mainly frequented the 'back bar' where they met up with the kind of women who were just out for a good time and free drinks. The local constabulary were often summoned to break up drunken brawls; the nastiest usually occurring between two jealous females, which almost always involved the worst violence accompanied by foul language.

Having lived a fairly sheltered existence, I knew nothing about town night-life. I was fascinated by the comical goings on, which I was able to watch from the safety of my room.

"There will be a large party of local government officials in the restaurant tonight chef; I think they'll all be after having the fillet steak, so make sure you'll have enough." Mr Mac gave me a cheeky grin followed by a little bow as he hurried out of the kitchen.

"You don't want to have any dealings with him," dad said when he saw the smile on my face; "they reckon he's queer."

"Who says *that*?" I fired back "he has been having a fling with that chambermaid, Janice, so how *can* he be?"

"I only know what folk are saying. Just don't get involved that's all."

However, get involved, I did!

J.O.M.

It wasn't long after moving into my new room; I had just finished supper and was making my way to the back stairs when Mr Mac walked in through the back gate. "Hello Miss Muffet, not going to bed *so* early are you? I'm going over 'The George' for a quick half, want to join me?" It was obvious he had already been drinking.

Still dressed in a morning suit of pinstriped trousers and black jacket, stood the rather overweight and slightly balding J.O.M; known by most as Mac. I was beguiled by the lilt of his strong Southern Irish accent, his impish grin and the cheeky twinkle in his bright blue eyes that were made even more alluring by enviably long lashes.

This was my first adult encounter of a 'chat up line' and seeing my wide-eyed look of amazement and before I had a chance to refuse, he was down on one knee imploring me to join him. He made me laugh, how could I refuse? I was so bloody gullible, but after the tormented past six years, this felt as though it was going to be an exciting new experience.

Against my father's advice, the involvement began.

Sitting on one of the high bar stools in the swish cocktail bar of the George Hotel, I was fascinated by the ambidextrous skill of the attractive, middle-aged barmaid as she served two customers at once, shaking a cocktail shaker in one hand whilst pumping a glass up to one of the various optics with the other. Dorrie, as she was known by her mainly male regular customers, was smartly dressed in a plain yet stylish black dress, adorned at the neck with a double row necklace of pearls along with matching earrings. I will always remember her expertly coiffured, silver-grey hair swept up from the nape of her neck into a fashionable bouffant. Expensive looking rings glinted as her well manicured nails, with polish matching her well applied lipstick, completed the picture. As she turned to face us, she gave me the impression that she felt a cut above those whom she was about to serve. I envied her elegant self-confidence.

It all felt so very different to the 'Hall Barn days' when I was made to feel so inferior. I now felt quite grown up as Mr Mac asked me what I would like to drink.

"Whiskey and ginger ale please" in my mind's eye I had a flashback of Leslies's voice saying "damned good whisky that" as I hastily added "Bells Please." 'Oh God,' I thought 'I hope I can drink it.'

It was as though Dorrie read my mind as she almost filled a tall glass with ice before adding the whisky " I'll let you add your own ginger ale, no doubt you know how you like it. Pint of the usual Mac?" she said as she pulled the first half pint of frothing ale in one downward sweep of the slender porcelain and brass beer pump, swiftly followed by the other half and without spilling a drop, stood the brimming glass in front of a beaming Mr Mac. "Slainte" he said peering at me over the rim of his glass as half its contents seemed to go straight down in one gulp.

"Cheers!" I said as I took a tentative sip of what turned out to be quite a pleasant drink. Was I finally growing up? I felt a surge of excitement as I soaked up the convivial atmosphere made even more pleasing as the second whisky slipped easily down and I got a knowing wink from Mr Mac.

"Come on, get that down you, I'm hungry." He said, downing his second pint.

Crossing the High Street we made our way through the Red Lion courtyard and out through the back gates into the dimly lit Culver Street, where his Red MG sports car stood in the small parking area next door to Humphrey's the greengrocers opposite.

"Where are we going?" I asked, feeling a little apprehensive.

"To get some supper, do you like fried egg sandwiches?"

Walking into the Marks Tey transport café, I felt a bit conspicuous as I was eyed by the rather rough looking lorry drivers occupying the tables.

"Hey Mac! Come and join us mate." A rather rotund jolly-faced man beckoned us over "Ello darlin," he said, eyeing me from head to toe, "don't be shy," patting the seat beside him. "See yer got a new lady friend," he laughingly said, winking at Mr Mac.

The fried egg sandwiches, oozing with tomato ketchup were delicious and the steaming mugs of strong sweet tea went down well. We chatted and laughed into the early hours. This was to be a regular venue for our late night jaunts. On the return journey, Jamie – as I now called him - had sobered up a bit and ended up in my bed.

Having finished a late shift, he would regularly knock on my door – I was usually asleep – and ask me to join him for supper. Having quickly dressed and let the night porter know that we would be late back; I would find him waiting behind the wheel of his car puffing on a cigarette. It was all so exciting – like nothing I had ever experienced before. He was always a little the worse for drink, but somehow it didn't seem to matter; I was having fun.

It was a strange courtship with both of us working different shifts; I worked from seven in the morning and finished around three in the afternoon, with two half hour breaks for breakfast and lunch whereas, Jamie worked two shifts, from ten in the morning until two in the afternoon and then from six until ten in the evening, depending on whether there was a function, which usually went on until after midnight. Some afternoons we visited 'Thorogoods' or 'Lasts' where we enjoyed jam doughnuts and coffee, then back to his room for sex and a nap. The sex was entirely different from what I had become accustomed to. He never showed the lustful urgency and dogged determination that I had learnt to accept as the norm in my past experience married to Leslie Lester; in fact, in this instance the effort was mainly down to me. He was usually too drunk or too tired to show much enthusiasm, whereas I craved love and attention and I suppose I just accepted what this happy go lucky, new man in my life had to offer. On Jamie's part, the relationship was very superficial. Looking back, I realise it was my neediness that kept it going – I needed him – there was no one else. My mother hadn't been in contact with me since the Leslie Lester episode when I was told never to darken their door again.

Dad was now married to Lil and my Brother Dick was wrapped up in his own family life with his wife Barbara and Bobby and Michelle his two children. I had chosen to take this new path of relative freedom and to quote Dad 'You have made your bed, now lie on it'.

I was good at my job and it wasn't long before I took over the linen keeper's job, who, due to ill health, had found it necessary to leave. I enjoyed keeping the linen in good repair and reorganising the linen room. I dealt with all the dirty linen from the guest rooms, kitchen and the restaurant as well as dealing with the personal laundry of the managerial staff.

It wasn't long before Dad, having been offered a better job, moved across the High street to The George Hotel where he made a great success of taking sole charge of the hotel's 'Buttery Bar' down in the basement. The then Manager Charles Macoy, remembered the Young Fred (Federico Oppezzo) from the days when they both worked at Frascati's Restaurant in London's West End, as waiters just before the war.

At Dad's request Lil was also offered a weekend job as his waitress. Unfortunately, the bar also provided alcoholic beverages to which dad was rather partial. Lil experienced many frightening journeys with a rather intoxicated Fred behind the wheel as they made their way back to West Mersea, usually after midnight. She often spoke of having to leave him in the car overnight, as he was too drunk to get out of it. He must have been most uncomfortable wedged in the cramped driving seat of the 'Fiat 500'.

Using the opportunity to visit Dad without the hostile presence of my stepmother, I often joined him in the Buttery

Bar for a drink. Having now become accustomed to drinking spirits, I was pleased to accept Dad's invitation to join him for "*A small tot*" (or two or three!) compliments of The George! I often found myself walking back over the road the worse for wear and very much alone. Jamie was usually working on an evening function and would almost certainly have ended up in the same condition – I don't know if he was always alone.

I hated the awful hangovers and repeatedly said 'never again', however, strong drink temporarily blots out unhappy memories.

It was around midday when one of the receptionists came up to the linen room and advised me that there was a lady asking to speak to me on the phone.

"A Mrs Prior; I think she said she was your mother. You know we are not supposed to receive calls for staff" she called over her shoulder as she dashed back down the stairs.

My heart took a leap as her words suddenly sunk in. My mother phoning me! Why? How did she know where I was? Questions raced through my mind as I made my way down to the reception desk.

"I have transferred your call to the side office" the head receptionist said; her usually baleful manner softened as she saw the look of concern on my face. "It will be more private in there."

"Hello." The soft leather seat of the chair behind the desk caught me as my legs weakened.

"Hello love," it was her; it was the familiar dulcet tones of my mother's voice, "how are you?" she inquired as though it had only been a few days since we last spoke.

I began to cry silently. "I'm fine thanks, how are you?" I gulped back the tears.

"Oh I'm OK love. What is your job there? Can we meet?" she said, hardly taking a breath, let alone allowing me the time to answer. "We are not far away, only in Witham you know. Daddy's job changed, he's now sales manager. We had to move from Rayleigh, you remember our nice bungalow in Rayleigh don't you." Oh yes, I remember the door of that '*nice bungalow'* in Rayleigh being slammed behind me, after *'daddy',* as she chose to call him, telling me never to darken their door again.

"How did you know where to find me?" I asked feebly, ignoring her questions.

"Oh it was easy, I just rang Leslie's Mother and she told me."

And did she also tell you how I left my little girl with her and just walked away because I had nowhere else to go and no one else to turn to; I wanted to shout down the phone at her; but I was too stupefied with the pure joy of hearing my mother's voice and too full of the need to run to her and bury my face in the bosom, which as a baby, I must have once nuzzled. I couldn't remember the last time I had experienced that kind of affection from either parent.

"Are you still there Darling?"

"Yes." I replied as I quickly gathered my jumbled thoughts, endeavouring to make a sensible reply. "No I haven't"

"Haven't what Darling"

"Got a car yet; although Jamie does let me drive his sports car sometimes so I am learning" I said with the eager voice of a child trying to please its mother. "I could get a train from North Station," I quickly added before she had a chance to interrupt.

"And who, may I ask is Jamie? Oh don't worry, you can tell me all when we meet."

Dressed in the only smart items of clothing I possessed; a metallic green, mock leather overcoat and matching stiletto shoes – purchased from 'Mansfield's Shoes' in the High Street – I thought I looked 'the bees knees'. As the train pulled out of the station, I was shaking with anticipation and excitement. 'You're going to see your mother, you're going to see your mother, you're going to see your mother' the train seemed to sing as it passed over the joints in the track.

What will I say to her? What will my stepfather say when we meet? Will she have changed? Will she see the change in me from the dowdy, downtrodden little nobody to a self-supporting, confident, working-girl? The signs announcing 'Witham' glided by as the train slowly pulled into the station. I tugged at my coat, feeling a little conscious of the shortness of its length. Checking for any stray wisps of hair that may have escaped the tight bun at the back of my head, I stood at the carriage door as the train came to a juddering stop. Stepping onto the platform, my eyes darted from person to person as I eagerly searched for the familiar face and then all other faces faded when all I could see was my mother as she hurried towards me; that vision then became blurred as the tears filled my eyes. "Hello Love," there was that much used, yet false term of endearment. My legs went to jelly and my stomach lurched as my arms reached out to embrace her. For what seemed like an age, I couldn't find my voice; I just clung to her, breathing in the familiar scent of 'Coty's Laimont' – her favourite perfume after the demise of Bourgois 'Evening in Paris' in 1969. I think had she known of its re-launch in 1992, she would have continued to use it. My mother was a creature of habit and found it hard to change.

"We can walk to The Avenue, it's not very far" she broke into my revelry. "I've made us some nice soup for lunch, would you like that? That's where my Johnny's office is" she said pointing to a drab looking building. "He won't be home to lunch today as he's got a meeting with his boss."

I began to wish that I hadn't worn my new stilettos as my mother hurried me along. She always had been a fast walker, even whilst shopping. She was still a very fit lady and certainly didn't look like a woman in her late forties.

"Here we are, come on in," she said, unlocking the front door of a very smart, semi-detached house. The unmistakeable aroma of lamb-bone soup greeted me as I stepped into the chequered tiled hallway. In the past, she always made soup using leftover lamb bones, in fact it was the only soup she ever made and it was usually swimming with fat. Having not had any breakfast, I was hungry and the thickly sliced, crispy new bread took the edge off the fat

"See you still enjoy your food, have some more love." Could this be the same woman who all that time ago, had stood beside my stepfather as he told Leslie to dump me in the river on our way home and that I was nothing but a little tramp."

We remained at the table and the mostly one-sided discussion began.

"You know dear Aunty Jess passed away. She had been very unwell for quite some time. It was very hard on us both; we were up two or three times a night in the end; well she was a great age, nearly ninety you know.

"How long ago did she die?" I was quite upset by this news. Aunty had always been there; it seemed strange to think that she had died and I hadn't known about it.

"Oh it must be nearly two years ago and that brings me to my other sad loss." At this her voice changed to a nervous quaver and tears welled up in her eyes. "I lost my Mark David six months ago," she said as she broke down and sobbed. "Your little brother" she whispered as she saw the confusion on my face.

Still frowning, I gently asked, "You mean you had a baby?"
She stood up and walked to the window, "Yes. We couldn't do anything until poor Aunty was gone. We had wanted to try for a child for a long time." She now had full control of her emotions as she made a pot of tea and sat back down at the table, "The cup that cheers, as dear Aunty used to say. Do you take sugar?" She asked handing me a pretty, china sugar basin.
"He only lived four months," she said as though reading what was going to be my next question. "My lovely gynaecologist Mr Marsh, David as we called him, said that I carried like a young woman and it wasn't my age, it was a one in so many thousand chances and could have happened to a woman of any age." Her voice broke again as she continued, "He was so beautiful, my Mark David."

"What went wrong?" My question seemed to be rather inadequately worded.

"There were multiple complications, which all seemed to be in the centre of his little body. He needed help with his breathing, his swallow was affected along with his digestion, he had to be fed via a tube; even his little legs were deformed." She was sobbing again and I got up from the table and tentatively placed an uncertain hand on her shoulder. Was this really the same woman who all those years ago had turned me away when I most needed her?

"He looked so like the photo of my father, we named him after him; although he did have his daddy's nose.

Poor thing I thought, as I pictured the image of my stepfather's huge nose.

During all that time she never once asked about the birth of my little girl, her granddaughter.

We went on to speak about my job and how I met Jamie. She told me how they had sold 'Redroofs' the bungalow in Rayleigh and all about 'Johnny's wonderful new job'. It was mainly her doing all the talking followed by my monosyllabic answers.

"What time is your train? You will stay and have some supper with us? I know Johnny would like to see you. Oh did I tell you my other bit of sad news? We had to have poor Peppi put to sleep, he did get very aggressive in his old age and used to hide under the bed and then bite me when I tried to get him out."

Peppi being the third black poodle they had owned over the years and was about five years old when I stayed with them, prior to getting married. It disliked me, the feelings were mutual.

"*Ah*! that sounds like my Johnny," she said as she excitedly ran to the door.

My heart pounded with the dread of meeting this man who for years, had shown me nothing but unkindness.

"Hello young Rita, nice to see you." His clammy grip wrapped itself around my shaking hand. There was no sign of the erstwhile malevolence from the time when I last sat in his presence.

"You are looking well. How is the job? What time do you need to get your train? You must stay for supper. I know your mum would like that wouldn't you Gwenny."

As he rattled on without waiting for a reply, I became lost as the tirade of questions seemed to suffocatingly engulf me, until I found myself asking where the toilet was; I needed breathing space; I wanted to leave.

"I must catch the next train back to Colchester as I am expected back at work by seven thirty," was my feeble excuse to escape.

I didn't hear from them again until I rang mum to tell her that I was moving to The Bull Hotel, Long Melford.

"Oh that's nice dear. I will be able to drive over to see you. My Johnny has bought me a lovely 'Isetta' and I have now passed my test, I only have a G license, I am not supposed to drive a car with a reverse gear and had to have the reverse blanked out, but I love it and it is so light, I can push it back if I need to. Have you passed your test? I don't suppose you have or you would have driven over here when you came to visit. Oh well give me a ring when you next get time off. Bye"

It was as though she didn't want to take a breath in case I tried to tell her about what was happening in my life.

Late Autumn 1966 when Jamie, having left the employment of Trust House Hotels, had taken a job at South Mimms as Assistant Manager at one of the first Esso Motor Hotels to be opened in Great Britain. I was rather disappointed when he told me that there were no vacancies offering living in accommodation other than that offered to the management team.

Having decided to remain with Trust House Hotels and take up the offer of management training, I accepted the job of running the bar at The Bull Hotel, Long Melford where I learnt bar and cellar management along with wine waitressing. I hardly saw anything of Jamie apart from his infrequent visits to The Bull. There wasn't time to miss him as I became engrossed in what turned out to be the most enjoyable six months of my training. At first I was very nervous as I had no experience of bar work.

I worked alongside the young barman Paul for the week before he was due to leave. With him having been very popular with both staff and customers, I felt that he would prove to be a hard act to follow.

"Hev you hed any esperiance at pullen a pint gell?" my first customer asked with a frown as I pulled the first half of a mild and bitter. "You shoulda put the bitter in first, as the way I likes it anyways." Noel was a giant of a man who came in for his first pint of the day just after opening time. It was his breakfast break and the kitchen sent up a plate of bread and cooked sausages at the same time each weekday morning. The same routine was repeated at midday, with the sausages being replaced by cheese and pickle. Opening time on Sundays was midday when Noel would arrive in his 'church going suit; brogues, cleaned and polished; his thick head of hair plastered down with brilliantine and a brightly coloured handkerchief sticking out of his breast pocket. I soon learned that since leaving school, he worked as assistant to his father who was head gardener on the estate of one of the local gentry. Noel, now in his fifties, inherited the job when his father was forced to retire, due to ill health, at the ripe old age of eighty. "Et wor the ol rhoomatics that got im in the end; looks like I'm a gitten the same," he told me holding up his huge, gnarled hands. "I hed to look arter im in the end, poor ol boy. When I asked him if he had a family, he told me that the right woman hadn't come along yet.

"But I'm still a hopen!" he said with a twinkle in his eyes.

After that informative conversation, Noel regularly presented me with dainty posies of flowers. One day he brought in a small bird cupped gently in the cornified palms of his cupped hands. "Poor little ol thing must a fallen out the nest. I'll take et hom along a me, at'll be company fer me." I became quite fond of this gentle giant.

Being proficient at pulling a cork without breaking it would have been a nightmare, had it not been for the expert guidance of Anthony, the head waiter and his gift of a professional wine waiter's corkscrew, which fitted neatly into the waistcoat pocket of my smart black uniform.

With my hair piled in neat curls on top of my head, and well manicured nails painted to match my lipstick, I thought of Dorrie, the barmaid at The George in Colchester, whilst endeavouring to emulate not only her immaculate appearance, but also her dextrous performance with beer pumps, optics and cocktail shaker. Noel taught me the art of gently pouring the temperamental 'Worthington's White Shield', so as not to disturb the sediment, also the skill of pouring a bottled 'Guinness', always aiming the neck of the bottle towards the thumb whilst patiently allowing the creamy head to top the dark rich stout.

The rotund wooden beer barrels, lying on their sides in their wooden supporting blocks, down in the cellar, beneath the floor of the bar, presented no problems after being shown by George, the hall porter cum cellar man, how to insert a tap. Having hammered in the small wooden spire enabling the beer to breathe and settle for twenty four hours; I went on to quickly master the knack of tapping by sitting astride the beer dampened keg with wooden mallet in one hand and brass tap in the other. My aim had to be perfect or I would have ended up with a beer soaked cellar floor and me. I hasten to add that my cellar duties were carried out first thing in the morning, wearing a pair of old jeans and sweater reserved especially for the job; hand-me-downs from Paul, the previous barman.

When the bar got really busy at weekends, George was usually sent in to lend a hand. It didn't take me long in building up my proficiency at managing the bar and wine waitressing duties. I met a lot of interesting local people along with coach loads of mainly American tourists for whom I had to learn how to make various cocktails, such as the whisky based 'Old Fashioned'; 'The Manhattan'; 'The Americano'. I even designed one of my own recipes when I ran out of Bourbon, which included Irish Whisky, crushed ice, Tia Maria and cream. Anthony taught me the art of floating cream onto

Irish and French Coffees. I learnt so much during the few weeks spent at 'The Bull', when the time came for me to move on, I was very sad to leave.

On the morning of my last day, I was surprised as several regulars and members of staff, gathered in the bar where they handed me gifts and 'Good Luck' cards.

"I didn't think you wor gonna match up to Paul when you first started, but *you're* gonna be a hard act to folla gell," Noel said handing me a large bouquet as he shyly kissed me on the cheek. I further embarrassed my gentle giant by giving him a hug.

Whilst on a visit to Jamie, where he was working at the brand new 'Esso Motor Hotel' in South Mimms, I found a Job working as general assistant at a classy public house/restaurant (the name of which escapes me) across the busy motorway from the motel. It meant me leaving Trust House Hotels before finishing my management training, but I was missing Jamie.

I hadn't been working there long and was running the bar when the actor Patrick McGoohan sauntered in and ordered a double Irish whisky and soda. I had been a fan of his since watching the television series 'Danger Man'. It just so happened that it was my birthday and not thinking twice I grabbed the card given to me by my colleagues and asked him to sign it; which he did, 'with love'!

I had been happily working there for approximately three months, when Jamie decided to apply for a job with 'Berni Inns'. Although we weren't married we went under the title of Mr and Mrs as the job required a husband and wife team to take over management of 'The Globe Hotel' Kings Lynn, Norfolk. I was completely out of my depth endeavouring to run this large and rather scruffy hotel which, to my recollection, had five or six different bars, four of which offered catering. The Fish Bar where I learnt to skin a Dover Sole and fillet a Plaice; the Steak Bar where I learnt the meanings of well done, rare and blue steaks; the Chicken Bar for 'chicken and chips' in baskets and the Pacific Bar, which served various cocktails to accompany rather questionable curries and bistro style food. The spit and sawdust Back Bar, frequented by sailors, dock workers and women who were locally known as 'dock rats', was where I had my first and not last experience of breaking up a fight between two of these very rough drunken women. Standing safely behind the bar, I shouted at the brawling pair, "Get out before I call the Police."

"Oh yeah, and who is going to make us?" the large masculine looking one shouted as she leaned menacingly over the bar, thrusting her clenched fist in my direction.

Shakily managing to stand my ground whilst looking straight into her bleary eyes, I called her bluff and hiding my fear, I shouted back 'Me'. She was a bully and from my past experience with my father's bullying temper, bullies don't like face to face confrontation. From then on she became my ally whenever trouble threatened. She awarded me with the title 'The little terrier'.

We stayed at the Globe for three months, during which time I had no choice but to learn P.A.Y.E, having to deal with tax and national insurance deductions from the weekly wages of forty members of staff. Whilst still at school, I was once told by an impatient teacher that I would never be any good at mathematics; a statement that I would believe for most of my growing up years. Yet here was I, dealing with the accounts system of a large commercial establishment. I think it was the extraordinary amount of paperwork involved in the running of a 'Bernie Inn', where every item of food and general supplies had to be accurately accounted for; even down to the measuring out of each portion of peas, that finally made Jamie decide to apply for another job. This resulted in yet another move to the newly built Skyway Hotel, Southampton where Jamie once again took on the role of assistant manager. I was thrilled to accept the job of assistant housekeeper; overseeing the running of the one hundred and twenty bedrooms; offering luxurious accommodation for passengers of the P&O cruise liners arriving and departing from Southampton docks.

There was one drawback; no living in accommodation,

resulting in us having to rent a flat nearby. With us both working different shifts, days would pass before we met up over a hasty breakfast. I was always asleep when Jamie arrived home in the early hours and he was asleep when I departed for work in the morning. We were like the proverbial ships that pass in the night.

I enjoyed the task of endeavouring to brighten up the shabbily furnished flat with the addition of fresh flowers bought from the flower seller on the way home from work. I washed the nicotine stained curtains and cushion covers and thoroughly cleaned a very dirty kitchen and bathroom.

Although I had not yet passed my driving test, the need to own a car was triggered one morning when, on my way to work, I passed a garage with second hand cars for sale. A blue Morris Minor convertible caught my eye.

"Thirty quid down and it's yours," the salesman said opening the door on the driver's side. "One careful lady owner, a district nurse, she's retired now. She's a good little runner, the car not the nurse," he said laughing at his own joke. "Want me to take you for a spin?"

I explained that I was on my way to work, but would call in when I finished my shift.

"You a nurse then?"

"No I work at Skyways Hotel."

"Mention me to Paddy the manager; he'll tell you, I'll see you right."

Two days later I was the proud owner of my own car, having paid the deposit and signed up with a finance company to pay the remaining balance over the next twelve months. I gave Jamie the money to pay for the tax and the insurance, which had to be in his name. For some reason he had found it necessary to sell his car when we moved to Southampton and was pleased when I bought the Morris. Although being in possession of a provisional licence and L plates, there was never any time for him to accompany me when I wanted to go out for a spin. We hardly ever shared the same days off, during which time he had the use of the car.

I was really enjoying my job until one morning everything changed when I was summoned to the manager's office.

Paddy O'Sullivan, a tall, good looking Irishman, sat at his glass topped desk, pen in hand and a pile of papers in front of him.

"Good morning Margherita, do take a seat. Would you care for a coffee?"

"Thank you and no thanks, bit early for me."

Coming straight to the point, he shuffled his papers and cleared his throat.

"I am sorry to have to tell you that I am going to have to let Mac go."

"What! But why?"

He had the nervous habit of clearing his throat before speaking."He's been fiddling the books."

"How do you know it's him?"

"There are always shortages in the takings when he has been on duty."

He could see how shocked I was and picking up the phone, he asked for a coffee and a tot of brandy to be sent in.

He poured the brandy into the steaming coffee along with two spoonfuls of amber coloured sugar crystals before passing it across the desk.

"Get that down you, you look as though you need it," clearing his throat loudly he went on to say, "I am going to be quite frank with you Margherita, you've proved to be a valuable member of my staff and you *could* have a bright future if you were to stay with this company," clearing his throat once again, he stood up and turned to look out of the large picture window behind his desk.. "Mac will only pull you down with him. His heavy drinking is another reason why I have to let him go."

I sat looking into my half empty coffee cup. I just didn't know what to say.

Turning to face me he gave me a warm smile as he reached across his desk with his outstretched hand. His handshake was reassuringly firm. "You don't have to make your mind up now, but please give serious consideration to what I have said.

"Now, you don't want to be believing what he says," Jamie said when, on my return home from work that evening, I questioned him. "I knew Paddy when he was a snot nosed kid working in his father's hotel in Dublin. He never liked it when I was put in charge of the staff quarters. Don't you be a worrying yourself; I'll soon get another Job, so I will."

One afternoon I returned home from work early feeling unwell. I expected Jamie to be sitting in front of the television watching the racing. The flat was empty, the bed hadn't been made; the previous night's empty beer bottles littered the floor and last night's supper dishes filled the sink. Opening the curtains I looked out at the empty space where the car usually stood.

"Hello Mrs Mac," my neighbour from the flat downstairs called through the door. "I thought I should bring your milk in for you, it's been sitting out on the step all morning," she said handing the bottle through the now open door. Mrs O'Flynn, a rather dishevelled, elderly Irish woman lived in the downstairs flat with her husband Billy who had recently retired, from his work on the docks, due to ill health. Both were heavy smokers and Billy liked his drink. We got to know them through another of Billy's addictions – gambling. Jamie used him as an excuse to 'have a little flutter on the horses'.

Inviting her in, I asked Mrs O if she knew where Jamie was.

"He left for work early this morning," she said as she rolled a cigarette, "don't mind if I smoke do you?"
I did, mind, but she lit up without waiting for a reply. "Your home early today," she said, coughing as she took her first drag.

"But he hasn't got a job yet," I said, hastily opening the window.

'Sure he has, he's had a job since he left the last one. He works at the Working Men's club where Billy goes at

258

weekends; he had a word with the manager for him."

The taxi took fifteen minutes.

Jamie spotted me as I stormed into the bar. A tall, overweight man stepped forward, stopping me in my tracks.

"Sorry lady, you aint allowed in ere, it's men only."

Jamie offered feeble excuses as we stood in the car park having a flaming row.

"I've been giving you money to pay the rent," I shouted through my tears, "and you've had use of the car; I have even paid for the petrol, you're a liar and a thief."

He just stood helplessly looking down at the ground.

"We are finished."

He looked, shocked fumbling in his pocket when I demanded the keys to my car.

Breaking the law, having not yet passed the driving test, I drove the car back to the flat. I then walked down to the Polygon Hotel where I had heard they were looking for staff. I was met in the spacious entrance hall by the smartly uniformed, head hall porter; standing beside him was a well dressed, middle aged woman who, giving me a broad grin, ushered me into a side office.

"Thank goodness, am I pleased to see *you*. How do you do, my name is Mrs Gaydie," she said offering me a chair. She must have spotted the puzzled look on my face as she went on to ask, as she sat wearily down at her desk with a sigh, "you *have* come about the position of assistant housekeeper haven't you,"

"Well yes, but how did you know I was coming?"

"You rang and made an appointment yesterday," again observing how puzzled I looked, she asked, "it is Mrs Jean Brand isn't it?"

"No my name is Margherita and no I haven't got an appointment. I just called in on the off chance that there might be a staff vacancy."

Letting out a loud groan, she gave me a sad look of disappointment. "This is the third time I have been let down by people not turning up for an interview, I think it's the prospect of having to live in. I must apologise for the mix up. Let me order us a tray of tea."

"Am I to believe you are looking for an assistant housekeeper," I asked excitedly.

"I am, but as you can tell, I'm not having much luck."
We neither of us could believe the coincidence when I told her that I was looking for just such a position and that I was presently employed as housekeeper at Skyways Hotel and looking to move jobs; in particular a job offering accommodation. The tea arrived and we sat chatting for nearly an hour. I got the job.

"When will you be free to start?"

"Now?!" I said expectantly.

Paddy O'Sullivan was very sympathetic when I explained why I needed to leave as soon as possible.

"We are going to miss you. It's going to be hard finding your replacement; but good luck.

THE REUNION

There were two Trust House Hotels in Southampton; 'The Dolphin', situated 'Below Bar' in the High Street and The Polygon – 'Above Bar' overlooking Watts Park.

(The origin of the term Below and Above Bar is said to stem from a Bargate which divided the north and south regions of the High street.)

On my first day, the awesome size and Victorian grandeur of 'The Polygon Hotel' filled me with anticipation, as Gadie – a name by which she preferred to be known – gave me a guided tour of the building; starting on the ground floor. I was told that the resplendent ball room, which accommodated up to four hundred guests, was regularly used for dinner dances and various receptions. Rococo style, ornate, gold framed mirrors lined the walls and large crystal chandeliers adorned the high ceiling. A third of the ballroom, when curtained off, was used as a dining area, seating up to two hundred people, some of whom were enjoying a late breakfast as we walked through into the hubbub of the huge, busy kitchen. I thought of my father as I watched the work force, dressed in their 'whites' and tall, stiffly starched, chef's hats. I thought also of Nonno Roberto, working in just such a large kitchen, of either 'Frascati's' or 'Monaco's' in London.

"Some of the girls will be joining us in the staff dining room for their coffee break at eleven," Gadie said as she whisked me up the main staircase, leading to some of the guest bedrooms on the first floor. "I thought this would be a good opportunity for you to meet the ones that are on duty today. They're a lively lot; all excellent workers, most of them having previously worked as cabin stewardesses on the P&O cruise liners. They get laid off when they either reach thirty or get married. Some have been with *us* for over ten years. You will probably find them a bit daunting at first; it does get easier once they get to know you," she said as she introduced me to Muriel, a tall attractive black woman who was pushing a trolley, laden with clean linen and cleaning equipment, through the open door of one of the rooms leading off the richly carpeted corridor. Inside the room, a canvas bag, containing dirty linen, stood beside freshly stripped twin beds; long net curtains, swayed by a fresh sea breeze blowing in through the tall open window; morning sunlight cast dancing shadows on the highly polished surfaces of the dark, oak furniture, giving the room an atmosphere of affluent antiquity.

"This is our new assistant housekeeper, Margherita; you don't mind the girls calling you by your first name do you?" Muriel gave me a shy smile before continuing with her work.

As we left the room, Gadie told me how Muriel, accompanied by her husband, journeyed from Nigeria to England in the hope of training to be a nurse. Having found himself a job on the docks, her husband was later to become the victim of a fatal accident. With no means of paying the exorbitant rent charged for a small room in a sleazy boarding house, and no money for her keep, she gave up all hope of a nursing career and, in need of a job that offered a roof over her head, she ended up working at the 'Polygon', where she has remained for the past eight years.

We went on from first to fifth floor whilst Gadie, having hastily made the introductions, showed me the rudiments of checking the rooms, which usually took place when the chambermaids had gone off duty.

"Once you get accustomed to what to look for, and providing all is satisfactory, you can complete the check in thirty seconds; starting by checking the lights as you enter the room; wardrobe, basin, towels and soaps; well you know what to look for. Oh and by the way, when you check Lizzie's floor, do the occasional spot check for hidden bottles! She is the most thorough of all the maids, and has been with us for the past ten years, but unfortunately she is alcoholic. Come on, it's nearly eleven, the girls will be waiting," she said looking at the pretty silver and marcasite fob watch pinned to her dress. "A present from my son, for my fiftieth birthday," she said, noticing my admiring glance, "that was five years ago."

The majority of female staff rooms running along the side of the main building were reached by a separate staircase; some overlooking the street and others, including the staff kitchen, overlooked the back yard. Gadie and I had sizable, neighbouring rooms overlooking the park. Male members of staff occupied the rather dilapidated building on the far side of the yard where crates of empty bottles, empty beer barrels and overflowing rubbish bins were stored. Heavy Iron gates, closing the yard off from the street, were usually kept bolted at night; that is when latecomers remembered to do so!

"Where is Maivie?" Gadie asked a somewhat overweight, masculine looking blond, as we entered the small, cramped staff kitchen. "She hasn't reported in today, is she still unwell?"

She told me later that Helga and Maivie had lost their jobs with P&O because they were caught making love in one of the guest cabins. "They share a room together here, but they are like an old married couple; always rowing. We turn a blind eye as long as their work isn't affected. Our head chef Brian, shares a similar relationship with one of the catering managers; both being very good at their jobs. There seems to be a lot of that sort of thing going on in the catering trade," she said with an unconcerned shrug.

I was introduced to Lizzie who grunted at me from behind the newspaper she was reading. Muriel gave me a shy smile as she asked if I took sugar. Christina, the last to be introduced, blew a plume of smoke in my direction as she nodded her dark haired head and winked one of her large dark brown eyes at Gadie. Lastly I was introduced to Agnes, a very attractive but rather overweight young Irish woman, who rushed into the kitchen just as we were about to leave.

"Sure I'm sorry to be late, "she said holding out her

hand as Gadie introduced us. "I dropped a tray and had to clear it up."

"They'll soon get used to you," Gadie said as we continued our tour.

The work was intensive; the unsocial hours were long, especially when there were late arrivals, due to a cruise liner held up whilst approaching the port or having been delayed by bad weather out at sea. However the job offered many compensations such as visits from famous people; Hughie Green overseeing auditions for 'Opportunity Knocks'; James Mason, with whom I travelled in the lift where he begrudgingly gave me his autograph; Jerry of 'Jerry and the Pacemakers' inviting me to join him at a party; being too cautious to accept the invitation, I gave the excuse of being on duty!

There were also entertaining episodes; for example, Friday evenings, when Lizzie went out on the town, dressed in a black suit (which she expertly tailored whilst working on the cruise liners), a snazzy black felt hat set at a jaunty angle over her well dressed, bleached, blond hair - now free of the usual hairnet; neatly aligned fine black stockings; black patent leather high heels and matching shoulder bag,. With her makeup immaculately applied she bore a remarkable resemblance to Marlene Dietrich.

If one just happened to be in the staff kitchen at precisely seven thirty, the clip clop sound of her high heels as she made her way down the iron fire escape -- visible from the kitchen window -- signalled her departure.

"We always make sure that a couple of us are in the kitchen from ten o'clock ready for her return," Gadie said as we watched Lizzie pull back the bolts on the back gate. "Will you join me this evening? You'll find it quite an experience!"

We sat drinking our hot chocolate and chatting to Helga as she unloaded the washing machine, when we heard 'clip clop trip, clip clop trip, clip clop, clip clop crash! Helga gave a knowing nod to Gadie as they hurried out through the kitchen door. Looking out of the window, I watched them as they made their way down the fire-escape stairs towards a very dishevelled Lizzie who lay on her back with both legs sprawled at a precarious angle up the first three steps of the stairs; with one shoe missing, a hole in her stockings and her hat now covering her face, she croakily sang 'It's a long way to Tipperary'. Picking up her bag and shoe, Gadie and Helga helped her up the stairs and seated her – still singing – at the kitchen table, where she was served a large mug of strong, black coffee; this being a regular occurrence, amazingly, as always, she was unhurt – apart from her ruined stockings injured pride!

Another amusing incident occurred when one evening I knocked on Muriel's door, needing to see her about working an extra shift, as Agnes, one of the maids, was off sick. She opened the door and stood there with her hair, in what I remembered as having been done to mine when I was a small girl. I found myself staring up at clumps of hair wound round strips of rag, standing up all over her head; bringing to mind 'Pansy Potter, the cartoon character from the Beano.

"I used to have the same painful procedure done to my hair to make it curly when I was little, but you already have curly hair," I said as she invited me in.

"I do it to straighten mine," she said with her usual infectious giggle, she went on to say as she pulled at a tight curl, unfurling it from close to her scalp, "otherwise it would all be like this al over. You want some green banana and yam curry?" she asked as she saw me glancing at the pot steaming on the small hot plate. She knew that staff were not meant to cook in their rooms, but it smelt so good and she was such a lovely person and with her room being one of the attic rooms – well what did it really matter. Our friendship grew over many a steaming plateful.

Whilst working out the following week's duty roster, I realised that Agnes Farrely, the maid in charge of the rooms on the third floor, had still not returned to work. I hadn't heard from her for over a week and knowing that she was friendly with Lottie, who worked on the second floor, I asked if she knew why Agnes had not notified me of the reason for her absence.

"Didn't you know," she said looking a bit sheepish, "I really don't know if it's my place to tell you."

"Well if you know anything, please tell me, because she is at risk of losing her job."

"She's pregnant," she blurted out, "she has come over from Ireland, with her brother, to have the baby adopted."

"I thought she was just overweight. Do you know where she lives?"

"No but Kathy the downstairs cleaner does; she lives in the room above where Agnes shares with her brother, she'll be able to tell you."

The house was dingy and smelt strongly of cat's pee. I knocked twice before I heard the sound of movement and muffled voices. The door opened just wide enough for me to see the unshaven face of a young man peering at me through the gloom. He didn't speak.

"Sorry to disturb you, is Agnes there? I need to speak to her. My name is Margherita; I'm the assistant housekeeper from The Polygon.

There was no answer.

"Is it alright if I come in? I need to speak to Agnes."

The door opened further as a bleary eyed Agnes, wearing a rather stained, pink, candlewick dressing gown, stepped out into the dimly lit corridor.

"Sorry, I was asleep," She said leaning heavily against the now closed door, looking very pregnant.

"I am sorry to disturb you, but I really needed to know if you intended to return to work, but I can see that's not going to happen."

A door across the hall opened and a scruffily dressed woman emerged and stood with arms folded across her ample bosom, nosily watching us

"Can I come in, I really need to speak to you in private, it is important."

The rank, stuffiness of the small, sparsely furnished

room, filled me with the desire to throw open the heavily curtained window, not only to let in some fresh air, but also, extra light from the outside street lighting. On the crumpled double bed sat two trays; one of which showed evidence of a half eaten meal. There were two orange boxes on either side of the bed on which stood candles in saucers, offering the only light to the room.

The young man gingerly took my outstretched hand as Agnes shyly introduced him as her younger brother

"We've run out of change for the electric meter," Agnes said apologetically, "otherwise I would have offered you a cup of tea."

As my eyes became accustomed to the gloom, I noticed a small kitchen area half hidden by a ragged curtain.

"I'll leave you two to talk," her brother said removing the trays from the bed. "I'll be fetching you a bottle of soda water so I will." The lilt of his softly spoken, southern Irish accent brought Jamie to mind.

As we chatted, I learned that Agnes had been sent over to this country in disgrace and that she was not to return home until she had given the baby over to the nuns for adoption. She was due to be admitted into the local convent the following week to await the time of her confinement.

"My brother will then be free to return home as we have just about run out of money."

This led to me telling her how my mother, at the mature age of forty eight, gave birth to a baby boy. Mark David, my half brother, who was born with multiple health problems and sadly died when he was four months old. I went on to tell her how devastated my mother was by the loss and how, two years later, wishing to adopt a child, she was refused by the adoption society, due to her being over fifty. I explained to Agnes how adoption would prove a possibility, if, through legal channels, I were to agree to act as third party to the adoption.

"But the nuns have arranged everything."

I found it hard to convince her until she finally agreed to meet my parents.

Speaking to my mother on the phone, later that evening, her voice was shrill with excitement as she relayed the story to my stepfather. "Johnny said that he will bring me tomorrow; by the sound of it we can't waste any time."

They arrived around midday and having taken the day off, I accompanied them when they met Agnes and her brother. It all happened so quickly. Firstly the visit to the convent where a promise had to be made for my parents to convert to Roman Catholicism before the nuns would agree to release Agnes from her commitment. "After all," to quote Mother Superior, "she is a grown woman, and therefore old enough to make her own decisions about the future of her unborn child." Our next destination was to Agnes' lodgings where my stepfather paid off the outstanding rent arrears. Her brother helped as we gathered their meagre possessions into two small suitcases.

We were all very relieved when at last we sat down to late afternoon tea in the convivial atmosphere of the Polygon foyer. Agnes' concerns about her brother's welfare were also allayed when my stepfather handed him more than enough money for his return fare to Ireland.

"How did it all go?" Gadie asked inviting me into her comfortable room.
Having thanked her for taking on my duties at such short notice, I went on to tell her of the day's events.

"So, she will be living with your parents until the baby is born?" she asked handing me a welcome glass of sweet sherry. "I think it must have been fate that brought you to the Polygon."

I must admit to having, what could be construed as selfish reasons for going out of my way to obtain for my mother that which she so dearly wished for. I hoped that this would at last give me what *I so dearly wished for* – the heartfelt love of my mother.

Agnes gave birth to a healthy baby girl in the evening of September 23rd at St John's Hospital Chelmsford. Three days later she returned to Southampton having handed her baby over to my delighted mother and stepfather. They named her Rachel Florence. Agnes never returned to work at 'The Polygon and I never saw her again.

As housekeepers, our tasks were many and varied, ranging from washing and re-hanging (all in the same day) the nets from all the guest bedrooms; dealing with the outgoing and incoming linen; ordering cleaning products; duty rosters, checking that cleaners and chambermaids had arrived for duty and were doing their jobs efficiently. Even collecting and distributing flowers from the flower room, having been made ready by the hotel's resident florist, for the dining room, ball room and reception areas; her work was endless. In all, both myself and Gadie each performed a full .day's work six days a week; which occasionally stretched into late evenings.

The hard work combined with managerial responsibilities enriched my life. I was in my element, dressed in my smart black dress with its starched white collar (removed for evening duty), and a bunch of master keys jangling from my belt as I went about my duties.

My contentment was soon shattered when, late one evening, I received a call over the internal phone. It was Robbie, the head night porter telling me that there was a very drunk Irish man, down in the foyer demanding to see me.

"Do you want me to tell him to sling his hook miss?"

Robbie was a giant of a man, sporting a ginger moustache, the ends of which were waxed and curled. Having served as a Sergeant Major and self defence instructor with the Welsh Guards during the Second World War, he was evidently still more than capable of dealing with aggressive situations

This took place every evening until I finally agreed to see Jamie. Robbie stood by whist I spoke to him and seeing that he was sober, I agreed to go out and have a coffee at the late night cafe, a short walk from the hotel. I found it very hard to believe most of his explanations and promises.

"Look, I realise what a fool I have been, I've let you down badly, but I promise I have learnt by my mistakes. I love you and want to be with you. We can even get married once your divorce comes through."

I began to weaken as I looked into his tear filled eyes.

"I've been for an interview with 'Watney Mann East Anglia'; they are looking for managers, please say you will come with me."

Gadie was devastated when I broke the news that I would be leaving in a month. The day before I left, I was summoned to join her for coffee in the staff kitchen. The usual noisy, coffee break chatter suddenly hushed as I walked in.

"We're all sorry to see you leave mate," Helga said burying my face in her large bosom whilst giving me a breathtaking hug.

"These are from all of us," Muriel said, handing me a large bouquet of flowers.

Gadie stepped forward and gave a little speech after handing me a card signed by 'all the girls'. I cried; not tears of sadness, but of pleasure, the pleasure of having worked and made friends with such nice people over the past few months.

THE LAMB INN

With the Morris Minor packed to capacity and Jamie at the wheel, we made our way out of Southampton. The early May weather was warm and sunny and with the morning rush-hour over, we made good progress as we headed in the direction of Norfolk. Having stopped just outside Luton for lunch, we finally reached the small town of Wroxham, on the Norfolk Broads, by mid afternoon. The landlady of 'The Kings Head' -- whose name escapes me -- after showing us to our room, invited us to join her for tea on the river terrace. It was a glorious afternoon, and we watched as various boats of all sizes cruised leisurely up and down the narrow waterway. I was enchanted as a family of ducks waddled noisily towards where we were sitting.

"People feed them, that's why they are so tame," our hostess told us as she threw a crust of bread into the water.

"It's better if the bread is wet, as dry bread could choke the young ones. We put that notice up to say as much, but unfortunately most people choose to ignore it," she said with a sigh.

We were then taken on a guided tour of the building, during which time it was explained what was expected of us as relief managers. We were introduced to several members of staff who all seemed quite friendly.

"I've put you in the spare bedroom in *our* flat, because it's a nice quite room, you can use our shower room and toilet. My cleaner Mary will look after you. I will now leave you to settle in; I must go and help the boss pack the car. Enjoy your stay."

For the forthcoming two weeks, most of my time was

spent running the busy bar; a fairly new building overlooking the river terrace. I didn't see much of Jamie, who seemed to hover between restaurant and office. We did meet up during the quiet period after lunch, when, having grabbed a quick snack, we were able to have an hour's rest in our room.

Jamie became friends with Keith, one of the chefs working in the main kitchen; they often sat outside on the river terrace, in the evenings, having a drink after the kitchen had closed. They were frequently joined by Keith's partner Peter, who worked at the Ferry Inn further down the river at Horning. I was always too busy to join them and by the time I had cashed up and closed the bar, all I wanted to do was go straight to bed, leaving them all where they sat drinking into the early hours. Knowing that Jamie had a set of master keys, I was concerned when I used to find empty wine and beer bottles the next morning, knowing that they had been taken from the bar and leaving no evidence of payment. Some evenings, Jamie would take over the bar, especially when a group of rather drunk Americans from one of the nearby air bases, having been drinking in the bar all evening, proved hard to evict at closing time. Dirty glasses and empty bottles that littered the bar tables when I came on duty the next morning, caused me to tackle Jamie about the lack of payment.

"Ah well, the till was locked, but look I have it all here," he begrudgingly said, handing me a fistful of crumpled notes. Paddy O'Sulivan's words of warning flashed across my mind, but worried as I was, I still didn't want to believe he would risk losing yet another job; I was so gullible.

The day finally arrived for our departure and as we handed over the keys, I was, both relieved and surprised when the landlady, having thanked me for looking after the place so well, handed me a gift of a bone china tea-set; I was also puzzled by the landlord's seemingly knowing wink as he shook Jamie by the hand. I never did get to know what that was all about!

The Two Bears, where once again we took over as relief managers for the following two weeks, was, in comparison to our last place of work, an ugly barn of a place in the centre of a heavily built up area of Great Yarmouth. The smell of stale cooking fat pervaded the entire building, especially the cramped room that looked out over the rubbish strewn back yard where an extractor fan continuously belched out greasy kitchen odours that drifted up through the widow of what was to be our bedroom for the next two weeks. The whole place looked badly in need of redecoration and refurbishment, especially the kitchen which in the main catered for the bar and the dilapidated ballroom where discos were held most evenings, both of which being generally frequented by American airmen. Jamie seemed to be in his element; however, I hated it, especially when I found out that the reason for my nausea during the final week of our stay was due to the fact that I was in the very early stages of pregnancy. Jamie seemed to take the news badly; I however, was delighted yet fearful with the memory of the appalling experiences I endured during the birth of my first child still clear in my mind. Not wanting to allow myself any misgivings about *this* pregnancy, I decided to go privately when seeking the advice of consultant gynaecologist, Mr Bentall who was based at The Norfolk and Norwich General Hospital. I did this with the knowledge that we would soon be taking up a permanent position as managers of the Lamb Inn in the centre of the city of Norwich.

"I don't want you to worry about a thing; I will take care of you, I promise," were the gently spoken, reassuring words from the middle aged, good looking consultant, gentlemanly holding the door open as I was leaving; my first appointment having come to a close.

The Lamb Inn was yet another extremely run-down, poorly staffed establishment. My nausea wasn't improved by the choking odour of stale frying oil and fried onions as we entered the bar area. Very few customers were sitting on the shabby bar stools; an elderly barmaid showed no sign of serving us as she stood chatting to a customer over the long wooden topped bar.

"What can I get you?" she said, eventually finishing her

conversation.

"We are the new managers, has the area manager left us the keys?" Jamie for once sounded official.

"Sorry I wasn't here when you arrived," a breathless Joe Caulton said as he hurriedly followed us in, "you're early, did you have a good journey, what would you folks like to drink?" he said shaking us both vigorously by the hand. "Ethel get your new bosses a drink, I'll have my usual. She's a bit deaf, but a good barmaid," he added as Ethel pumped a glass up to the Bells Whiskey optic.

"Slainte," Jamie said as he downed half of his pint of Guinness in one; I tentatively sipped at my Orange juice as I walked through to the Griddle Room where a sole diner sat tucking into a plate of egg, sausage and chips. I gagged and quickly went back to ask Ethel where the ladies room was.

"Take Mrs Mac upstairs to the ladies loo and then take her and show her the flat will you Ethel."

"It hasn't been cleaned today as Audrey, our cleaner is off sick, it's her job to do the flat and the ladies loo and cover for when the pot man is off duty or sick," Ethel said, opening the door to what was now to be our living quarters.

The Flat was littered with debris and as we went from room to room, I realised it was going to take more than the efforts of one woman to make it at least habitable.

"Just let me know what you need," Joe Caulton said, following us into the small kitchen, "as you can see the previous managers did 'a moonlight', taking most of the equipment with them, including the cooker and washing machine; but don't worry, it's all in hand. They even took the bed and all the bed linen. Replacements are being sent over from our storage depot later today, so at least you can have a good night's rest before you start tomorrow; however, I expect you will want to supply your own bed and linen, knowing what will come out of the warehouse, it's all second hand stuff that people have chosen to leave behind."

Seeing the state of the mattress of the divan double bed, when it arrived, all I wanted to do was rush out and buy a new one; instead of which, I decided on an emergency shopping trip into the city, in search of two sleeping bags, two pillows and some towels. That evening, having thoroughly cleaned the bath, I was glad to have a relaxing soak, before climbing into my new sleeping bag; it was just after eight thirty and I almost instantly fell sound asleep. I presumed Jamie was still where I left him, down in the bar.

The next morning I was awakened from a deep sleep by a knock at the door. I could see by the unmoving mound in the sleeping bag beside mine, that Jamie was still asleep. Still confused by sleepiness, I momentarily wondered where I was; then another knock brought me quickly to my senses. "Hang on, I'm coming," I called out, pulling a jumper on over my pyjamas.

"Mornin' missus, sorry to disturb you," a large, middle aged woman stood wiping the sweat from her lined, sallow skinned face. "I'm Audrey, your cleaning lady, sorry I wasn't here yesterday but I've been unwell; it's me joints, they plays me up sometimes." I found myself wondering how this overweight and obviously unfit woman was going to be able to help me with the imminent workload.

Over the next few weeks, we had to make staff changes; one of which was Ethel. Realising that there were regular discrepancies in cigarette sales whenever she was on duty, Jamie, having set a trap by counting the amount of packets sold compared to the amount showing on the till receipts, found it necessary to give her notice to leave, saying that he would now be running the bar. She left without any argument. Ethel's son in law was also given his marching orders due to his insubordinate attitude when asked to clean the grillroom equipment where he worked as grill chef.

Being in the centre of the city, it became obvious that with a limited time for lunch, office workers and staff from the large stores were going to need speedily produced light meals and snacks. With this in mind I had one of the function room trestle tables brought down to where I soon had it set up in the bar where I served various salads, cheeses and cold meats along with crispy French bread. I became adept at carving the joints of cold meats, especially ham from the bone. Ends of various joints were minced and made into large plate pies, portions of which were served with a portion of chips for either 'take out' or served in the grill room. Lamb and ham bones along with chicken carcases provided the stock for making soup. Nothing was wasted. My catering venture became very profitably popular. Joyce, who usually worked as a waitress in the grill room, proved to be a good cook and became my right hand woman. The large function-room kitchen upstairs became her domain where she made the salads and pies and cooked the meats ready for the snack bar. We served the homemade soups along with Jean's speciality – Sheppard's pie - from the grill room. She also made wonderful apple pies. Thankfully the demand for burgers soon faded into oblivion. Word of the reorganised catering services soon spread and the popularity of The Lamb flourished, not only the lunchtime trade, but also the function room came to life. Bookings for parties, wedding receptions and dinner dances flooded in.

There wasn't a lot of time for socialising; however we did manage the occasional visit to the local night club. The doors of the Washington 400C club opened at 11pm every evening offering late night drinking, dancing, gambling and entertainment by smutty comedians and strippers. My desire for alcoholic beverages had waned somewhat since falling pregnant; I didn't gamble and by that time of the evening, after a busy day's work, I was too tired to join in the dancing. Sitting at one of the tables that surrounded the dance floor, we were entertained by the various performers, two of whom were strippers. It was the first time I had ever seen a completely naked woman. One of the club's regular strippers was a rather well built black woman who went under the name of Tropical Linda; her ungainly performance left very little to the imagination. Christine Etoile, on the other hand, whose name translates from the French with the apt meaning of 'the star', was indeed the star performer. Her only props were a scruffy raincoat hanging from a stand, topped with a battered cloth cap. As the French style burlesque music played through the sound system, she stood facing the raincoat whilst threading her slender arms into the sleeves which immediately sprang into life. It was as though an old man was slowly undressing her. She performed her act with the balletic charm of a true professional.

As time went on, the late evening excursions to the club became less and less. My days were taken up with the increase in trade; also most weekend evenings involved running the function room bar along with the supervision of various functions. Although he was not playing a huge part in the general running of the place, Jamie was spending a lot of time out, supposedly drumming up trade from other drinking establishments; I, however, was enjoying the responsibilities of, most of the time, being in sole charge. Audrey was not only proving a conscientious worker, but also a reliable ally. She had never married and to my knowledge, had no relatives. She came to look upon me as a daughter figure and was always there for me when I most needed her, which was becoming more frequent with the progression of my pregnancy.

I had my first experience of cooking game when a group of young farmers delivered twelve brace of pheasants in readiness for the end of the shooting season party. I was horrified as I found small metal pellets embedded in the flesh of the oven ready birds. Before attempting to cook them, I rang my butcher who laughingly informed me that it was lead shot and not to worry about trying to remove it.

"But isn't it dangerous, people could break their teeth."

"No, it's to be expected when eating game birds."

"What, breaking teeth?" I said, trying to match his humour.

"No, being aware of the presence of shot"

"Do they always use shotguns to kill them, isn't there a kinder way?"

Again, the phone resounded with hoots of laughter. "Well what do you expect them to do, run after them and ring their necks? Now, shove a piece of onion and a bay leaf up their bums; wrap them up cosily in streaky bacon; sit them in a little water and snuggle them together in a large roasting tin; season with salt and freshly ground black pepper and cover them over with buttered greaseproof paper. Don't overcook them and leave the worrying about shot to those that will undoubtedly enjoy them." My first lesson in cooking Game birds was a huge eye-opener, resulting in a great success. With the help of Joyce in the kitchen and two of the casuals who helped out at various functions preparing the tables and serving.

THE BIRTH OF MY SECOND CHILD

Time flew by until early one morning I was awakened by pains in my lower back. I knew that my time had come. My gynaecologist Mr Bentall was spot on with the predicted date – 27th February. It was a leap year and I wondered if my baby would be born on the 29th which would have meant only having one birthday every four years. I found it difficult to wake Jamie who had had a heavy nights drinking. He wisely rang for a taxi after ringing the hospital to let them know that I was on my way.

"I'm sorry mate, you're gonna av to come wiv the lady cos we aint sposed ter take expectant mums unaccompanied, specially at five o-clock in the mornin," the rather rotund, elderly taxi driver called out to Jamie who was hovering in the doorway still dressed in his pyjamas.

I was under the impression that as a private patient I would have a room to myself; however when I was shown to my room by an auxiliary nurse, I was dismayed to find that I was to share. My roommate appeared to be in the final stages of labour and as I entered the room she was being escorted to the delivery suite by a stony faced midwife. The room smelt strongly of cigarette smoke and I noticed two packets of American cigarettes on her bedside table along with a half full bottle of Bourbon, which I presumed, had been left there by her husband.

"It's Mrs MacDonald isn't it, we *are* expecting you," the auxiliary nurse said looking at a clipboard. "Sorry about this," she said picking up two dirty glasses from the other bedside table, "Mrs Brae's husband stayed quite late last night." She tutted as she smoothed the cover of what was going to be my bed. "Get into your nightdress and into bed and I'll be back shortly with a nice cup of tea."

"Hi there, my name is Sharon," my roommate said in a strong American drawl. "It was a false alarm after all, it's all so damned boring," she said reaching for the cigarettes. "I'll be glad when it's all over and I can get back to the base."

I was both shocked and annoyed when she blew clouds of smoke my way. "Are you supposed to be smoking in here?" I said trying to hide the disapproval in my voice.

"Aw I aint gonna worry, any way this is why Hank is paying privately; he's an officer an there aint nothen he won't do fer his little ol Sharie." She lay back on her pillows letting out a contented smoky sigh.

I thought about mentioning the effect smoking was having on her, as yet , unborn baby; however, realising it was too late for that, I let the matter drop.

"Hello Mrs MacDonald, My name is nurse Thornly, I'm one of the midwives on duty today." She turned out to be the stony faced one I had seen earlier.

"Mrs Brae, please put out that cigarette, I'm sure Mrs MacDonald doesn't want to breathe stale smoke all day," she raised her eyes as she pulled the screens around my bed.

"Now dear I need to examine you. How often are your contractions," she asked as she prodded my bump with cold bony fingers; as she did so I felt a strange, painful movement as though my unborn child recoiled from the unwelcome action.

"Try to relax my dear," she said as the dull ache in my back worsened. "Hm, I am now going to give you an internal examination; place the soles of your feet together and let your knees fall apart and please try to relax. Oh good you've had a shave."

Yes, I thought, I didn't want to go through the same experience as with my first child and judging by what I was now going through as 'stony face' dug into the depths of my private parts causing me to yelp, things were not going to get any easier.

"Try to relax; I am going to try to turn the baby as she is

facing the wrong way." Pain and fear took over from then on.

"Hey Honey, don't take on so," Sharon said as 'stony face' left the room. "She's an old dragon, I bet she aint had no kids or got no man in her life for that matter; come on dry your tears," she said, handing me a tissue as she sat on the side of my bed.

"I felt my baby turn when she first started to examine me, she was so rough," I said through my worsening pain. Sharon gently placed a comforting hand on my swollen belly as tears rolled down her cheeks. "Don't worry," I said, picking up on her anxiety, "I'm sure we'll both be alright."

"I'm awful worried," she said burying her face into my bedcover, "they say my baby is way too small and if it won't come natural, I'll have to be induced."

"Come along Mrs Brae," Stony face had re-entered the room, seemingly summoned by the sound of Sharon's wailing. "Mrs Macdonald has to get some rest after I've examined you both." Not long afterwards, Sharon's waters broke and I heard her cries of pain and fear as she was whisked away in a wheelchair. My contractions were coming with increased intensity and regularity and by mid afternoon I awoke to the sensation of wetting the bed; my waters had broken. I prayed 'stony face' didn't answer my call for help as I hurriedly pressed the buzzer.

"Hello Mrs Macdonald," relief quickly swept over me when I looked into the pretty face of a young nurse. "I'm Nurse Hall and I will be taking care of you for the rest of the day," she said with a friendly smile. "Now, if you can manage to sit in this chair while I change the bed, then we'll see how your baby is doing."

It was around nine thirty in the evening when I was finally taken to the delivery suite, where Mr Bentall was there waiting for me

"Can you lie on your back so that Mr Bentall can get a closer look at you?" Nurse Hall, who was now joined by another nurse, said as they tried to get me to change my position. Now painfully lying on my back as requested, a glorious gas and air swoon distanced me from the searing pain as I clasped the mask over my face.

"Your baby is lying in an awkward position," Mr Bentall said trying not to alarm me, "with the crown of its head pressing against your spine. I am going to endeavour to turn it. Take some good deep breaths into the mask."

I seemed to be floating above the extreme pain and my cries sounded as though coming from a long way off. I heard the distant sound of Mr Bentall's voice saying that I had suffered seriously during the birth of my first child and how he had promised me that he would not let it happen again. The words 'forceps' and 'anaesthetist' broke into my gas fuelled revelry which seemed to be going on forever, until the mask was taken out of my grasp.

"Mrs Macdonald," Mr Bentall's face, now very close to mine, "I am going to call in the anaesthetist, you have been a very brave girl but both you and your baby are getting very tired.

Coming round from the anaesthetic I was aware of Jamie standing beside me, his tear stained face smiling into the face of our new arrival. "You have a bonny baby girl" Nurse Hall said, handing me my beautiful baby daughter.

Theresa Lorretta was born 11.50pm on the 27th February 1968.

A new era was about to begin. The work on this section of the tapestry has now been completed. Whether it is I who once again picks up the needle at a later date, or the task is undertaken by another, the *Unfinished Tapestry* must continue to be worked on, therefore contributing to the legacy for future generations.

ABOUT THE AUTHOR

Margherita Lydia Oppezzo has had an eventful life in which she has met a host of colourful characters who populate the pages of her memoir.

Unfinished Tapestry covers the decades, from the history of her paternal Italian family, and the Jewish family on her mother's side, who were German/Polish. This volume dates from the 1830's to the birth of her second child in 1968. It is called *Unfinished Tapestry* because there is more to tell.

From all of her experiences of sadness, disappointments and loneliness, there is in equal measure, joy, humour, and a great deal of learning.

Margherita has many and varied interests which include yoga teaching, aromatherapy, dowsing, painting, singing writing and cooking. She has managed to combine these interests with motherhood and a varied working life in the hotel trade, and nursing.

She has found the writing of this book a cathartic experience, enabling her to explore more fully her own identity. She also hopes that those close to her will understand the making of the character of Margherita.

She now lives in Essex in an idyllic cottage where she enjoys cooking for family and friends; making preserves in aid of 'The British Red Cross' and 'Save The Children'; writing; painting and attending her local church where she sings in the choir.

ACKNOWLEDGMENTS

I would like to thank Anita Belli, for her expertise, advice and patience in helping me to get this book into print;

Alison Macdonald, for her ongoing support and enduring friendship;

Ian Petrie and Linda Furtado, for their patient listening;

Brian Jay for helping with local photographs and information;

The Harwich Writers Group for their support, encouragement and patience whilst listening to excerpts.

All my family and friends who have supported me throughout the writing of this book and are eagerly anticipating its publication.

86207618R00176

Made in the USA
Columbia, SC
10 January 2018